SUCCESS IN FILM
A Guide Funding, Filming
And Finishing Independent Films

JULIA VERDIN
MATT DEAN

"This is a must-read for any first-time filmmaker. I will be recommending this book to my students, and wish I had read it before I made my first film. This is a book for filmmakers, written by filmmakers. One of the best books I have read in my many years in the industry. Highly recommend!"

> **Cynthia Riddle** - WGA member, produced screenwriter and producer, former studio executive, film/screenwriting professor at the New York Film Academy

"An invaluable guide to fully prepare any filmmaker with all you need to know about producing your own film. Success in Film is one of the best books I've read on the subject as it provides a comprehensive set of tools for filmmakers of every skill level. It is jam-packed with information on all aspects of the process -- from pre-production, all the way through post-production and distribution. DO NOT pick up a camera before reading *Success in Film* from cover to cover."

> **Peter Hunziker** - Director, WGA member, Produced Writer.

"Thank you Julia and Matt for your insights and roadmap to accomplishing success in the very unpredictable world of independent film making!"

> **Christine Peters** - Producer *How to Lose a Guy in 10 Days, The Out-of-Towners*

"In a time when everyone is producing content from web films to theatrical releases, this book covers it all and inspires you to produce your own movie."

> **Farhad Mann** - Emmy Award Winning Television and Feature Film Director *Max Headroom, Lawnmower Man 2, Face of Fear, Aaron Stone, Painkiller Jane, Knightwatch*

"Don't hesitate to buy this book! Now every filmmaker can benefit from their decades of successful hands-on experience from script to delivery. Couldn't have made it across the finish line on our movie without Matt's cost-efficient post-production expertise."

> **John Alan Simon** - Director/Producer, *Radio Free Albemuth*

"Success in Film is a must read at a time when the digital revolution has enabled so many more artists to enter the field, Never have more people made independent films. But what do you make? How do you start? This book covers everything from ones philosophical and practical reasons for making a film to the actual nuts and bolts. How to avoid easy mistakes. How to plan. How to research the marketplace. These are just a few of the topics covered. The author Julia Verdin is one of the most knowledgeable and creative producers I've ever worked with. This book shows hers and Matt Dean's generousness of heart in giving away many tested and helpful trade secrets."

Jonathan Heap - Oscar Nominated Director

"I've been a film director for many years, but I'm always looking for new things to learn. This was the perfect book to fill in all the gaps. I highly recommend it to any film maker young or old."

Jason Satterlund - Director of film and television and the award winning feature film *The Record Keeper.*

"After 23 years in the business, I have never met someone who is better connected than Julia Verdin. Her strategic mind & expertise have been a big insight for me in film production & independent distribution. I always feel more confident making decisions after Julia's imparted pearls of wisdom."

Kristanna Loken - Actress, Producer

"Excellent, practical guide to making and marketing independent films. A great refresher for seasoned producers and a handy guide for those starting out."

Elizabeth Karr - Producer "Radio Free Albemuth"

"This book simplifies the complex, solidifies the abstract, and takes the fear out of filmmaking. I would highly recommend it to anyone with a passion to get their stories on the screen."

Chris Christenson - Graduate of Bethel University Minnesota, Independent Filmmaking Major

About the Authors

Julia Verdin - is an experienced film producer and indie film consultant who has produced 30 feature films and has extensive knowledge in all areas of producing, casting, financing, selling a film and taking films to the festivals. Many of Julia's films have had theatrical releases and played in major film festivals such as Sundance, Toronto and Venice. She has worked with top talent such as Al Pacino, Jeremy Irons, Danny Huston and Sienna Miller to name a few. As well as producing her own films, and running her production company Rough Diamond Productions, Julia has consulted for numerous filmmakers and through her expert advice and guidance helped them get their films made. Julia is a consulting producer for filmmakers group Raindance LA, has given seminars and participated on panels on film production for numerous organizations including Woman in Film, WGA, BAFTA LA, AFM, Story Expo, Raindance film festival, LA Femme film festivals and many others. For full resume and further info on films produced see http://www.juliaverdin.com.

Credits include: *The Merchant of Venice, Riding the bullet, Two Jacks, Stander, Slipstream, I Witness, Contaminated Man*

Matt Dean – An adjunct professor of editing and post production, Matt has a career in film and television spanning 25 years. Starting in Broadcast News for ABC in Virginia, Matt went on to produce and direct TV commercials and then documentaries and TV shows. In 2007 he worked as the Art Director for Unistar International Pictures and then expanded his career into producing and post supervising feature films. To date he has worked on 24 feature films and 80 episodes of TV. His production company Matt Dean Films helps deliver feature films to international markets and his broadcast clients have included ABC, FOX, Discovery, Nickelodeon, Bravo, Disney, MTV, OWN, ESPN, PBS, Redbull Media House, TLC and HGTV. http://www.mattdeanfilms.com

Credits include: *Radio Free Albemuth, Across the Ice, Fighting for Freedom, Undercover Cupid, Creators of Tomorrow, Two Jacks, The Devil Within*

DISCLAIMER

The material in this book is the opinion of the authors and should not be considered legal advice. Before beginning any film project it is recommended to consult an attorney to insure that proper procedures are followed to mitigate risk and keep within any applicable federal and state laws.

Knowledge and best practices in the field are constantly changing. As new research and experience broaden our understanding, changes in research methods and professional practices may become necessary.

The material in this book is the opinion of the authors and for educational purposes only. Nothing in this book should be considered business, financial or legal advice. Before beginning any film project it is recommended to consult an attorney to insure that proper procedures are followed to mitigate risk and keep within any applicable federal and state laws.

Practitioners and researchers must always rely on their own experience and knowledge in evaluating and using and information, methods, compounds or experiments described herein. In using such information they should be mindful of their own safety and the safety of others, including any parties to whom they have a professional responsibility.

To the fullest extent of the law, neither the publishers nor the authors assume any liability for any injury and or damage to persons or property as a matter of products liability, negligence or otherwise, or from any form of use or operation of any methods, products, instructions, or ideas contained herein.

CONTENTS

"Happiness is not in the mere possession of money;
it lies in the joy of achievement, in the thrill of creative effort."

– Franklin D Roosevelt

THE DREAM

FADE IN:

EXT. HOLLYWOOD BOULEVARD -- NIGHT

Twin spotlights cut through a cloudless night. Set strategically between historic Hollywood landmarks, the twin beams sweep back and forth hypnotically as they beckon all to gather.

Amidst the neon lights and the flashbulbs of the press, an elegant-looking man, JOHN, steps from a black limousine and onto the red carpet. John pulls closed his black suit jacket as he takes a deep breath and walks side by side with several world-famous stars toward the theater.

Displayed on the theater marquee is the title "THE DREAM" - John's first big film. John glances at the title and then back to the reporters snapping his picture.

Surrounding the building is a large crowd that has

gathered in hopes of catching a glimpse of one of the famous stars John assembled for this great film.

As John nears the end of the carpet and is about to be ushered into the theater, a reporter calls his name. John turns to the chorus of a dozens of flashbulbs exploding from photographers' cameras as the reporter extends her microphone.

> REPORTER
> How do you feel?

John looks out at the throngs of people staring back at him, and smiles.

> JOHN
> It's a dream come true.

> REPORTER
> Where did you get the idea for this film?
> Where did it all start?

John raises an eyebrow.

> JOHN
> That's an interesting question.
> It all began ...

FLASH CUT TO:

INT. APARTMENT NEAR HOLLYWOOD BOULEVARD - NIGHT

An alternate reality.

The same man JOHN, this time in a dingy T-shirt, stares out the dirt-covered window of his studio apartment. In the distance, twin spotlights pierce the night, and the muffled sound of a gathering crowd rumbles like a party he wasn't invited to.

In the corner of the room is an old and scratched wood desk, a worn chair, and a lamp with a flickering bulb. Beneath the lamp is an unfinished script with a scratched-out title that once read "THE DREAM."

At the back of the desk, a hard drive sets dormant. A white piece of tape covers the top of the drive with the scratched out title "THE DREAM" along with - "Directed by John Anderson."

As John stares at the script and then back out to the wandering lights, he wonders to himself where he went wrong. His dream was real, his passion was palpable. Why did the person under the lights succeed and he did not?

                    JOHN
          What did I do wrong? What else could
          I have done?

His questions hang in the air unanswered as he sits back down at the desk. Tossing the old script in the trash, John opens up his old laptop and turns it on.

Determined to finish his new film, John begins typing. This one, he hopes, won't be like the last one.

                                        FADE TO BLACK

JULIA VERDIN and MATT DEAN

Forward

Success in film. It may seem like an ambitious notion when you consider all the road blocks and difficulties that any film faces. From finding the right script to attaching a great cast, getting the film funded, technical problems or completion issues and struggles with distribution, films are fraught with difficult decisions and daily challenges. But in all honesty, so is any new business.

The great thing about making film your business is that the producer has a chance to create something that can be experienced by people around the world. Your ideas, dreams and creative inspirations can influence people you will never meet and have an impact on lives long after you are gone. Whether you are creating something of great social merit or just fun entertainment, every film has the potential to give people an emotional release, fill them with inspiration, or even move them to take action.

Like all great storytelling, films can remind us of who we are or inspire us to fulfill our potential. They can lead us on a great adventure or take us home. They can give us strength, make us laugh, make us think, ask us to question, or strengthen our beliefs. Filmmaking can be a noble profession, a way to make a difference and create debate, a way to make money and pay the bills, or for a lucky few, all of those things. In an era where everything is possible, where special effects can help you achieve whatever dream you can come up with, it's up to you, the filmmaker, to decide what is important to you. What story do you need to tell, and what new way can you tell it?

The way before you is challenging. Many have tried, but few have succeeded. That is where we hope this book will help. Once you have an idea of what that success can look like, you should be able to more accurately find, complete, and distribute your project in a way that meets your goal for success.

So how then does a producer plan for a future in filmmaking that will give them the best chance for success? There is a simple question any filmmaker should ask before beginning the difficult task of developing a picture: **Why do I want to make this film?** Some filmmakers may think this question is too simple and skip over it. But consider all the films that are made yearly that never make a profit for the investors, win no awards, and don't even give the filmmaker a good demo reel to send out for future work. Whether the filmmaker is a writer, producer, director, or an actor, it is important that the filmmaker understands their objective so that they chart a path to achieve it.

Indie filmmaking is very hard work and rarely financially rewarding. For every "against all odds" indie film success story, there are thousands of other indie films that don't find success. To help give the filmmaker a better chance of succeeding, we will explore in this book the basics of producing and share the methods that we have learned along the way that have helped make our films a success. The rules here are not hard and fast, so you may discover that additional methods will also help you find the success you're looking for. Nevertheless, everyone needs to start somewhere, and it is the goal of this book to give you, the filmmaker, that starting line.

The approach we take was designed to be helpful no matter the filmmaker's background or how much experience they have in the film business. The ideas and principles we present are meant for both ultra-low-budget films and those of larger budgets. This is possible because whether the filmmaker distributes their film to one person on the Internet or to a thousand-seat theater, they will have to consider the exact same basic building blocks for the movie. What is the story? How will it be funded? Who is the audience? Will that audience justify the budget? How is it going to be shot? What talent works best creatively and will help the film's visibility? How does the finished film get to the audience? How is the funding recouped (or is it)?

Our hope is that when you finish this book, you will have a better handle on how to complete and find success for your film.

PART I
DEFINING SUCCESS

"All you need in this life is ignorance and confidence,
and then success is sure."

– Mark Twain

"Only those who attempt the absurd
can achieve the impossible."

– Albert Einstein

Chapter 1

Why are you doing this?

In the battle between Art and Business, which is more important? Often we've had to try to balance the two sides, sometimes more successfully than others. The artist asks, "What should I make?" but the producer needs to ask, "Why should I make this?" Though art is an intricate and essential part of making a film, art may operate without regard for the overall success of the project. A film can be considered highly artistic and still fail commercially. For this reason, a producer must decide why they are making a film.

When you think about why you want to make a film, what is the first truthful response that comes to mind? Do you want to entertain an audience, make money, find fame, make a statement on a topic or idea, win awards, create a calling card to get yourself work, or, show off your skills as a director, cinematographer, actor, writer, or producer? There is no wrong answer to the question of "Why do I want to make a film?" but answering that question will set the course for everything else that happens from this point forward. If the producer doesn't ask "why," then there is no way to plan pre-production, no clarity for the production, and no way to measure

1

if the film is a success once it is released. People fail in their path to success when the goal and the project don't match.

What we see most often when defining success are the following five categories: entertaining an audience, self-promotion, promoting an idea or topic for audience awareness, making money, and winning awards.

Some of the goals or definitions of success for a film may not work well together. For example, if a producer's goal is to show off their skills and create a "calling card" for future productions, then they may not be concerned whether or not the film makes any money. This is often the case for short films. Instead of returns on the investment, the producer may focus on the art and character of the short film so that the film gets noticed and they get a chance to produce something bigger. On the other hand, the producer may only be concerned with making money back for the investors and so they chose a popular genre and make a feature film as inexpensively as possible to maximize profits. Neither of these answers is right or wrong, but they must both be handled in a completely different way during production to achieve success.

Some people may think their film can be the one film that does it all. It's possible that your amazing film could be one of the few Academy Award-winning films that is visually stunning, wildly entertaining, promotes a topical international debate, and makes tons of money. However, as those films are extremely rare, we recommend that people start with the basics to ensure that at least their most important objectives are met.

Entertaining an Audience

It's doubtful that anyone sets out to be boring with their film. There are, however, a great number of films produced ever year that are rather questionable in their ability to entertain. Does then a film's entertainment quality depend on the number of good reviews or the number of people who pay to see it? As this idea of "entertaining" is rather subjective and what is entertaining to one person is boring to someone else, you will likely need to pair this goal with one of the others (e.g.: making money or winning awards).

A good standard to set when planning to make an entertaining film is to look at which films are the most popular in the genre you wish to produce. When you want to watch something "fun," which films do you pull off the shelf or rent over and over? What is it about those films that made them so memorable? What is the element that captured the heart and minds of the audience and made them want to see the film again and again, and then recommend it to their friends? Usually, these films invoke an emotional response from the audience whether that be laughter, tears, or terror. As this can be subjective, the best way to find out whether your film makes that emotional connection is to share it with an audience and gauge their response.

Self-promotion

Self-promotion (i.e. showing your skills as an artist) can be a very useful tool in finding further work, building credibility, or securing investors for a larger project. Many short films, Internet videos, and even some features are made purely as tools to promote the individual's skills. Whether you are an actor, director, writer, director of photography, or a special effects artist, the self-promotion piece is a great way to show what you do. It is important, however, that investors are made aware from the beginning that the project's main objective is to display the filmmaker's talents. Earning back money may be a second or third goal, or may not be important at all.

For a filmmaker, the self-promotion piece can help build credibility in the industry. To do this, the film needs to not only be of good quality (directing, acting, production design, etc.) but it also needs to come in on time and on budget. If you are looking to promote additional skills, then you need to be sure that the script gives you the chance to show off those particular skills. For example: the producer/writer, the film needs memorable characters, catchy dialog, and should display a good understanding of the genre; the producer/actor needs a role that best shows the type of acting they want to promote (whether that is a leading actor of a character actor), and it would also be wise for them to hire a strong, even recognizable co-star to help elevate the scene; the producer/director needs a film to stand out with a uniquely creative style of storytelling.

Promoting an Important Idea or Topic

It takes great balance when promoting an idea or topic. When the film is too one sided, it can feel preachy, making the audience think they are being talked down to. Ideas and morals can be inserted into any style or genre of film, but if the entire purpose of the film is to promote an idea or topic, it is important to find an entertaining way to accomplish this so that the audience will stay engaged. Of the top-200 films of all time listed on IMDB (Internet Movie Database), most of them convey ideas of family, social injustice, hope, freedom, sacrifice, or duty. Films like *The Shawshank Redemption, 12 Angry Men, Schindler's List, One Flew Over the Cuckoo's Nest, Seven Samurai, Forest Gump, City of God,* and *Mr. Smith Goes to Washington* are each wildly popular and convey their ideas in an entertaining and memorable way. Many good films have something to say about the human condition. This can be as simple as character choices made by your protagonist or as in depth as a documentary focused solely on a particular topic. Documentaries are a great way to discuss a social injustice or promote a thought or moral, but keep in mind that unless a documentary is topical and socially relevant, it can be difficult to sell.

If you are strongly driven by the need to promote an idea to the public, then talk about that idea with friends, acquaintances, and strangers and see how they react. Once you gauge their acceptance or rejection of the topic, look at creative ways to get that idea across. If the idea can be considered educational, you may be able to get help from a grant, institution, or Public Broadcasting to produce your film.

Making Money

Making a profit in films is tricky. The needs of the market place change yearly, as does the desire for certain actors. To have the best chance for success, the producer must determine how much the market will pay for the film they want to produce by talking with distribution companies and gauging current market trends. The difficulty in market planning is that in the time it takes to make a film, the market may change its mind about what is popular. This is where a strong business plan and a grasp of balance is important. There are certain genres that are always more difficult to sell to the general public (e.g. dramas usually do not make as much money as action films); however there are still ways to make money with films that are not as popular with the general public.

If you want to make money while still making a less popular genre film, you have to determine if the cost of making that film is less than the market will pay to see it. In an ideal scenario, a good distribution company can give examples of current market prices in multiple countries around the world, allowing the producer to determine the possible value of the film. In today's market and changing economic conditions, however, it can be difficult for even the most capable distribution companies to give accurate forecasts. It is important therefore to include a degree of uncertainty through a best-case/ worse-case scenario in the business plan to take into account that this value can go up or down depending on the cast attached and the final quality of the picture.

Winning Awards and/or Getting Festival Play

Each year, thousands of film festivals take place all over the world, and for the emerging producer, the festivals can be a wonderful place to meet their audience and gauge reactions to their work. If your film gets into a larger festival, it may increase your chances of distribution and getting the press to talk about it. Many of these festivals cater to a specific genre, like horror, sci-fi, documentary, short film, gay and lesbian, women in film, and action. The festival circuit can be an important venue for independent films to market to their specific audience, but the producer needs to know that festivals and distribution companies have very different criteria for picking up a film. As vital as festivals can be for some films, festival play and awards do not necessarily mean that a distribution company will pick up a film or that the film will see a large increase in sales.

While distribution companies want a film that is viable to the general market, festivals want films that are viable to their particular audience. When considering producing a film for festival play, the producer should look at other films that were accepted at those festivals to determine if their film is similar. Casting, story, and style will all determine the film's ability to find an audience in the festival circuit. Festivals can also be political. If the goal is to get into festivals like Sundance, Tribeca, or Cannes, it's important to hire a good publicist or a good producer's representative who has

5

relationships with those who select the films for the festival. (i.e. festival programmers).

The more prestigious festivals will require that the film has not yet premiered to the public or premiered at another festival. If you feel your film is strong enough to get into a larger festival, you will want to apply to these first before playing at any smaller festivals.

By attending multiple festivals, the filmmaker can better get to know their audience, what their audience likes and what they don't like, and obtain as much press as possible to further promote their project. In addition, festivals can be a lot of fun as the producer has a chance to meet people who are extremely passionate about the types of films promoted at that festival.

"To fulfill a dream, to be allowed to sweat over lonely labor,
to be given a chance to create, is the meat and potatoes of life.
The money is the gravy."

– Bette Davis

Chapter 2

What is a Producer, and What Do They Do?

Many people get into the film business to fulfill a dream. Often they have read books on how to make their own movie for under $10,000 or they've watched the latest indie hit and thought, "I can do better than that!" Having met a lot of people who came to Hollywood to become a great writer, actor, director, or producer, etc., we've seen how frustrated people can get when after years and years of work they still haven't achieved their goal. If that's you, and you have grown tired of waiting for someone else to make that dream come true for you, then it's time for you to produce your own project and take charge of your own destiny. But what is a producer, and what are they supposed to be doing?

For a long time in Hollywood, the term producer meant one thing: The producer was the one who controlled every aspect of the film. They were the one responsible if the film failed or succeeded. Today, however, after years of being diluted by handing out titles like "co-producer" and giving studio heads and investors "producer" or "executive producer" titles, the term "producer" has become a nebulous term. There are many variations of the title "producer" as it often takes more than one person to produce a movie, each with a slightly different role. This can easily be seen during the credits of many films when the term "producer," including all variations of that term, is used by anywhere from one to a dozen or more people.

According to the Producer's Guild (PGA), producer titles change their definitions depending on the media that you are working on (i.e. video games, Blu-ray's, Internet videos, etc.). The Producer's Guild has worked hard to create a definitive guideline for producers to protect producer credits, and a more detailed list of definitions can be found on their website (http://www.producersguild.org/). In an attempt to simplify the definition of a producer and the variants of that title, we're going to start with some traditional definitions.

Executive Producer (EP)

The executive producer is usually the person who has financed or helped to acquire financing for the movie. Sometimes the executive producer credit is given to distributors, foreign sales agents, or a representative of the distribution company. Often, if the producer is partnering with a studio, the studio will give an executive producer credit to whomever they assign to oversee the production.

There may be more than one EP on the film, but a producer should be careful about how they hand out this title. If someone brings in $50,000 on a $5 million film, they would not normally be given an executive producer title, rather - they are considered an investor. The title of EP should be left for those who make a large percentage contribution to the funding or packaging of a film. (Packaging a film refers to putting together the team of lead cast and department heads who have committed to the film.) In the world of independent films where you may need to hand out titles to skilled actors or key crew members who are donating a significant amount of their time and energy in return for little or no monetary compensation, you may need to use the EP credit as a reward for their contribution. For example, if

8

your lead actor, (who is well known) agrees to lend their name and talent to a film with little to no pay, they may require an EP credit.

In regards to fundraising, the producer and the EP may work with a "finder" (i.e. someone who finds funds but isn't directly funding themselves). It is customary to give this person a finder's fee (a percentage of what they bring in). They are not, however, an executive producer unless they bring in a significant portion of the budget and this title has been negotiated with them.

Co-Executive Producer

Co-executive producer is a newer title, often given to those who have introduced a financing source, put in a smaller amount of financing than the executive producer, or brought in an element that made the film financeable, like a director or an actor.

Producer

A producer is traditionally the person who has optioned a script, developed the script, attached a director, hired a casting director, or has themselves packaged the talent, and assembled the key creative team needed to make the film. They are also usually the one who finds the executive producers, or they find the financing sources themselves. The producer is almost always the person who is involved in the decision making on a film from start to finish. They are also the person responsible for the film's success or failure. Due to the large number of responsibilities, a producer who is relatively new to the business would be wise to bring on a more experienced producer with a strong track record to help them.

Co-Producer

Co-producer is a fairly new credit that is sometimes given to someone who has donated their services to a lower budget project for less than their normal fees. It could be the writer, one of the principal cast members, casting directors, line producer, or anyone who has contributed services, or an element that helped move the film forward.

Associate Producer

This is a credit that is given to someone who has worked to set up the film in a lesser degree than the producer. They may have helped attach talent, secured production deals or a limited amount of the financing.

Line Producer

The line producer handles much of the day-to-day nuts and bolts operations on the film. They are brought in to set up and manage the budget, hire the below-the-line crew members, secure production deals, and manage equipment.

Supervising Producer

The supervising producer is a title usually given to someone brought in by a studio, distribution company, or those funding the picture to oversee the film on location. Depending on the contracts, this is a person the producer may have to report to directly.

What is a Producer Supposed to Do?

For the purpose of this book, we will mainly talk about the "Producer" function of filmmaking. At times, this may encompass some or all the other producer titles, depending on the size of the film. From time to time, we will discuss some of the other producing functions, but these will not be the main focus of this material.

The role of producer is both practical and artistic. The producer must balance the business needs of the film as well as the artistic needs. This is not easy. On one side is the director who leads the artistic vision for the film. The producer's job is to support the director and give them the best resources available given the budget constraints. On the other side, are the investors or the studio that demand to see a return on the money they've invested in the film. Sometimes, those two sides line up, other times they are directly opposite of each other and the producer must use their best judgment to determine how to complete the project giving concession to both sides. To this end, the role of the producer encompasses many jobs: visionary, storyteller, manager, cheerleader, diplomat, and networking expert. A great producer knows how to be each of these and has the ability to use their diplomatic skills to handle each of the various personalities both on set and off. They also understand how to help keep the team running smoothly, the actors happy, the studio happy, and the investors glad they invested. For those who like to multi-task, this can be the ultimate job.

The Producer as a Visionary

What does it mean to have a vision? Every great business venture starts with an idea of what that business will look like and passion for that idea. This idea and passion must inspire others to spend their money and/or their time helping the entrepreneur achieve that vision. In film, the producer must likewise be able to inspire people around them to invest in something not yet tangible.

In working with numerous crews on various-sized budgets, we have found that people want to work on a project they can put their creative energy or their financial resources into and feel that they will see a return on that investment. On lower budget films, the producer may need to pull favors for things like equipment, costumes, and locations to name a few items. They may also need to hire a cast and crew at less than their normal wages. Each of these "donations" of time and resources are investments into the vision. If the producer has a strong vision and a passion for the project, they will find it much easier to attract others to their cause.

If the producer doesn't have a strong vision and passion for the film, then they should reconsider working on it. Most feature film projects take a minimum of one year and up to five years or more to develop, produce, and release. At some point along the way, something will happen to challenge that vision and the producer may be the only one keeping the project together.

The Producer as a Storyteller

Great films often have a producer who is a great storyteller or at least understands the story process. The producer doesn't have to be a great writer, but it's important for them to know the basics of great storytelling so that they can guide the writer, the director, and the editor through the entire process. If you don't feel like you have a strong storytelling background, it would be wise to study the conventions of genre and story before attempting to break the mold and try something new. Some recommended books for understanding thoughts on structure and script writing are Christopher Vogler's *The Writers Journey*, Robert McKee's *Story*, Steven King's *On Writing*, Blake Snyder's *Save the Cat* series and the all-important book on grammar and style *The Elements of Style* by Strunk and White. Regardless of the genre, key items to look for in a script include: relatable themes and characters, an emotional hook, and a story structure that fits the genre of the film that is being produced.

Taking time to research as much as possible will help the producer find the type of storytelling that best fits their style. For the diehard storyteller, there are lecture series and books available that cover these topics by Robert McKee and Blake Snyder (Blake's lectures are now given by his students and colleagues since his passing).

The Producer as a Manager

We have found that that majority of producing time is spent on preparation and management. As a manager, the producer needs to understand funding and the budget, cast and crew, production resources, time limitations, trouble shooting, and marketing. Managing problems or "trouble shooting" is an area that may take much skill and patience. Unless the project is a short film or a made for the web video, the producer will live with the film (and with many of its partners) for several years. In that time, there will be an onslaught of issues that will get in the way of completing the project, including funding issues, staff problems, availability of cast, technical issues, bad weather, tapes lost or hard drives crashing - the potential problems are endless. The producer may not be able to account for every possible disaster that may befall the set, but with careful planning, they can know what to do when something goes wrong.

The producer will also be required to set an example both on set and off of how everyone should behave. The production team takes their energy and tone from the producer and the director. If the producer works hard, the team will work hard. If the producer encourages the team leaders, those leaders will encourage their staff.

To help avoid problems with your crew and to make your job as producer much easier, hire the right people for the right jobs. A good manager will meet with at least three people for each of the key production positions and make sure to check references. Each person should be skilled at what they do with at least several credits to their name, a great attitude, and strong work ethic.

The Producer as a Cheerleader

We have found that on any film (but especially on lower budget films where the cast and crew may be underpaid), motivating the cast and crew requires the producer to become a cheerleader to make the team feel excited about the production. Money isn't everything when it comes to creating films. People want someone to believe in and a project they can care about. They need to feel wanted and appreciated, and both of these are up to the producer. We've found that if the producer encourages everyone, thanks them for their hard work, and makes them feel like an important part of the project, the production team will go the extra mile ensuring a quality film.

Producer as a Diplomat

Diplomacy is the key to any smooth running set. It would be nice if everyone just got along on set, but the reality of life on a film production is that the producer may work with a large staff and long working hours. In this mix of artists, managers, and crew members, people get tired and personalities and egos clash. A good diplomat can stand in the middle of a disagreement, translating ideas and actions into solutions that best serve the film. Creative differences between departments, hot tempers or hurt feelings between actors and staff, conflicting schedules, and moving shoot days are just a few examples of issues the producer may face.

From time to time we've had issues with members of the production team, and in such cases, we've found that it's important to pull the relevant team member aside and deal with the issue in private, not in public. Remember that these people have come out to support your vision and should be treated with respect, even if they don't behave that way themselves. There are times, however, that after a confrontation it may be better to ask an uncooperative team member if they really want to be part of the project and if not, ask them to leave.

Producer as a Networker

First and foremost, the movie business is a people business. Officially it's called "networking," and it's one of the most vital duties of a producer. The producer needs to be able to interact with people, throw parties, lead meetings, have lunch with investors, and build relationships with production companies and studios.

When developing a film project, the producer often needs a large list of friends and acquaintances to call on. If you have a hard time networking, it's important to try a few things to break out of your shell. Start going to industry events in your areas. This could be as simple as local writers meetings, film festivals, or business management conferences. Every community has business development meetings, art events, or other social gatherings that you can attend. You don't have to live in a big city to start networking. Any event that gets you out into the public, meeting new people and potential partners, is good. While at the meetings, take notes on what you learn, whom you met, and in what area their skills may complement yours. Always bring a handful of business cards to give out, and don't leave without getting cards or contact info from people you may need   later.

PART II
DEVELOPMENT

"Talent is cheaper than table salt.
What separates the talented individual
From the successful one is a lot of hard work."

– Steven King

JULIA VERDIN and MATT DEAN

> "[I]t is the wine that leads me on, the wild wine
> that sets the wisest man to sing at the top of his lungs,
> laugh like a fool – it drives the man to dancing...
> it even tempts him to blurt out stories better never told"
>
> – Homer, The Odyssey

Chapter 3

How to Find a Story

Introduction to Development

Often producers will have multiple projects in development simultaneously. From a horror film, family film, true crime story and even a war picture, it's hard to know which one is going to find funding first, so many producers will consistently have several balls in the air at once. Development can take months or even years, and the battle for a successful film is won or lost in the development and pre-production stage. Development begins by finding a story you are passionate to produce. You then refine that story into workable screenplay, raise the development funds, assemble the key cast and crew, and build a business plan. As each of these areas is filled with a large amount of detail, we've broken each topic into its own chapter. We start with finding the story.

How to Know What to Look For

Development begins by finding a great story. Rarely is a good film made from a bad script. So how do you know a good story when you find it? We aren't going to go into the finite details of script writing as there are numerous books on the subject. Instead we suggest that the best way for a producer to get an understanding on the difference between a good script and a bad one, is to take time to read a few of these well-written books. Two books we suggest are *Save the Cat* by Blake Snyder and *Story* by Robert McKee. *Save the Cat* has great method for creating script structure. It lays out a 15-point beat sheet that any good story should include. *Story* will tell you what to look for in the details of the characters and the depth of the meaning behind the images and between the lines of text. This is a great way to add depth to the structure set up by Snyder. Other great books are *Screenplay* by Syd Field, and *The Writer's Journey* by Christopher Vogler.

The next way to recognize a great script (and this may seem obvious to some) is read great scripts. You can find every script that has been made into a film on the Internet or available for purchase through a bookstore like the *Writer's Store* in Los Angeles. Look for *Academy Award*-winning films and scripts that were big-budget or micro-budget indie hits. Find ones that fit closely with the style or genre you want to produce, and read as many as you can get your hands on. The more you read great scripts, the more you will know a good one when you see it.

Next, find out what other people think about the script. Trust your script to people whose opinions you respect, then listen carefully to how they respond to the story. If they say things like "it was sweet, cute, touching, depressing, some funny moments," or "interesting read," then your readers are being nice to you and the real feedback is that it wasn't any of those things. If you get that response as feedback, your script needs a lot of work. If, however, you hear "exciting! couldn't put it down, hilarious, I couldn't stop laughing, it was a page turner, provocative, can't stop thinking about it, heartbreaking, made me cry, I was so touched by the story or great concept!" now you have something worth spending your time and money developing.

Finally, get professional coverage. Coverage is when a film industry professional gives you notes on the script, telling you what works, what doesn't, and what might improve the script. This is a vital service that you may have to pay for. Numerous companies offer this service.

Once you have educated yourself on the basics of script writing, you can better trust your own judgment when reading a script. Once you've read dozens of great scripts, you begin to notice when an element works and when it doesn't, and you'll have a better feel for whether the audience might connect with the characters.

Submission Release Form

Before you look for a story from other writers, you need a submission release form. You will send this document to the writer to protect yourself from any possible future legal action. This will be used for any completed script, article, or story you received from an author or screenwriter. Over the course of your career, you may receive scripts with similar ideas, situations, or characters and it is important that you protect yourself from those who might think you have stolen their material. To help guard against that, the submission release form should state that the material submitted to you is original, that you don't guarantee you will produce their material, and that you may have already received or may receive in the future similar work. You can get a submission release form from an entertainment attorney. With your submission release form now in hand, you can begin to look for story ideas and scripts.

Where to Find a Story

1. The WGA (Writers Guild of America)

Most produced writers, or writers with a certain level of experience, are members of the Writers Guild of America. If you plan to option a script or hire a WGA writer, the company making the film needs to be WGA signatory (http://www.wga.org). You can look on the the WGA site to familiarize yourself with the rules associated with becoming signatory. If you plan to hire a WGA writer, there are set payment structures, depending on the budget level of the film. Even with a limited budget, you may find ways of working with union writers that won't exceed your budget constraints. With small-budget films in mind, the WGA has created new contracts that help a producer work with writers on low budgets and stay within union guidelines.

2. Non-union Writers

There are many talented writers who have either not yet been discovered or have not yet joined the guild. With non-WGA writers, you can dictate the terms of what you are willing to pay or optioning or purchasing material.

3. Literary Agents

Before good agents send you their writers' material, they want to know that the producer has the ability to finance a movie in addition to being able to pay option money for their client's script. If you are a new producer, look for smaller agencies with new writers who may be more willing to take a risk on someone without a track record.

4. Literary Managers

If you aren't an established producer or production company, then a writer's manager is often a little easier to deal with than agents. Managers have fewer clients than agents and likely have a little more time to talk with and send scripts to new producers.

5. Pitch Festivals

A pitch fest is an organized meeting between production companies and writers. They are often put together in larger cities and can be a good opportunity to meet prospective writers. At the pitch fest, production companies are given tables where they sit and listen to short pitches from writers. To qualify to be pitched to at these events, you need to be an established production company. For those starting out, it can be difficult to qualify. If you are qualified, this can be a great way to find new up-and-coming writers as you have the advantage of hearing pitches before requesting the material. To find out about qualifying to hear pitches, contact the pitch fest you wish to attend.

6. Magazine or News Articles (True Life Stories)

Current news can be a great place to find raw material for a script. If you want to use material you find in a magazine article or on a website, you must acquire the rights from the appropriate parties. If the publisher purchased the article from the author, you have to work through the publisher. To cover yourself, you should contact both the author and the publisher to make sure you have the correct information on who owns the rights to the story.

A script taken from actual news accounts of a true story may be considered in the public domain. A producer may risk a lawsuit, however, if the script is written using speculation or hearsay about an individual or if the life rights to the story are not purchased. Whenever the rights to a story are in question, a producer should always seek legal advice to insure they are protected.

7. Books

Literary properties can be great basis for screenplays. If you find a book you are in love with, you need to contact the publisher and see if the film rights are available. If the publisher is not handling the film rights, they can usually direct you to the appropriate person. Sometimes the writer has an agent or lawyer who handles media rights.

8. Public Domain Material

A good option for anyone who does not have funding to obtain rights to a current book is to look for material that is public domain. This can be a poem, song, book, or other material that has gone past its copyright date or was created prior to copyright laws. Books like Charles Dickens' *Christmas Carol*, and portions of Sir Arthur Conan Doyle's *Sherlock Holmes* series, for example, are both in public domain and have made great films. An advantage to well-known public domain stories is that the material already has an audience, which gives you built-in branding. It also gives you a ready- made story and characters that you just need to adapt for the screen. There are long lists of public domain material online, and you can often get *Kindle* versions of public domain books for free.

9. Script Web Services

Another way to obtain scripts is to register with one of the web services like *Virtual Pitch Fest* or *InkTip*. These services are free to producers. Through these web services, writers submit a synopsis to producers and ask if they would like to read the script.

10. Script Competition Winners

Writing competitions have scripts where the winners or finalists have already been read and considered of merit by industry professionals. For access to this material, contact festivals that feature the genre of scripts that you are looking to produce and tell them you would like to talk with their finalists. If you have trouble getting through to contest officials, you may be able to find a list of their finalists on the contest's website. You can then use IMDB or other industry tools to locate contact information for the writer or their agent. In the past, we have found that competitions like the Academy *Nicholl Fellowship* through the *Academy of Motion Picture Arts and Sciences* are extremely helpful in finding great talent.

11. Industry Networking Events

In many cities around the world, writers and industry professionals get together to discuss the world of film and television. These events can be helpful to producers to connect with writers who are actively seeking producers for their material. If you find someone whose script fits what you are looking for, go through the same process of sending him or her a submission release form, or make a request through his or her manager or agent.

12. Scripts from Known Writers

If you can afford to hire a known writer, go through the movies you like and research who wrote the script. You can find the writer's agent or manager through IMDB pro and contact them to see what other material they have available. As is the case with any agent or manager, you will most likely have to show that you are a proven producer with the ability to fund the type of project that can afford that writer.

13. Film Schools or Writing Courses

Film schools and writing courses can be a way to access writers who are looking to see their material on the screen. A good way to get submissions is by contacting the school or tutoring service and post a message on their website message board or physical message board at the school if they have one. If you have a very small budget, you may be able find someone talented who is at the start of their career and willing to option their project for a low fee.

14. Personal Experiences

Some of the best stories can come out of your own personal experiences. Family members, people you grew up with, stories from your home town - all of these can lead to insightful stories that may resonate more with an audience than something completely fictional.

Writing Your Own Script

Not everyone is meant to write the script that they will then produce. There are a significant number of producers and directors who don't write the movies they create. If this isn't for you, then skip ahead, but if you want to know a few things about creating your own script, here is where you start.

First, create a log-line for the film. The log-line is one sentence that sums up the world, the main character(s), and the main character's desire and conflict. This tool is often used in the sale and marketing of a film and can be a great way to tell if you have a compelling story. Before pounding out the entire script, tell that log-line to a few people and gauge their reaction. If you can't sum up your premise in one sentence and get people interested, then you may struggle to find an audience for your story down the road.

Once you have your log-line, develop the idea a little further by writing a paragraph that sums up the story and again, read it to some friends or family, or better yet a stranger. Your friends and family may not be honest with you, and the best way to tell if your story is interesting is a stranger's reaction.

Once you have a paragraph that sums up the film, you are ready to lay out the structure. There are several forms of structure used by many Hollywood writers. One good structure is the 15-point method laid out in the book, *Save the Cat*. A second is in the book *A Writer's Journey* by Christopher Vogler. Whether you use either of these or some other method for structuring your script, you need to know that structure is not the enemy of creativity. It is the guideline that frees you to create a story that is relatable. When you release a film to the audience, you are trying to communicate with them. Communication relies on your audience understanding or at least following the story they see on screen, and that type of understanding needs structure. Confusion over your characters, plot lines, and themes will alienate your audience.

Once you've laid out the structure, you're ready to fill in the gaps by adding the action and the dialog. Be sure to use script software like *Final Draft* or *Screenwriter*. Using *MS Word* or a similar program will not give you a professional-looking script, and it will take time to format that should be spent on creativity.

We'll leave most of the script writing instruction to the books we've suggested, but here are a couple of things to look for when you write. First, don't explain the action with the dialog. Talk about it or show it, don't do both. Second, don't include a huge description of something that is going to be left to the art department. Make your descriptions short and sweet so you can get to the main point of the story. Finally, make the dialog sound conversational. Listen to how other people talk and emulate that with the script and then have a few friends read through the dialog with you so you can tell if it sounds real or not.

Now that you have a finished script, rewrite it, and then rewrite it again. Once you've made it the best you can possibly make it, it's important to get coverage on it as you would with any script from another author as this is the only real way to find out if your film is viable or not. If you treat your script like you would any other and not like a precious child that cannot be altered, you will have a much better chance to finding out if it will truly reach your audience.

A Script for a Lower Budget Film

If at the beginning of this process you already know that your film is going to be a low-budget project, it would be wise to create a story and script that can be completed in that budget range. You won't know the exact cost until you do a full breakdown and budget, but there are several ways to help keep the costs down. The ideal scripts for low-budget films are what we call "four people in a room" scripts. These are films like *The Breakfast Club*, or in the horror genre *Saw*, where there are a limited number of actors in a limited number of locations and a limited size to the scenes.

First, keep the cast to a minimum. The more people you have in the script, the larger your crew needs to be to accommodate them.

Second, keep the number of locations to a minimum. The more locations you have, the more the entire film company has to move, requiring time to tear down, relocate, and set back up again.

Third, keep the number of scenes down as each scene will require a new set up for the camera and crew. Even if you are shooting documentary style with little to no lighting and a hand-held camera, you still need to reset your crew and actors for each scene, which takes time. Also, be careful about trying to shoot too many large scenes. A scene with two actors standing on the side of the road talking may only take a few seconds to set up, but a scene on a large set with 40 extras, a rain storm, and a car crash could take hours or even days to set up.

Each additional cast member, crew member, and company move adds to the total cost of your film. Keeping the script to around 90 pages (each page represents around one minute of screen time) keeps down both the amount of time needed to shoot the film and the amount of time needed to finish the film in post-production.

JULIA VERDIN and MATT DEAN

"There are no rules in filmmaking, only sins.
And the cardinal sin is dullness."

– Frank Capra

Chapter 4

You Found a Story, Now What?

Over the years we've looked at thousands of ideas for films and read hundreds of scripts. Of those few gold nuggets we've found over the years, how did we decide which film we wanted to produce?

Are You Passionate About This Story?

You are about to spend anywhere from one to five or even ten years on developing, shooting, and releasing a film. You need to ask yourself if you really love the story or if it's something you are going to be tired of a few months down the line.

Is There an Audience for This Film?

Knowing your audience is key to determining if you are going to be able to make your film a success. Everyone wants what is called a "four quadrant film," which means it appeals to pretty much everyone. (The four quadrants are: female under 25, female over 25, male under 25, male over 25.) The problem is that usually only the studio blockbuster films reach this audience. Indie films normally hit a very specific audience depending on the subject and genre, and you need to know who that is so you know the potential value of the film and how to market it.

Does the Story Have a Leading Role That Will Attract an A-List Actor?

Actors love a great role, especially if it's something they haven't done before. To attract a name actor to your film, they will either need a great role, a good paycheck, or, ideally, both. If you don't have a lot to offer financially, then the story needs to have an amazing role to offer instead.

Is the Script Strong Enough to Attract a Good Director?

Many known directors look for a film that attracts them on a personal level. They want a project that challenges them and gives them the best chance to express their artistic style and ideas. They also need to believe that the film has a chance to be both a critical and commercial success, as their next directing job depends on the performance of their last film. If the script or basic story is not strong enough to interest them, you need to take another look to determine if the story is as good as you think it is.

How Marketable Is the genre?

Both your investors and the distribution company are going to want a film that is easy to sell. The biggest sales point on a film is the genre. In the past, action films have been the highest valued films for the film market place. Depending on the region you sell to, the second highest may be science fiction, horror, or family/kids films, followed by dramas and comedies. Why don't dramas and comedies do as well? Because each territory you sell to will have different ideas on morals, values, and humor, and often the language differences can be a barrier. For example, a comedy written about the streets of Detroit may mean very little to someone in Germany because comedies often don't translate well into foreign language. A drama based on and around Japanese culture may work well in Japan, but it will not have as much value in South Africa or other territories. Along with this, some territories and broadcasters have content restrictions for anything from nudity to story content and certain propaganda. These restrictions may limit where your film can sell and thus how much it can make back given those restrictions. If a producer has an audience-specific film, this does not mean they won't find funding. They would just have to limit the budget to a level that can be supported by that audience and look for funding sources who want to reach that audience.

Does the Story Have Great "Trailer" Moments?

The first marketing tool for any audience is the poster and the trailer. As you look at the story, can you see great moments in the script that will give you the scenes needed for the trailer to sell the film to your desired audience?

Does the Story Fit with Your Idea of Success for This Picture?

Your goal for the success of your film must be considered as you judge the viability of the script. Does this script lend itself to the type of film you know that you need to make to be successful or are you finding excuses as to why it will work even though it doesn't fit? If it fits, move forward. If it doesn't, change the story or change what type of success you expect it to have.

The Idea Works, Now What?

To produce a film, you need to have the rights to the story and the script. To do this, you have to "option" the story and or screenplay rights from whoever owns the rights (an option means that you temporarily own the rights to the story and the cost of that option is negotiable). We recommend that you option material for at least two years. It can easily take two years (or more) to develop an existing screenplay, and you may need one or more rewrites, which can take months to finish. During that time, you will need to create a budget and schedule, secure the main cast, find possible locations, make a business plan for investors, and raise funding for the project. If you option the property for less than two years, your option becomes a ticking clock where you have little time to complete all that is needed to close your funding and start production on your film.

It's wise to have an option extension clause in the option agreement in case funding takes longer than anticipated. For an additional payment, you have the option to renew the script or story for a further agreed time period. Along with the extension clause, you should also include a paragraph giving you the right to purchase the screenplay and/or story rights for an agreed price once you receive funding for the film. The total purchase amount will be worked out between you and the writer or their manager/agent, and is often based on the overall budget of the film. The WGA has guidelines concerning purchase prices for scripts according to various budget levels, and you should consult with them for the current rates.

Basing your script on pre-existing material can be a little more complicated. For example: If you find a short story in a magazine that you like, you might option that material from the author for two years (with the option to purchase upon receiving funding for an agreed amount), and then hire a writer to write the screenplay as a "work for hire" so that you have the rights to the underlying material and own the screenplay. You then shop that screenplay to production companies or studios, or to your investors. Upon obtaining funding, you purchase the rights to the story from the original author so that the entire underlining property and the script is now yours. If your option runs out before you obtain funding, the screenplay is still yours (as it was a work-for-hire), but you cannot do anything with it unless you renew the option with the original story author.

If you have optioned a completed script, then you are ready to move on to the pre-production stage. If you are optioning a short story, book, or magazine article, you have to hire a writer to write the script.

Hiring a Writer

The "Where to Find a Story" list we shared in the previous chapter can also be helpful for finding a writer. As you interview writers, it's important to identify one with the correct style for the screenplay you want to produce by asking to see writing samples. This is necessary because not all writers are good at writing all genres (e.g. a great comedy writer may not necessarily be able to write a really good dramatic thriller).

After you see a writing sample, try to get the writer to give you a detailed "beat" treatment. The beats are the main story points in the script. The beat treatment describes the key characters and outlines and describes the key storyline. This sample will show you what to expect from the script when the writer delivers it. You may need to pay a writer before they give you a beat treatment. It would be wise to sign a work-for-hire agreement with them at this point so any story developed at this stage belongs to you.

Choosing a Title

The title of the film is the first thing people will see and is one of the most important elements of selling the film. People need to at least have an idea of what to expect from the film when they read the title. *Texas Chainsaw Massacre* is a good example of a title that tells what to expect from the film.

Everything you do from here out will be tied to that title, your business plan, website, posters, etc. As you make a list of possible titles, ask your friends and the distribution company if any of the titles fit. Also check to see if there have been other films with the same title in recent years. Try to find something that stands out so that you don't get lost in the many films coming out this year named "Love" or "Awakening." (To date, there are thirty-four films on IMDB named "Awakening" and 70 films named "Love.")

In the current marketplace, naming your film with a number or starting with the letter "a" helps it get better placement in the video-on-demand (VOD) market, but don't use that as your only reason for naming your film. As the VOD market becomes saturated with films named in this manner, sellers will find new ways to randomize the film selections.

Fine Tuning the Script

In our many years of producing, we've had to ask over and over again for script rewrites to help us achieve our objectives or because of studio notes on what they would like to see. Fine tuning the script doesn't have to be a touchy subject, provided that you have had a discussion with the writer at the beginning of the process letting them know that rewrites may be expected.

Your agreement with the screenwriter should detail the writer's compensation and what is expected of their writing services, including a provision for rewrites, notes from the producer(s), the studio, production company, sales company, lead actor, or the director. If you expect them to do rewrites, include how much they will be paid for rewrites or how many rewrites you get under the initial amount paid to the writer.

If the budget is tight, talk with the writer to see if they are willing to work on rewrites for a deferment (payment is made when the film receives financing) so that the script meets the standards required by your financiers. Don't count on using this method, however, when dealing with a seasoned writer.

When setting up the agreement, make a timeline for completion of each draft of the script so that the writer knows when each draft is expected and the producer knows when the script will be ready to send out to desired cast and directors. Even when you get to a point where you like the script, the financiers, the production company, or studio you are working with may ask for additional rewrites. This can lead to an endless number of rewrites that the producer has to pay for.

If you are working with a studio or a production company, ask if they would be willing to pay for any further rewrites. While this is not always easy, it avoids a situation of the producer incurring more cost without a firm financing commitment. If the studio truly likes the film, they may be willing to option the story from you and pay for additional work on the script. Keep in mind, however, that the studio owns what it pays for unless you have a contract with them that allows any rewrites revert to you if the studio drops the picture or fails to come up with the funding. The option from the studio or production company should be for a clear length of time and should also contain a reversion clause that if they did not end up financing the film in a set period of time, the rights of the material reverts back to the producer. When negotiating the deal, try to ensure that this reversion does not contain any further obligation to the studio, nor should the contract contain an amount to be paid to the studio as a refund for what they spent on the project. Though this may not always be possible, it is worth asking for so that if you have to go elsewhere for funding, you are not encumbered by a heavy cost attached to the project.

Chain of Title

"Chain of title" is an industry term for having all the rights to your screenplay and is one of the most important items to keep organized when finding your material. This list of paperwork begins with the option of a screenplay or script and ends with a copyright giving you and/or your production company ownership of the film. To prove ownership, you need to keep track of where you found your material and who you paid. You should retain copies of all the agreements. It's important that nothing ties up the rights to the script or the story and that no one but the owner can legally claim the material belongs to them. There have been many great film projects that were never produced because of chain of title problems. To keep from having a chain of title problem, here are a few tips:

1. If the screenplay is based on a public domain book, the script should be registered with the WGA (Writers Guild of America). This keeps the rights to the particular screenplay adaptation of the book clearly in the hands of the producer.

2. If you have written your own screenplay and you hire or ask other writers to do additional work or any type of polish or creative work to your screenplay, get them to sign a work-for-hire writing agreement. You should pay them something, even if it a friend doing you a favor. Just paying them one dollar helps you keep a clear record that their work was a work for hire and that you own all work done on the screenplay. Keep track of all receipts and all work-for-hire agreements.

3. If you've optioned a script from a writer or from another producer who owns the script, you should have an option agreement with that owner. The agreement should clearly state that the owner has all rights to the material in all media in perpetuity and that there are no liens (money owed) against the project from anyone who previously optioned the material. A lien can exist as a result money owed to previous option holders for payment of rewrites, additional writers or other development costs.

4. Make sure to get what is called a "Certificate of Authorship" from the writer which says that the writer is the sole author of the material.

5. If you have optioned true story rights, or a magazine article, news story, or any other life rights from an individual, you need to include that agreement and rights purchase as part of the chain of title paperwork. If a story came from a news report and is public knowledge, you may not have to option the life rights from the people involved. It's important, however, to consult an attorney before proceeding without any rights to a true story.

6. Keep all your original chain of title documentation in a safe place. Any financier or studio or bank may want to see all the chain of title paperwork before spending money on the film. You will also need to provide it to the insurance company and to the bond company if you have to get a completion bond on your film. SAG-AFTRA and other union guild may want to see this paperwork, too, if you enter an agreement with them.

7. Get legal advice on making sure your chain of title is in order before proceeding with the project.

Clearance Report

The final item needed is a script clearance report from a clearance company or your legal counsel. A legal consultant creates this report by looking through every aspect of the script to let you know if there are any copyright or clearances issues that need to be dealt with prior to filming. By noting any problems with items like characters' names, products used, defamation of character etc., the clearance report helps you determine if there are any changes that need to be made before you go into pre-production on your film.

"It's clearly a budget.
It's got lots of numbers in it."

– George W. Bush

Chapter 5

Development Funds: Why You Need Them

Whether the producer is using their own money, getting a loan, or has raised funding from investors, they almost always need a development fund. If the producer is working on a film that requires investors, they will need to have enough money or resources to put together a business plan. To do this, they may need to spend money to hire a writer, hire a lawyer, pay someone to breakdown the script, prepare a schedule and a budget, get sales estimates, do market research, build a website, pay for an LLC (Limited Liability Company), and possibly pay to attach an actor to the film.

Some of the expenses a producer may run into are:

1. Research

The story you have selected may need further research. For many true stories or documentaries, research can take months or years. This could be accomplished free online, or you may need to purchase books, visit a location, interview experts. You need clarity as to what research your particular project needs and budget accordingly.

2. Optioning or Purchasing a Script

If you want to use someone else's script for your film, you have to either purchase or option the rights. Purchasing means you own the script until you sell the rights of the film to a distribution company upon finishing the film. Optioning means that you own the rights for a limited time after which the rights revert back to the author. If you have a relationship with a writer, you may be able to option a script for little to no money. However, for a good script, you will likely have to pay for an option, which could range from a few hundred dollars to thousands of dollars, depending on the status of the writer.

3. Hiring a Lawyer

It is advisable to consult an entertainment lawyer on every matter of film production, including contracts, clearances, and setting up the business entity to make the film. During development, the attorney will help you secure rights to the property (film script, book, or idea), making sure that you retain the rights until you are ready to sell the film, and they will help you with any legal advice and paperwork as you work on the business plan and bringing in investors.

4. Hiring a Line Producer

To create the business plan, you need to create a breakdown of the script, an initial budget for the film, and a tentative shooting schedule. If you don't know how to do those things and you have a budget for it, you should hire an experienced line producer.

5. Business Proposal/ Business Plan

The business proposal outlines the details of what film you are going to do, who is part of your team, the costs involved, how you are going to raise the money, and how it is going to be paid back. In the chapter on business plans, we explain how to put together the business proposal, which some producers do on their own. You may, however, chose to have a more experienced producer help you put this together as well as have your legal team look over the documents and add any needed legal disclaimers. A full business plan will contain greater details than the business proposal and include additional material required by investors and government regulations.

6. Play-or-Pay Option for Actors

If you want to attach a "name" actor to your film (someone whose name is recognized by the general public and can usually fill a theater), you need money for "play-or-pay." This means that the producer guarantees payment to the actor whether the film happens or not, and the actor guarantees they will appear or "play" in the film if the picture happens within a certain time frame. Like the option payment, this fee range depends on the status of the actor.

The standard play-or-pay payment for actors is 10 percent of their agreed fee and usually comes with a date when the remaining 90 percent will be paid. If possible, the producer should try to make the remainder payable after closure of financing. This way if the film does not happen, you only lose 10 percent rather than the entire fee.

7. Limited Liability Company (LLC) or Other Business Entity

Normally a film needs to be run through a separate legal business entity for the receipt of funding, payments of expenses, and possibly the payouts when the film is sold, plus it gives the producer a layer of protection from any legal issues that might arise. The legal structure and contractual arrangements for each film as well as associated costs can vary from state to state and country to country, so it is important to seek appropriate legal and accounting advice to determine the best way to set up your business.

8. Website

A website is a great source of information for the investors, actors, and studio partners. Purchase a domain name that fits the name of your film, and set up a website using images, sound, or video that conveys the artistic vision of your film. Include the names and info of your team members, any cast that has been attached, a summary of the film, and a "lite" version of your business plan. You should be careful, however, about giving out all the financial information on the film. Rather than giving all the details on your website, you can save the detailed information on a secured website, or in a PDF that can be downloaded by your investors.

9. IMDB Pro Membership

As you begin to research writers, actors, directors, and production companies, you need to have easy access to their contact information. One of the better sources for this is IMDB pro. Their yearly fee is reasonable and will give you easy access to much of what you will need to find later, plus it's a good source for researching information that you may want to include in the business plan, like the box-office gross on films similar to yours.

Accounting

To be able to give account for every dollar spent on the film, keep track of every receipt from the beginning. As payments are made for anything related to the film, the producer should keep both a hard copy of every receipt and every check paid and a digital ledger to hand off to the bookkeeper or accountant once in pre-production. Since you will likely be the first investor in the film, you want to insure that each dollar you spend is recorded and then recouped out of the film's budget when the film is funded. Also, keep a copy of any agreements made in a file that you will later need to hand over to the distribution company.

Development Funding Sources

Funding for development can be really difficult, especially for the first-time producer. There are, however, some places to go to that can get you started. In addition to going to production companies or other professional investors, other good sources from which you can raise funds for development include crowd funding websites, angel investors, family and friends, a fundraising party, government grants, local film commission incentives, and filmmaking contests and awards.

In our chapter on funding, we talk about many of the principles that can work for development funding. However, there are a few areas that differ, one of which is development grants. To help promote film production, some governments and film commissions offer grants for development. For example, in England, the *British Film Institute* has offered various development grants for British filmmakers, and in Canada various regions have offered regional development funds for Canadian production companies. The best way to find out about any government programs is to find a film commission close to you or in the country or state where you want to film, and ask about any programs that may apply to you and what is required to qualify.

Another source of funding can be film festival script writing contests where your script could win money toward developing your film. The Sundance Institute offers a writers lab that has produced many great screenplays that often get made into films. Before you enter, find out the details of entering and restrictions. If you win, be sure that those restrictions fit with what you want to do with your film.

Trouble Finding Funds

If you have an extremely low budget or are having trouble raising development funds, there are some creative ways to put together a team with limited or no resources. There are many wonderfully talented writers, directors, actors, and technicians who are struggling to be discovered. Attending short film, music video festivals or film school showcases are great ways to find fresh talent eager to break out and looking for a producer to take a chance on them. Working with an eager but unchallenged team may not give a producer the large budget they were hoping for, but it's a great place to start, and that team may be willing and able to take risks that another team may not.

"None of the pictures I take a risk in cost a lot, so it doesn't take much for them to turn a profit. We don't deal in big budgets. We know what we want and we shoot it and we don't waste anything. I never understood these films that cost twenty, thirty million dollars when they could be made for half that. Maybe that's because no one cares. We care."

– Clint Eastwood

Chapter 6

Breakdown and Budget
(The Value vs. the Cost of the Film)

Determining the Monetary Value of the Film

Before you decide how much you can spend on your film, you need to get an idea of how much it has the potential to earn. It's all about value vs. cost, market research, and budgeting. For those of you who just want to do something creative, the business part of filmmaking can all be a bit like pulling teeth, but don't skip over this. Understanding the value vs. cost is something we have come to increasingly appreciate as our careers have progressed.

Value vs. cost is the difference between a producer making money and losing it. Simply put, if you make a film for $1 million and get less than $3 million in total sales, you've lost money. For those of you who feel that the math doesn't add up, here's the explanation. Rule of thumb for any film that you sell through a distribution company is a ratio of 3 to 1. Three dollars earned equals one dollar back to the production company and the investors. For example, if your distribution company makes a sale to Amazon, and Amazon sells the film for $10, Amazon takes 40 percent, leaving the distribution company with $6 out of which they take their fee of 30 percent plus any marketing fees (possibly another 10 percent). This leaves you with around $3.60 out of a $10 sale, which is just over a 3 to 1 ratio. If you are able to calculate that the film will likely give you $1 million in sales, you should think about making the film for $330,000 or you could risk not making the investors' money back.

How then do you know what your film is worth? It comes down to three simple things that every distribution company is going to ask. What is the genre? Who is in it? What does it look like?

What is the genre?

The first question deals with the genre of the film. As we mentioned earlier, certain types of films have a better chance of selling than others. Though this fluctuates year to year, you can still look at the overall trends to determine probable sales, plus talking with distribution companies will give you what genres are selling well. Action films are usually a safe bet, but only if you can keep the cost down, which can be difficult if you want to include all the fights, chases, or explosions that an action audience expects. Horror films sell well unless the marketplace is saturated with them, which happens from time to time. Family films do exceptionally well, particularly for holidays and primetime TV sales, but they often require a major A-list actor to boost sales. Dramas, on the other hand, rarely do well even if the film has an A-list cast and an award-winning script. If you are thinking about producing a drama, be extra cautious about the budget level and be sure your script can attract A-list talent. If you want to make money with your film, don't produce a drama unless the script is brilliant and has been vetted by several reliable coverage companies. Does this mean that no one should ever produce a drama? Of course not. It just means that the producer should know what parts of the market like dramas and how much they usually pay for them and then keep the budget in balance with the sales potential.

Who is in it?

Increasingly, distribution companies are chasing after the same named actors for each film as few and fewer actors are able to attract an audience by their name alone. A great actor and even a great director cannot guarantee a great film. They can, however, give the distribution company a better chance of selling the film than a cast of actors with no following. The problem with hiring a well-known director is that their fee is going to be much higher. That, paired with the cost of the A-list actors, may add up to more than the distribution company says the picture is worth. To solve this you need to work with the distribution company to determine how much any particular director will help the sale of the film and adjust the budget accordingly.

We'll talk about casting in more detail, but for now, the best thing you can do is make a list of the lead characters in the script and name four or five actors who would be great creatively in each role. Talk with your distribution company and get their suggestion as to which actors they think will help the sale of the film and which ones will not. This should not be an unrealistic list of actors that you have no way of contacting, but a list of people you will be able to reach through their managers, agents, or through the casting director. When we get to casting, we'll talk more about how to contact A-list actors and what they are looking for. Does this mean you can't make a film with all unknown actors? No, but you are going to lower the potential value by casting unknown actors. If this is the route you want to take, look for actors with star potential, meaning that they have the charisma, the drive, and the work ethic to break out or be discovered. If the actor gets cast in a major TV series or larger budget film down the road, then your film will benefit from the actor's increasing name recognition and career achievements. Often, a great casting director will have a good idea of which young actors are on the fast track to become notable stars.

What does it look like?

Simply put, quality matters. Competition around the world grows every year, and there are brilliant directors and cinematographers in India, China, Spain, Japan - everywhere you look, new filmmakers are leaving their mark on the industry. The chance of a film with low-quality production value making money in today's market is extremely slim. To add value to your film, you need to shoot with a style and a format that the distribution company thinks is sellable. In addition, you need high-quality audio and the ability to add foreign a language track to the film. We will talk about this more in the segment on post-production. Even if you are filming a found footage movie, your best bet is to shoot on the highest quality format available given the budget level you are restricted to. You can always degrade the footage later if needed, but if you don't shoot the film on an acceptable format, you will lose a large number of foreign sales.

Here's how you add all of this up to determine the potential value of the film. Let's take the example of a political thriller where you have a strong male and female lead and an unknown director. Let's say that the story and the budget aren't quite strong enough to attract A-list actors, but you were able to bring on board several fairly well-known B-list actors. This at least gives you minimum returns in foreign countries. If for total world market for TV licensing, DVD and Blu-ray sales, VOD and SVOD, and pay TV, the distribution company was paid $900,000 for all the rights and sales, the return to the producer would be around $300,000.

The distribution company can tell you the possible best-case and worst-case sales number scenario for each market. Whatever numbers you end up with, you will want to use the distribution company's worst-case scenario to minimize the risk to your investors. The truth of the performance of any film is going to depend on how well your director executes the picture and how well the audience reacts to the film. With such a large number of variables, there are no guarantees that a film will do well. However, with experience and planning, you should have a good idea what the potential sales are of a film in any genre.

To raise the value of the film, you can shoot a more widely appealing genre, hire a known cast, buy a really strong script, and hire a director with a good track record of successful movies. In addition, finding a U.S. distribution company willing to get behind the film and willing to give you a certain level of theatrical release along with a good marketing campaign will help boost sales numbers around the world and could mean the difference between good sales and losing money.

By using this method to determine the potential value of the film, you'll quickly see that to minimize risk with an unknown director and cast, you need to keep the budget down. If the director does an amazing job and the film is well reviewed, you may get good offers for distribution and do well financially. But if the opposite happens, at least you have minimized the risk to the investors.

The Cost of the Film

Now that you have placed an approximate financial value on the picture, it's time to find the cost of your film. This is referred to in industry terms as the budget. For some of you on an ultra-low budget, this is going to be the cost of pizzas and a case of water for your friends. For others on a larger budget, this is going to be hundreds of thousands if not millions of dollars. No matter how large or small your film, you need to go through this process to determine if your film's costs fit the value. If the cost is higher than the value, you need to adjust the script and the budget or lower your expectations for the picture.

To create a budget for your film, you need to create a full breakdown of all the elements needed in the film, as well as a pre-production, production, and post- production schedule. Each of these items will later be included in your business plan, which will outline the elements of your picture in a way that can be presented to investors or production companies. If you don't know much about a film crew and who or who not to include in the budget for a particular film size, we've created a full list and breakdown of crew positions and duties in chapter 10.

The Breakdown

The first step to creating your budget is breaking down the script. The breakdown is a list of items that the producer or a line producer creates that shows everything needed in each scene so that you can go back and make an accurate schedule and a budget. From the actors to the locations to the props, this list has to include every detail. If you don't have experience doing this, you can use the following list to help. If you can afford it, however, it might be wise to hire an experienced line producer who can more accurately assess the elements needed from each scene.

The breakdown includes:

1. All characters

Main cast first, supporting cast, "under fives" (characters with five lines or fewer), and extras

2. All locations and how many scenes are at each location

3. Props

These are the items that your characters touch during any of the scenes.

4.Special effects

These are the in-camera effects that will be shot on location and require a special effects team (e.g. fire, water, explosives, squibs, etc.).

5. Visual effects

These are effects created in post-production that often require special planning during filming and a VFX team (e.g. compositing, green screen, animation, etc.).

5. Stunts

This includes any specialty items, props, and or vehicles that are used in each stunt, how many stunt performers are involved in each stunt, and if any special construction is needed.

6. Sets that need to be built

7. Set dressings

This means everything you need to bring to your set to make it look how you want it to look like, including paintings on the walls, lamps, chairs, etc.

8. Costumes for each character

Even if you have your cast bring their own clothes, list what they will need: T-shirt, jeans, suit and tie, dress, etc. When characters are in scenes involving stunts, you need wardrobe for the stunt doubles, too, and usually two-three sets of that wardrobe in case the stunt needs to be repeated.

9. Animals

If any animals appear in any scenes, you need to make a list of all animals and also hire an animal wrangler.

10. Special equipment

A list of any special equipment needed for camera or lighting such as a car camera mount or underwater camera

11. Picture vehicles

Any cars, helicopters, or special trucks

The breakdown is usually written on a single page for each scene. This form includes each of the items listed above as well as the production title, date, producer's and director's names, contact name, and who it was prepared by. You can see a sample breakdown in our resource guide. Sample breakdowns are easy to find online and can be imported into a Word document. If you can't find one, you can write the items in a list like so:

Scene 1, EXT - Street Outside Old House - Day

Karen comes running out of the house as Tom smoking a cigar, drives slowly up street, as he sees her, he speeds up and runs her over. Jill jumps out of another passing car and rushes to Karen's crumpled body. Tom drives off with his foot hard on the pedal.

Cast: Jill, Tom, Karen
Stunt coordinator
1 stunt double for Karen
1 stunt driver to double Tom
Extras: 10 passers-by on street, upscale area type
Jill's wardrobe
Tom's wardrobe
Karen wardrobe x3 as will need extra doubles of wardrobe for stunt double and assume you may need to do more than one take
Props: Tom's glasses and cigar
Vehicles: 2 action cars, 6 other cars parked on street
Medic on set and ambulance standing by
Special car camera mount to shoot Tom's POV of Karen

As you can see, the breakdown gives you a precise count of characters, locations, props, and everything you will need to properly budget and schedule the film. If you only have two characters in one scene for a short film for the web, it will take you five minutes to breakdown whereas a 90 to 120-page script will take much longer. The reason this is important for any size project is that even if you are getting your cast and props and costumes for free, you still have to know exactly what you need. This breakdown will also be used to get the right information to every department on the film. The location manager, casting director, props department, etc. - all need to know what is needed and when. If you have hired a director already, have them go over the breakdown to be sure that everything they need is included.

The Schedule

Once you have a full breakdown, it's time to schedule the production. This is not necessarily the exact days you want to shoot, (e.g. Jan. 5 to March 7) but instead is the number of days you are going to shoot. In addition, this includes the number of days you need for official pre-production, (not including the producers development time) and post-production. By using the cast list, number of scenes, locations, and other breakdown information, you can determine how much time you will need, various actors, crew members, studio space, locations, and how long you will need to rent any equipment.

This will not be your final schedule, just a rough idea of what you are going to attempt. Your final schedule will be put together with the line producer and first AD during pre-production. To help with scheduling, it's recommended that you buy an industry-standard scheduling program. Currently, the industry standard for budgeting and scheduling is *Movie Magic*. Make sure to write off the cost of the software as part of your development costs. This software inputs the list of scenes from your script and gives you what are called "strips," which is one line for each scene. You can then take each strip and move them around to different days of shooting to line up filming the same locations at the same time. If you don't have or can't afford the software, you can print strips of each scene, cut them out, and place them on a cork board with thumbtacks. This, by the way, was the way scheduling was done for decades prior to the software version.

Pre-production

How many days do you need to prepare prior to shooting? One day? One month? Six weeks or longer? Do you need to round up a large number of costumes? Does the location need to be prepped? Do your actors need rehearsal time? How long each of these things will take depends on how many people you have helping you and how big your film is.

If you are shooting four people talking in a room, it may only take you a couple weeks to find and rent the location, prep the actors, gather the costumes, and schedule your crew. But if you are filming a war epic with hundreds of people, massive sets, and a lot of costumes, it could easily take you six months of preparation. Using your breakdown of what is needed, estimate how many days it will take each department to do its job. That becomes your pre-production schedule.

Production

You need to determine how many pages you can shoot per day and how many days you will need to complete production. An average indie feature with a budget under $500,000 can afford to take 12 to 18 days to film, and shoots four to eight pages per day. On larger studio pictures, you may have a lot more time to film so you may not need to get through as many pages per day.

The number of pages depends on how many of those scenes are action sequences with numerous setups, (a setup is a camera move from one position to another usually with lights being moved as well) and how many of those scenes are dramas with fewer setups. (Dramas are often filmed with fewer setups for the camera so that the actors can be the focus and not the camera movement.)

To determine how many pages you can shoot per day, talk with the director and the DP to discuss what they think can be achieved. If the director wants to take longer to set up each shot, your schedule may be more like three to five pages per day. You may find, however, that this schedule puts you over the budget, so you may have to ask the director to make adjustments to the script so that you have fewer pages, or adjust the shooting style to get in more pages per day.

Post-production

It will be helpful to create the final version of this with your post supervisor, but for now, you can give a general guess as to how long it will take to complete post-production. Most likely, you will need four to eight weeks for the "string out" edit, another six to 10 weeks for the director's cut, two to four weeks for the producer's notes and changes, four weeks for sound, eight to 12 weeks for music, one week of online and color grading, anywhere from a few days to several months for VFX depending on what you need, and four to eight weeks for delivery. Many of these items can and will overlap, so you don't necessarily have to string them all one after the other. (e.g. The sound designer may gather sounds and the music composer may start putting together possible themes while the editor is still cutting.)

The Budget

Now that you know what you need and how long you need it, you are ready to put together the preliminary budget. Like the schedule, this is not your final budget, but a rough idea of how much it is going to cost. Here again, it's a good idea to use a line producer to help you create the budget. They should be someone who has relationship with production houses and post-production houses so that they can get good deals on each item that is needed for the film.

It's important to be as accurate as possible with the film budget, especially when the producer is working on a low-budget film as there is very little room for error. If you are working on an ultra-low-budget film, you may not be able to afford a large crew so it's important to know what each person does and who you may or may not be able to live without on your film. By using the info we've included in chapter 10, you can see which personnel will be needed and which ones you may be able to skip. Knowing the duty of each crew member is vital to knowing who a producer can afford to cut without losing key positions. Crew costs add up quickly, especially if you are out on location where you have to supply travel and housing on top of the salary and food for each day. Each film has to take into account the total budget and the complication of the shoot before it can be determined what crew is needed.

If you plan to create the budget yourself, use a program like *Movie Magic Budgeting*, which is the industry standard. Trying to create the budget on a Word doc or a Works template is going to take time and effort that should be spent elsewhere. In addition, when you do hire a line producer to take over, they will use *Movie Magic Budgeting* and *Movie Magic Scheduling* and have to recreate everything you already did. If you can't afford a budgeting program, you may be able to use *Excel* to create the budget by using the list of cast and crew we gave you in chapter 10 and enter in costs for each person you are going to need, or if you are a student, you may be able to get the educational version. Cost can vary from department to department and can vary depending on the skill level of the person you hire. For most experimental and lowest level budgets, it's important that you stay within the current minimum wage requirements for the state or country you are filming in. Different parts of the world have different costs, so check with a local film office to try and find the general cost for crew members.

Traditionally, film budgets are divided into "Above the Line" and "Below the Line" costs. This is where you input the cast and crew member needed from the list we gave you in chapter 10, and add in the additional production costs. Often, the above-the- line costs are very high because of salaries for the actors, director, and producer along with the cost of purchasing the story rights and the script. The below-the-line costs are traditionally the cost of the actual production and post-production.

Below is a list of the items that may need to be added to your budget. Using the schedule, you can add in the number of days you will need for the cast, crew, equipment, locations, props, etc. and their associated fees. You want to include approximately a 15 percent contingency for anything you may have missed, or anything that could go wrong during the production.

Above-the-Line Costs

1. Story rights

Did you have to option/purchase the script and what is that cost? The cost of getting the script clearance report should also be added here.

2. Producer

What are you paying the producers, yourself included? Producers usually get a set fee. The industry standard is often 5-10 percent of the cash budget split between all producers, excluding the line producer. The producers will most likely also be getting a percentage of the profits of the film.

3. Director

This is usually a negotiated fee for their services, and if appropriate you might also decide to include a percentage of the profits. If the director is in the DGA (Directors Guild of America), you will have to pay the director according to the union rules.

4. Actors

For well-known actors you will have to work out a deal with their agent, and they will often ask you to pay the actor's current rate. This fee is called the "actor's quote." You or your casting director can get an actor's quote from their agent so that you know their asking price. From there, you can try and negotiate the best deal they are willing to give. If an actor loves your script and director, you may be able to negotiate a lower rate and sometimes give them back end points or a deferment that they will get upon sale of the film.

For other union actors, the total budget of your film will set the day rate as the minimum required by the union. If the actor is willing to work for a "SAG/AFTRA scale rate," that means they will accept the current union fee for the day given the budget of the film. This can be anywhere from $100 per day on a SAG ultra-low-budget contract or an experimental film contract, to $900 per day on a multi-million-dollar budget. See SAG/AFTRA website for current indie day and weekly actors film rates (http://www.sagaftra.org/production-center/theatrical/signatory-information).

For non-union actors, your rate will be negotiable, but cannot be under minimum wage.

Another cost to include in the budget when working with union (SAG/AFTRA) actors is that the union requires you pay into the pension and welfare fund. The pension payments are a percentage of your total payment to the actors. For example, if you were to pay an actor $100 for one day, you would have to pay an additional percentage into their pension fund. At the time of this book's publication, that payment is 16.8 percent. You should check with your SAG/AFTRA representative for the current amount.

To make sure that the production company makes the payments required, SAG-AFTRA may ask that you pay the estimated budget for the actors into a holding account called a "bond." If you estimate that you have three actors for three days at $100 per day, that amount would be $900 plus $151.20 for the pension fund. SAG-AFTRA does not pay the actors from this account; instead they return those funds to you once they have confirmation that you have paid all the actors what they are due, and the pension and welfare percentage on all SAG/AFTRA members' salaries have been paid into the pension fund.

If you have already attached a named actor, look at their contract to see if they have asked for any additional expenses from the production company, including first-class flights, trailer, assistants, etc. All of these costs need to be included in the budget.

Below-the-Line Costs

1. Production Staff

This includes your camera crew, production manager, assistant director, script supervisor, location manager, office staff, and more. This is often calculated at more than just the scheduled shoot days, as you will need most of these people to be on staff for pre-production.

Using the crew list we have in chapter 10, enter the cost per person, per day for pre-production, production, and post-production. If you've hired a line producer, they will know the rates they can get for the crew. If you are doing a budget yourself and aren't sure what to put in for each person, contact department heads you are interested in hiring and ask them for their rate. You can find a list of production people through your state's film office or through production guides from LA or New York, as well as online. On smaller budget films, you may be able to find some crew members willing to come out for $100 per day. However, rates for most professionals are going to be much higher than that.

2. Production Expenses

This includes - all office expenses including: office space, phones, Internet, photo copies etc.; location expenses including catering, transportation, trailers, location fees, permits, etc.; rental equipment including cameras, lights, chairs, tents, portable toilets, studio space, vehicles, props, costumes, etc.

Using the breakdown of needed items and locations, list the cost of everything. Go through each department listing how many of each item is needed and for how long. If you don't know what the costs are for some of the items like camera and light rentals, call rental houses in or near where you plan to film to find out those rates. If you are already talking with or have attached a DP, ask them for a list of gear needed and costs associated with each of those items.

If you know where you are filming, you should be able to find local prices for studios, props, costumes, and other items. If those items are not available where you are filming, be sure to include the cost of shipping those items into that location.

You may be able to find a DP who has their own camera and even their own grip truck. Sometimes this will save you money, but don't settle on a decent DP just because they have equipment. Get the best DP you can afford and then find a good deal on cameras and lighting equipment by talking with rental houses in major cities near where you are filming.

With the list of crew you need for the film, decide how many people you need on location for each day. You need to determine how you are going to feed, house, and transport these people. For each location you need to include the cost of permits, location fees, transportation to and from that location, toilets, and any hotel costs.

3. Post Production

This includes: the edit suite, editor, special effects, music, color correction, and delivery costs. Some of these items will be determined by how you deliver the film. If you send the video straight to the web, you won't need to run it through quality control (QC) at a place like Technicolor. If you plan to sell your film to foreign and domestic distributors, you will need to make sure the film passes QC. Ask your distribution company which QC companies they will accept and get bids from three.

To help keep your post-production costs low, it's helpful to have a post- production partnership where all of your editing, audio, VFX, and delivery needs can be taken care of in one place. Check with local post houses to see what they are capable of doing and if they will give you a bid for your film.

Editing Costs

Editing costs may include: the edit system, editor, assistant editor, and mastering. To get current rates, contact local post-production houses. A less expensive route would be to use a local editor with their own edit system. There are numerous websites where a producer can find freelance editors.

A good editor should have experience on multiple editing platforms. An even better editor should be able to prep the video for color correction and have the audio sent to the mix house.

Music Costs

If you want an original score for your film, you need to consider the cost of hiring a composer. Composer rates vary significantly depending on experience, and credits. New or less expensive composers can cost between $1,000 to $5,000. High-end music composers for larger budget films can range between $15,000 to $200,000. Electronic scores are usually much cheaper than orchestral scores.

If you don't have much budget for a composer, you have a couple of options. First, you can purchase pre-recorded library music. There are a number of large music libraries willing to work with low-budget films and can provide you with access to their library for a flat rate. Second, you may be able to get a musically talented friend to compose the music for you. If you go this route, make sure they know how to record the tracks properly as you may need a specific mix from them when you do the final audio mix of the film, especially if you want to do a surround sound mix. Third, find local bands that want to be promoted along with your film. You may be able to get great songs from them at no cost and in trade you promote their band along with your film.

Special Effect Costs

If you have special effects in your film, get a rate for each shot depending on what the shot involves. Simple compositing shots can cost around $500 per shot while 3D modeling, shading, and extensive multi-layer compositing and motion tracking can cost thousands of dollars per shot.

Online Edit/Color Correction/Color Grading

Online editing and color correction are often done at the same time, at the same place. This stage of the process takes around a week to complete. Contact several post-production houses to get quotes on finishing your film. Cost for a session for a lower budget film is usually around $1,000 per day with two days to online and three days to color. Higher quality films with longer color sessions and a more experienced colorist may cost more.

Quality Control

Quality control costs can usually range between $3,000 and $10,000, depending on who you use. Your distribution company may require you use a particular lab, or in some cases, the distribution company will take care of that for you. To be safe, include this in your post-production budget.

Delivery Costs

All distribution companies require that you to have what are called "delivery items." This may include the video and audio masters, Digital Cinema Package (DCP), art work, trailer, behind-the-scenes video, a delivery binder of all your paperwork on the film, and much more. You will need to include in your budget the cost for someone to copy and prepare these items. To get a full list of possible requirements, talk with your distribution company to see what they expect to receive as part of the delivery.

It can cost you thousands of dollars to put together all the delivery items and will depend on how much of the film you prepared for international delivery when you finished the post production. The physical delivery items l depend on the agreement you have with your distribution company.

Marketing

If you have chosen self-distribution or even a smaller distribution company, chances are you will have to market the film yourself. From social media to festivals to posters and advertisement, the more money you can set aside to promote your film, the better chance you have to make a return on your investment.

It's rare that a small distribution company has the resources to do any promotions of the picture, so even if someone picks up your film, you will most likely have to do the advertising yourself. Larger studios often spend half of their budget on advertising and marketing. As you may not have the same depth of resources, start by setting aside 10 to 15 percent of your total budget for marketing to hire a publicist to do social media outreach for you. If you plan on self-releasing the film, set aside half of your total budget to market, promote, and release the film.

Festival Costs

If you plan to enter the film into festivals, you may be able to get the distribution company to take care of these costs for you. If not, you should put aside a small budget for festival entry fees, postage and shipping, travel and accommodations for yourself and possibly your lead actors and director. (Some larger festivals pay for transport and accommodation for a director and name talent.)

4. Additional Costs

Additional costs include: legal fees, insurance for the productions, and for some films, a completion bond and banking fees.

After you enter each item and person needed for the film, you should have a grand total. Take this budget number and compare it to the projected sales number. If it's three to one, sales to budget, then you are set! If not, you need to adjust your budget to fit. A good place to start when trying to lower your budget is to trim the number of locations, combine scenes, or combine characters. To do this without compromising the film, talk with the writer and director and see what scenes, locations, or characters might be combined to help lower the costs. The next big cost is the actors' fees. If you have an A-list cast, you may have fees way above the range your film can handle. If so, you may need to talk with the actor or their agent to see if they are willing to take a deferment or a producing credit and percentage of sales if they lower their initial fee. Another big cost is post production. A good way to lower post-production costs is to partner with a post-production company that can handle everything you need rather than parting out each service to individual companies. However you achieve the budget, you will have to include those details in the business plan.

> "He who is best prepared
> can best serve his moment of inspiration."
>
> – Samuel Taylor Coleridge

Chapter 7

The Business Proposal

We have worked with many different funding sources over the years, and one of the things we are often told in private by people who get approached to fund films is that they wish more filmmakers understood how to put together a properly organized business proposal (aka: business presentation). After years of pitching films to various investment groups and studios, we've put together what we consider to be a concise proposal that seems to appeal to funding sources.

What we are describing here is not a full business plan which you may need to have for your investors and should be reviewed by your entertainment attorney. Instead, we are describing a business proposal or presentation (a.k.a. prospectus) which contains the basic elements needed to get someone interested in your film. This, like the rest of the book, is our opinion and is not to be taken as legal advice. Depending on the type of fundraising you are considering using this proposal, you may be offering what the state or federal government considers to be a "security" which in the US, is regulated by the Securities and Exchange Commission. When dealing with investments and offering a return on money given to you, you must consult with an attorney to insure you follow all state and federal regulations. It should also be noted that film investment is high risk and very speculative and we strongly advise against giving any type of guarantees.

Just like any other business, the filmmaker has to know what they are selling, who they are selling to, what the film costs to make, and how much they can sell it for. As you build the business plan, you will use each of those elements to prepare a business proposal to show potential investors, producing partners, studios, and production companies. This will include everything anyone would need to know about your production, and it should do it in as few pages as possible.

A business proposal should include a synopsis of the story, bios on all the above-the-line players, and if you don't yet have cast attached, some realistic casting ideas for each of the lead roles. It will also include an outline of the schedule, the top sheet of the budget (i.e. the first page of the budget with the total budget numbers), realistic options for distribution, comparison numbers of other similar films and how they performed, how much money will be needed from investors, how much money will be provided by other sources (tax breaks, bank loans, distribution rights advance, etc.), how your investors will recoup their money, and appropriate legal disclaimers.

Along with the details of numbers and projected earnings, the proposal should also contain art work that helps convey the tone of your film. Starting with the cover, the art should grab the interested parties and instantly tell them the type of project you are presenting. To us, this is one of the areas that sets the business of filmmaking apart from a standard business proposal. Though film is a business, it is also an art form that should be conveyed throughout the process. Your art should be well thought out. If necessary, spend some of the development funds to hire a good artist or Photoshop poster designer who can help you come up with artwork that will stand out. The proposal should not, however, sacrifice substance for the sake of art. Those who invest in films are used to seeing business proposals on a regular basis and know the form and detail that should be included.

Below is an outline for the business proposal and what should be included. The following page numbers are a guideline and you may need an additional page or two for some of the categories listed. It's generally not a good idea to make your proposal more than 20 pages long. Any proposal should be able to be presented in an artistic and orderly fashion in 10-15 pages.

Page 1

The Teaser Image/Poster

Create a poster-style cover that gives your readers a sense of the film. Think of this as a teaser poster. For the film *Pirates of the Caribbean*, it was a skull and crossbones. For *Fast and Furious*, it was a race car. You should not have any actors in the image unless they are already attached to the film. Don't include who you would like to be in the film. That comes later. The title and the log-line should also be on the image (see a sample in the resource guide).

Title and Log-line

The title and the log-line should give an increasing level of clarity to what you are presenting and what the audience is going to see. Your title should be as clear as possible. If your title can't sum up your story as well as needed, your log-line has to. For example, *Raiders of the Lost Ark* nicely summed up the story. The producers of the film added log-line of "The return of the great adventure" as a throwback to the classic adventure films (that George Lucas and Steven Spielberg grew up watching) and now the audience knows what they are in for. The title *Joe* does not convey the same idea. Since there have been at least 10 films named *Joe* since 1924, you may want to find a better title.

The log-line is one sentence. This is what is on the poster just under the title and it summarizes the movie as best as one line can.

Page 2

Summary

This should be two or three paragraph summation of the entire picture. Talk about the character goals, the obstacles, and end it with a summary of the theme. Is this good vs. evil? Is it social issues wrapped in a comedy? What is the theme and what can the audience expect to get out of the film?

Additional Images

Along with the teaser poster, include several more images throughout the proposal to help convey the overall tone of your film. These do not have to be on every page. This is the "art" of the proposal. Film is a visual medium and this is your chance to convey a brief idea of the setting and the look of your film.

Page 3

Explain who the audience is and why the investors should get involved with this film.

Is your film a comedy aimed at teens? A romantic comedy designed for women? An action film designed for a wide audience? Here is where you can list similar films in your genre and show how well each of them did in the market. This step is also a good way for you to look at other pictures similar to yours and see if any of them have made money. If you find that there are few to no films in your category that have made money, then you may need to rethink the film you are asking people to invest in. If you decide to continue with this type of film, you need good evidence that there is an audience for it and why you think it will make its money back.

As examples of performance for your film, it's best to list at least three films in the same genre that have come out in the last five years. Also, stay away from films that are not the norm. For example, listing *Paranormal Activity* is not a legitimate example to back up your justification for funding a "found footage" film. The year that *Paranormal Activity* was released, there were dozens of other "found footage" films in the market that were never seen by a wide audience. When *Paranormal Activity* was picked up by Paramount, the studio spent hundreds of thousands of dollars promoting the film, which ultimately was what made it such an enormous success. Very few people would have ever seen it without such a huge advertising campaign. Instead, use several examples of more standard films in the genre of your film so that you present a realistic outlook for possible sales.

Page 4

List who is attached to the film.

Here is where you list each of the main cast and crew who are attached to the picture. This is called the film "package," and we will go through this in more detail in chapter 9. Using small publicity-style photos of each person, list the main producer(s), director, and any A-list or recognizable cast who are attached to the film. If you don't have cast attached yet, list them as "possible cast" so your investors can see the level and creative type of talent you are thinking of attaching, who you would like to approach, and/or who you are already talking to.

If you already have relationships with actors who are right for the part, and if you have already sent them the script to consider the part, you can include in the document that you are "contacting" that person, but do not say they are attached unless you have signed paperwork that they have agreed to do the film. Saying people are attached who are not attached is risky as investors may check this with the actor's agent or manager and this may injure your chance to work with legitimate actors.

Page 5

Budget

Next, include the top sheet of the budget you created. Do not include the full detailed budget, only the first page or two, which outlines the totals of each major category. If the investors want a detailed budget, you can get that to them later in the full business plan.

Page 6

Schedule

This is a summary of planned shoot dates and how long each phase will take. (On a micro budget, your schedule will likely be much shorter.)

> For example:
> Pre-Production: 8 weeks. Jan. 6 - March 2.
> Principle photography: 6 weeks. Scheduled to begin March 3, wrap shooting on April 12th. Pick up shots: 2 days. April 14-16.
> Post production: 30 weeks. Scheduled to begin April 21 – Nov. 3
> Film ready for delivery: Nov. 6

It's not necessary to include your full production breakdown and schedule, but you should have those details ready for any investors or production companies who want to see them.

Page 7

Finance Plan

Following the budget should be a list of how you intend to raise the money for this budget. This could be angel investors, (e.g.: large sums of cash from individual investors) loans, tax breaks, studio co-production, or for smaller budgets, you may be raising the funds online using one of the many crowdfunding sources like indiegogo.com or Kickstarter. Include what percentages will come from each source.

Page 8

Marketing Plan

Outline any plan you have to get the film into festivals or any specific types of marketing for the film that will help increase its value. This includes TV, Internet, social media, hiring a PR agent, or any other marketing plans. If you plan to begin marketing the film prior to shooting, or if the film has a built-in audience from already- popular material or characters, include that here as well.

Page 9

Distribution and Return on the Investment

If you plan on giving the investors a return on the investment, here is where you list the potential returns on the investment plus the amount of interest. Industry standard is 10-20 percent on top of the original investment amount.

Do you have a distribution company attached? Do you plan to approach a distribution company or will you try to distribute the film yourself? Outline what your distribution plan looks like and an estimate of how long it will take to see the potential return on the investment. To give your investors an idea of possible numbers and to show that you have done your research, it's a good idea to have a sales estimates from a reputable sales company attached.

One avenue of possible early recoupment for the investors may come from the tax breaks from one of the many states or countries that offer them. Some places offer an income tax break directly to investors while other states or countries offer tax break incentives on goods and services used during production. Those tax rebates could be used to return some of the investment unless the producer is using them to help fund post production or secure bank loans. Another avenue of returns for the investor is pre-sales or an advance from the distribution company.

Page 10

Investment/Legal Information

It's important to include a legal disclaimer if you are getting funds from individual/angel investors. Federal and local governments place restrictions on businesses asking for money, and you must include the regulations in the proposal as required by your state or country. To be sure that you've met all the requirements, you should consult with a local entertainment attorney. By law, in the United States, you must also have a document in the proposal outlining the risk of the investment. The federal government can pose stiff penalties on producers for not adhering to the law. A clear statement should be included that says that investing in a film is a risky business investment and that no one should invest in a film unless they can afford to lose the entire investment.

Depending on the type of investment you are requesting, (in the United States) the federal government may consider your business proposal a securities offering which is heavily regulated. We cannot emphasize enough how important it is to consult with an attorney when seeking investments for your film as breaking any federal or state laws may result in heavy fines or even jail time.

Formatting

Finally, if you are sending the proposal to people digitally rather than presenting it face to face, we recommend that it be formatted as PDF file, not a doc, not a Flash presentation, and not a Power Point. (You may want to create a Power Point or Flash presentation if you present it to them live, but not if sending it via email.) A PDF is readable by everyone and can be made small enough to email by using Adobe's *Acrobat Pro* or other PDF software. Most document-creation programs can save as a PDF and some can compress the PDF to a smaller size.

The entire document should be less than 8 megabytes so it can be easily emailed as most email software cannot send files more than 9.5 MB. (You should aim for under 2 MB so that it downloads quickly.) Arranging the photos and words on a document can be easily accomplished using Microsoft Word or Mac's Pages. If your software won't compress the PDF, you may need to buy Adobe *Acrobat Pro* (the PDF creation program) or find another PDF compression solution.

Website

If you have not yet built a website, this is a good time to build one so that you can direct potential investors to it. Purchase a domain name that uses the name of your film. Keep the title as simple as possible, and if the name is taken, add the word "movie" or "film" to the name and see if that is available. Use the visual material you created for your business proposal to populate your website. The cover image with the title and log-line along with the synopsis of the film and the information on the cast and crew is a good start for the content of the website.

This site should have the best imagery possible to convey the look and feel of your film. As you may not always get to meet face to face with investors and distribution companies, it is important to have a website to send them to look over the material. Don't post all of your funding numbers on the site. Save that for the proposal. You can send through email or give them directly.

Additional Material

The website is also a good opportunity to create additional promotional material. Depending on the type of film you are producing, additional materials may be useful to help sell the idea of the film, or the creative power of the team. Some films create what the industry calls a "look book." This is a series of color images or photos, similar to a storyboard. A storyboard is a sequence of images, often hand drawn, that uses desired camera angles to show the progression of a scene. The look book may or may not contain character images, but will often show the look and feel of each scene as desired by the director. This can be as few as a half dozen images for the film to several images per scene.

If the film has a complicated look or visual style, like a science fiction film, you may also need to create pre-visualizations of the effects you want to see in the film to show the financial partners or studios you can accomplish the type of film you are describing to them. This can be very costly and if done poorly, can do more harm than good, so if you have a very limited budget, stay away from showing your pre-vis to investors.

"There's nothing creative about living within your means."

– Francis Ford Coppola

Chapter 8

Funding

Though on larger films, funding usually comes from multiple sources, all it takes is one person, one investment source and your dream can become a reality. Though this may feel like playing the lottery, and you cannot rely on pure luck to fund your vision. This is where the hard work of the last several chapters begins to pay off as you now have a well-prepared business proposal to present to the right funding source. It may take a while to find the right source(s), and along the way you may find that because of the subject matter or genre you chose, the film is more or less difficult to fund. This is why we recommend developing several projects at once. If one project is rejected, you have another one ready to present.

There are numerous sources of funding, but not all are right for a particular project. Before you approach a funding source with your project, find out if your film is the type of project they are looking for. As you present your plan to investors, look for ways to improve it with each person or group you pitch to. If your proposal is turned down, try to find out what was not appealing and look for ways to improve your chances with the next investor. In a difficult economic climate, you may find that to fund your film, it is often necessary to combine a variety of different types of funding to get to the total investment needed, particularly on larger budget projects.

Below is a list of some possible funding sources.

Self-Funding/Family and Friends

Many first-time filmmakers fund their first project themselves, or through family and friends. This can be an easy way to get started as family and friends already know and believe in you. However, this also puts them at great risk. If you are being funded by family and friends, do them a favor by giving them a proper business plan and make them aware of the risk of investing in a film. Don't let family members put up their life savings or home, just so you can make your film. Many films don't make money and if your family and friends are not independently wealthy, it's safer to go with the crowd funding option so that you spread the risk to a lot more people for a lot less cost per-person.

Crowd Funding

Crowd funding is a concept where people donate money to your film project through a website like Indiegogo or Kickstarter. Because these are considered donations, people who give to you do not own a piece of the project. Instead, in return for their donation, you send them whatever reward or gift you have promised. This type of service does not allow you to sell "shares" of your project as shares are regulated and considered an investment.

When we have done crowd funding campaigns, we found that the majority of donations come from family, friends, and fans of the genre or the actors. Campaigns are most successful when the filmmakers and actors involved in the project have a large number of followers in social media outlets prior to starting the campaign.

It's easy to set up a page on one of the crowd funding sites and then promote the project through social media. For best results, record a video or a trailer, post photos, post a synopsis of the project, and include much of the same information that you have in your business proposal. Each crowd funding site has regulations on how short or long the campaign can run. It's a good idea to run a campaign for a long enough period that people have time to explore and donate, but not so long that they lose interest. While the campaign is running, continue to post new information every few days.

One of the best (and least expensive) ways to expand your following during a campaign is to find websites and bloggers who like to talk about the genre of film you are producing. These individuals may respond to and write about your film and are often connected to hundreds upon thousands of followers who may also be excited about seeing a film in the genre they love. This is especially effective within the horror and fantasy film genres.

Unless you are extremely fortunate, count on the majority of your donations being small amounts. In our experience, we've found that contributors rarely give more than $50. For each donation, you need to have "awards" or gifts to give to the donor. Keep the gifts in balance to the amount given, as some of the money donated will be spent providing those gifts to your donors. Gifts can be signed photos or posters from the cast and crew, DVDs (if they still exist by the time you finish your film), downloads of the film, a pass to visit the set, dinner with the cast and crew, etc. Where possible, keep your costs low by making your rewards digital downloads which will limit your hard costs in creating the rewards and shipping. Tax laws are currently changing regarding this type of fund raising, so be aware of any possible tax implications and get professional advice from a tax expert.

Angel Investors/Equity Investors

Angel investors (aka financiers/equity funding) are people with sizable sums of money who invest in your film. This can be a friend or family member, but is often an entrepreneur who has an interest in film and looks for production companies or producers to invest in. There are angel investor groups all over the world, and you may be able to find one near you by searching for investment companies or angel investors online.

A good way to find angel investors is to contact the business development center in your town or city. There are often organizations that are set up to help businesses get started. Some of these businesses are tied to investment groups that look for up-and- coming products or businesses to help. Some of these groups prefer to work with a company who has at least a small track record of developed films, while others will work with start-up companies. In larger cities, there are meetings and conferences for business development. Attending these conferences is another tool for you to meet prospective investors.

Sometimes, investors come from the most unlikely sources. Some accountants represent high-net-worth individuals who can be open to speculative projects like films. Put the word out to all your friends as you never know which of them may be connected to people with a lot of money who may be interested in investing in films. Investing in film can be a fun prospect for a doctor, lawyer, dentist, or other individual with disposable income. Getting the chance to meet famous actors and have great stories to tell their friends while golfing or meeting over dinner are often the reason angel investors want to get involved with film projects.

Hedge funds

Sometimes, as part of their portfolios, hedge funds will invest in feature films or in production companies. Hedge funds are represented by a manager who oversees the investments of a group of people who are looking for ways to diversify their investments. To present your project to a hedge fund manager, you need a clear business plan and detailed budget with sales estimates from a reputable sales company. Hedge fund managers aren't going to be as interested in the creative aspect of your project, but rather the business plan you present and in your track record of past projects.

Lawyer and Accountant Contacts

In addition to helping you with legal paperwork, good entertainment lawyers and especially larger law firms may be able to introduce you to investment sources. Your lawyer, or one of the lawyers in the firm, may have dealings with larger businesses, investment groups, or individuals who may have interest in investing in films. As you look to hire legal counsel, inquire as to their ability to help you raise funds, or at least put you in touch with possible investment sources.

Likewise, an accountant may also have high net worth clients or know of individuals who like to invest in film projects. Taking time to meet with and befriend numerous lawyers and accountants in your area may help you find the investors that you're looking for.

The Studios

If your movie is a "big budget, epic, studio tent pole" type of movie, your first port of call should be the companies that are actively financing those types of movies. These are the "major studios" or the "mini-majors" and they will have the best chance of releasing a large-budget film and recouping money, as they have their own distribution output deals worldwide.

There are several major studios in the United States such as *Warner Brothers, Fox, Sony, Disney, Paramount, Universal,* and *DreamWorks.* The mini-majors are companies such as *Lionsgate* and *Relativity.* To get your project to a studio or one of the larger production companies, you need your agent, manager, or lawyer, to send your script to a production executive or development person at that studio. You may be able to get around this if you have a personal relationship with someone at the studio, but most studios do not accept unsolicited material.

Production Companies

There are dozens and dozens of production companies that also finance films located around the world. A good way to identify the right company to work with is to find a movie in the same genre as yours and search for the company that produced it. Some of these companies may have distribution output deals with a studio. Contact their development department and find out what type of films they are looking for and whether they are accepting material from outside sources. Ask for their submission requirements and who to contact. See if they will give you a time frame to expect a response and then after you send in your materials, give them time to look it over. If they like your story idea, they may ask for a meeting or to read the script. If you do get a meeting, be prepared to share storyboards or visuals you have created and discuss budget and business plan.

Tax Incentives

There are several different types of tax incentives, depending on which country or state you are working with. One is a "tax credit," which is a payment from the government to the production company as a refund for taxes paid during production. In some places, tax credits can be transferred to other third parties. Another tax incentive is a cash rebate or refund, which is paid to the production company as a percentage of qualified expenses. Another is sales tax exemptions, and another is direct income tax breaks to investors.

The percentage of refunds or credits may change every year, so it's a good idea to contact the film office in the location where you plan to film to get the current rate. You also want to know at what point in the process the rebate or credit will be applied. Usually, the rebate comes after the shoot is complete and you've handed in your paperwork and passed the government audit. However, in some places, it may take several months to receive the tax rebate.

To help initially fund the film, a producer can sometimes get a bank, financing entity, or an equity investor to fund the tax credits. They will take a percentage of that rebate or tax credit as a fee for this service, but it may be worth the fee for the producer to have the funding needed to start production.

You will also want to be sure to be very clear about the basis on which these tax credits are handed out. A certain number of people on your production team and cast may need to be hired from that location, or a certain percentage of your budget spent there, so be sure to check all the regulations carefully. A simple mistake may disqualify you from receiving a much-needed tax credit. Often, you can get a pre-qualification for the tax credit based on your budget and spending details, which will give you a good idea as to what to expect in return.

Foreign Production Incentives or Tax Rebates

Tax rebates and production incentives may also be available in foreign countries. Similar to the U.S. tax rebates, these vary from country to country and often require you to have a co-production deal with a production company from that country. As with U.S. tax incentives, certain restrictions will apply. The local film office or government body can give you details on what is required for your project to qualify. If you have trouble reaching the local film offices, you may be able to reach them through a film market like AFM, Cannes, or Mip-con. Often, film offices from countries that offer good incentives attend film markets to promote their country.

Foreign Sales or Domestic Distributors Minimum Guarantee

If your film is packaged with an A-list director and A-list talent, you may be able to get a foreign sales company or a domestic distributor to give you a minimum guarantee as an advance toward your budget. The minimum guarantee is based on sales the company is able to secure for the film from specific territories, and collections on deposits from those territories or from a domestic distributor it might be an advance against the domestic rights.

Bank Loans

Based on the pre-sales numbers and estimates for the rest of the foreign territories on the film, some banks will give you a loan for a certain portion of your budget. If you are thinking of working with a bank, it's a good idea to find out which sales companies the bank is comfortable working with so that you can target those companies first. Banks like to work with sales companies that have a good track record and will be able to deliver on their sales estimates. You also need to equate how much the interest on the bank loan will cost you.

Funding Websites

There are some funding online platform/market places that have been recently launched such as *Slated*. Websites like this try to connect legitimate filmmakers with legitimate funding sources by requiring the filmmakers to be vetted by other members of the website, and the investors are required to be accredited. Each country has different regulations for accredited investors, but in the U.S., the U.S. Government's Securities and Exchange Commission (SEC) oversees the accreditation of investors in an attempt to legislate who can invest in certain types of higher risk investments including films. Projects for these types of funding websites often have to fall within the site's parameters and be budgeted between $500,000 - $15 million for features and $250,000 - $2 million for documentaries. To have the best chance of success on this type of site, your project should be as fully packaged as possible.

Talent Agencies

Some of the larger talent agencies now have independent film departments that work with film funds and production companies with financing, and will help structure and arrange financing and distribution on for films.

Additional Funding Requirements

Completion Bond

Some funding sources require that you get a completion bond. A completion bond on a film will ensure the investors, bank, or financing entity that the film will be completed and delivered for distribution, so their investment is protected. If for some reason you are unable to complete the film, the bond company will take over the project and either complete the film so that the investors can recoup their investment or they will payback all the investors if the film is abandoned.

If you work with a bond company, you need to send them a script, shooting schedule, production schedule and budget, chain of title, and the details of your film's financing. The bond company often requires resumes on and will likely want to meet with your director, producer, line producer, and key heads of departments.

Bond companies employ a team of experienced professionals who know filmmaking. They look for clear and precise budget numbers and justifications for those numbers. They often require specific detailed budgets from each department and tend to look particularly closely at special effects, visual effects, and post budgets. They may also want to sit down with the producer and line producer and go through how you arrived at all your numbers. Before the bond company is willing to put up a guarantee to the investors, they want to be convinced that your business plan, budget, and schedule, are realistic and achievable.

Once they are happy that you have a realistic budget and product plan for your script and feel confident that your director and production team have the capability to deliver the picture, the bond company will give you a "letter of intent" saying that they will go forward subject to your meeting their various conditions.

You will need to negotiate a fee for the bond with the bond company. This may be anywhere between 3 to 6 percent of the budget. As this is subject to change, check the rates with the bond company you intend to use. Along with their fee, bond companies require that you set aside at least 10 percent of your budget in cash as a contingency for any problems that may occur.

Before beginning production, the bond company wants to see a cash flow chart on what you will spend each week. To do this, you or your accountant can take the budget and the schedule and plot out what will be spent each week. (A cash flow chart is a good idea for any picture even if you are not working with a bond company.)

When prepping for production, bond companies can help steer you away from bad suppliers, ineffective crew members, and troublesome actors, any of which could injure the film. They will have a list of suppliers they have worked with in the past and will help you find the right team, for the right price. If you have stated a low price in your budget for certain items like camera rental or grip truck rentals, they will want to see proof that this is indeed a rate you can secure.

Once you start pre-production, they will monitor your progress and usually ask for weekly cost reports. Upon beginning production, they will ask for daily reports to make sure that the director and DP are on schedule. It is very likely that they may send a representative to your set to see that everything is running smoothly. If you are going over budget or are behind schedule, the contract with the bond company states that they can take over the film and complete it themselves. (This is a worse-case scenario, but it does happen from time to time.)

If the bond company does need to take over the picture, they usually have the right to fire the director, producer, and/or line producer if film is not being properly managed. To avoid this, it's good to hire a line producer and production accountant that the bond company recommends. The bond company would rather not take over your film so they will usually work with you to make sure that doesn't happen.

Using a bond company is a lot of work, but it can be for the benefit of the film. Even if you don't end up working with a bond company, the requirements we have listed here are a great checklist for any producer to be sure that you have a solid business plan.

Setting Up a Company to Manage the Funds

To raise and disperse payments, it's a good idea to set up the company that will oversee the production. Usually, this is done in the U.S. by creating a Limited Liability Corporation (LLC).

If you have limited development funds, you may want to wait to set up the LLC until you know that the film is going to get financing as the cost can range from $600-$1,200. (Cost depend on where you are setting up the business, and whether you have someone else set it up for you.) This will be one of the last expenses for your development fund. Setting up an LLC can take several weeks to several months, depending on the backlog of work the state government has to go through. If you don't want to put funding on hold and if you have enough development funds, you may want to set up the LLC as you are starting the business plan. Even if you are producing an ultra-low-budget production of under $100,000, you may still need to set up an LLC in the state you are operating in.

Some investors may not want to deposit funds into your personal bank account in which case you would need to set up a business account. A business bank account through the LLC is also recommended to disperse money to your cast, crew, and vendors, during filming and then disperse any return on investments after distribution. (In foreign countries, you need to look into which type of business entity is best to use to control the film. For this, you should consult with a local entertainment lawyer.)

To form the LLC, you need your production legal team to draw up an operating agreement between you, your production company, and all your investors. Most production lawyers have standard templates for this that can be adapted to the demands of the individuals concerned.

Bank Account

To set up a business bank account, the bank will require your LLC paperwork and usually the operating agreement of the LLC. You may need to give your accountant, and possibly your line producer, access to this account so they can set up any services needed for payroll or payments to vendors.

Collection Account

Some investors or financing partners may want to set up a 3rd party collection account and have all revenues from a film paid into that entity. That entity would then pay out all investors, sales agents commissions, marketing fees, deferred payments, profit participation. Freeway and Fintage House are 2 of the bigger ones commonly used. A collection account agreement is then made outlining the terms and order of the recoupment of all parties involved who are due payments or profit participation from the film.

.

"Coming together is a beginning.
Keeping together is progress.
Working together is success."

— Henry Ford

Chapter 9

Partners:
Assembling the Key Team
(A.K.A. – Packaging)

There is nothing better than having a great team to help you with the film. Skilled artists and hard workers have made many of our films so much easier to complete and so much better to watch. But there have been a few projects where the teams weren't right for the task at hand. So how do you know who are the best people to partner with to make your film a success? To help answer this, we've broken this section into two chapters. Chapter 9 introduces the key team members (i.e. the film package). These include additional producers, the director, cast, etc., and will be included in the film's business plan. The producer needs the development fund to hire and use the services of these team members for the purpose of obtaining complete funding for the film. The second part of building the team is in Chapter 10, which includes the titles and duties of the rest of the crew.

There are two important questions to ask when assembling your team: What do you need help with and what can you afford? The assumption at this point is that the producer is going to attempt to raise a certain amount of money so that they can pay for talent, crew, production, and distribution of the film. It really doesn't matter if you are trying to raise $10,000 or $10,000,000 - the principles are the same. Every business venture has to create a business plan, and its success is largely determined by the key team members who will execute it. On a film, these key team members are the producer(s), executive producer(s), director, talent (actors), a distribution company, and any co-production partners, including production and/or post-production houses. Along with those key team members, the producer (unless they have the skills to do themselves) also needs to hire a casting director, line producer, first AD, and a location scout to complete the requirements of a good business plan.

Why do you need all these people to help? Very few producers are brilliant at absolutely everything, and a good producer knows where they need help. If you decide to take on a partner, you'd be wise to find one with skills that complement yours. You'll find that some people are great at raising funds, others are great at putting together the technical side of filmmaking. Whatever your area of expertise, it's important to know where your weaknesses are and find others to help. If you don't know how and don't have the relationships to get a good cast, hire a casting director. If you don't know how to raise funds, partner with a producer who does. If you don't know how to budget a film, hire a line producer. It is important, however, when attaching partners to the film, that you find a balance between skill and voting rights as too many partners may slow down the decision-making process, and if those partners do not have enough expertise, they may advise you to make the wrong decisions.

When you have the right team around you, everything you may have been afraid to do before becomes a much simpler and a much more enjoyable part of the process. The following is a list of the key team members and why you need them.

Executive Producer

If you are not skilled at raising funds, you need to find someone who believes in your script and can help you raise financing. Look for someone with experience in financing for businesses or who has worked with raising capital for other types of ventures. Since raising money for films involves slightly different risks and a different financing structure than other business ventures, your EP should have experience in raising funds for films. Anyone raising funds for you will expect a small fee or percentage of the money they raise for your picture.

Additional Producing Partner(s)

As you tackle the challenging role of producer, you may decide that you need to bring on a producing partner who has a set of skills that complement yours. If you are just starting out in producing, it would be good for you to partner with someone who is more experienced as they may have connections that will make it easier to assemble your team. It may be that they have relationships with financing sources, can get steep discounts on goods and services, or have great relationships with actors who are be willing to attach themselves to the film.

If your budget is large enough, the simplest way to create a partnership is by paying for the service provided rather than giving them any additional stake in the film. If your budget is not very large, you may be able to give them a deferred compensation or profit participation to make a lower upfront fee more palatable to them.

Even when working with friends, it is a good idea to have a clear agreement in writing covering each party's responsibilities and their share of ownership. Friendship can quickly dissolve once a project is underway if expectations are different from the results. The same applies if you are hired to work on someone else's project. You should have a clear agreement of your responsibilities, credit, level of ownership and payment.

Line Producer

The line producer is one of the most important people on your team as they handle all the below-the-line requirements of your shoot. A good line producer should have contacts and relationships with crew members, production houses, and rental houses that are able and willing to work with the budget level you've established for the film.

The line producer should be familiar with the union rules and requirements, as well as labor laws for your budget level and your shooting location. As each budget level changes the pay requirements, and each state and country has different labor laws, they will need to have contacts and relationships where you are filming and be familiar with those requirements.

The line producer works closely with the production accountant to insure that everything stays within budget, and that invoices and fees for items and staff are as agreed. If, however you don't have the budget to hire an accountant, hire a line producer who has great accounting skills. The line producer should understand how to make a schedule, as they will help make the initial schedule for the film. This job will eventually be given to the first assistant director (1st AD) during pre-production.

On smaller budget films, the line producer may also act as the production manager overseeing not just the rental of the equipment, but also the management of that equipment on set. They may also be asked to handle location management as they have responsibility for arranging the location agreements. Be careful, however, not to give this person too many duties. Their first priority needs to be keeping track of your budget so that you don't go over or something doesn't get over looked.

Check the line producer's references to find out if on previous projects they've been able to come in on budget, properly handle paperwork, properly wrap the set by assuring the return of rentals and the closing the production offices.

Director

For films other than ultra-low-budget, the director should be "bankable," meaning they are well regarded in the industry and have had at least some box office success and some critical success. It is extremely helpful if your director has worked on several pictures in the same genre of film you are producing. This shows that they can handle the type of material you want to cover and that their work has been embraced by an audience and by the industry.

If you are a first-time feature film director, or a producer who has hired a first-time director for your project, you may still be able to find funding, but it will be more of a challenge. It's important that the director has had some sort of directing experience whether in commercials, TV, short films, or music videos. Many great directors have come up through the ranks this way, and there is a good argument to be made that many well-known directors' first movie was one of their best.

The challenge with a first-time director is getting the cast to attach themselves to a film when they are unsure of the director's work and their ability to translate the script to screen. Professional actors may have a rational fear that an unknown director will make them look bad on screen, which is something no actor can afford. Getting an experienced director of photography (DP) and editor on the film to help support the director will help instill a confidence level of both talent and investors, showing them that though this person is a first-time director, you have attached a competent team that will make everyone look their best. If the director needs to show that they have experience, it would be advisable for them to direct a short film with good actors so they can prove that they have command of the craft and can work with talent to get great performances from them.

It's important that both the director and the producer have a similar creative vision. The producer entrusts to the director much of what makes the picture great, including creating the look and feel of the film, the flow and clarity of the storyline, as well as the performances of the actors, the wellbeing of the crew, and the totality of the edit. This should not be someone who the producer is going to constantly second guess. If the producer feels like they have to direct the film, they should direct rather than hang over the director's shoulder and tell them how to make every decision. The director is hired because they have a skill that the producer recognizes and values. If the producer has made a good choice in the director, they have to trust them to do their job. However, if the producer notices the director making errors that could jeopardize the film, it is up to them to reign in the project and, in a worse-case scenario, find a new director if needed.

Prior to hiring the director, take a look at their previous work. Do they get good performances from the actors? Is the story well told? Was it well paced? Do they seem to have a good sense of timing? Does their work show they are a good fit for the genre? (i.e. is their comedy funny or their thriller suspenseful?) When possible, check with the people they worked with in the past. Did they work well with the producer, actors, the DP, and the editor? How were they in the editing process? Did they get all the shots necessary to cover the story properly (coverage), or were there many reshoots and compromises required to complete the film? How was their film received? Did it play well at festivals? Did it earn back money for investors? Did it come in on time and on budget? This is one of the most important team members you will bring on to your film, so it's important to do your research and reference check well.

If you have decided that you want to direct and produce, we strongly recommended that you have at least one skilled producing partner. You need someone to take care of the day-to-day operations of the picture while you work on the creative side. Without a sensible business partner, production problems will distract you from the job of directing, and the film will suffer as your time with the actors, the DP, and the art department become compromised.

Casting Director

A great casting director can increase the value of your film by having relationships with agents and managers who represent known actors. Even if you are shooting a low-budget film, you may still be able to afford a few known actors. There are some wonderful, working, recognizable actors who, if they love the script, will work for SAG scale, and even name actors will often work on indie films for less than their studio quote if they love the material.

Partner with a casting director who has relationships with actors and their managers. This person can send out your script and get a response, which can often be difficult to achieve on your own. A good casting director can reach the level of actor that fits and enhances your film according to the size of your budget.

As with any position on the film, if you are on a very low budget and can't pay the casting director's normal rate, a possible solution is to ask if they will work for a lower rate, in exchange for a co-producer credit and some profit share. This approach can be applied to other key team members most typically name actors, the line producer, and highly qualified individuals who are working beneath their normal

A good incentive on smaller budget films is to give the casting one fee for general casting and an additional fee if they can attach a known actor who enhances the sales value of your film.

When checking the references for the casting director, make sure that the actors on their resume actually came into the project through them, and not through one of the other producers or the director. Just because they worked with someone on a film, does not mean they necessarily have a relationship where they can contact them again.

Cast

The ideal in packaging is to attach a cast that works creatively for you and the director, but also has strong market value. A good way to increase the value of the film is to attach an actor for one role that is popular domestically, another actor that is popular in the foreign market. After that, hire as many other recognizable faces as you can afford, depending on the budget of the film. If you think your project will appeal to a target demographic group, you might want to cast an actor who is popular with that group.

To get an idea of how popular an actor is at the moment, the IMDB pro "Starmeter" can be a great resource. If an actor is in the 0 - 1000 range, this indicates that there is a good public awareness on that actor, and odds are, this actor will have some sales value. A 1000 - 5000 rating is also decent. Usually, film distributors and financing companies have lists of their current favorite actors, which can vary from country to country.

Co-production

Production partnerships are essential in any film and you may be able to lower many of your budget costs through a co-production or a goods and services deal. On a low-budget film, this means that you borrow a camera from a friend. On a larger budget, it means you show your budget, schedule, and your business plan to a production company and see if they will partner with you either financially, or with goods and services. This could mean they will donate the gear and production services for free, or it

.y mean they will charge you half rate for a camera package, lighting package, and edit suites. Either way, this can help take what could have been a $1 million budget down to a $500,000 dollar budget, and it may make all the difference between making your film happen or not.

A production company considers those production deals an investment, and they want a return on that investment when the film is sold. The amount of that return and credit for the company on the film is determined by the deal you can make with them.

In this same way, you can make a similar deal with many of the people working for the production. If the director of photography really likes you or your script and thinks the film can make money, they may be willing to come in at an ultra-low cost granted they get a profit percentage or a deferred fee from the returns on the film.

When possible, it's a good idea to work with a production company that also handles post production and can help you from pre-production all the way through delivery. They handle your workflow, provide you with a post supervisor, and have the gear needed to run through most or all of your post process, including any needed tape decks, edit systems, color correction, sound design, etc. If you can keep all of your work in one place, the work flow will be much smoother and the company will likely make a deal with you that is usually less expensive then parceling out each piece of the production.

Location Scout

Before you can decide where you can shoot your film and what costs and/or benefits you will have by shooting there, you need to at least have the major locations scouted. Until you know what state or country you want to shoot in, you won't know what tax benefits, crew availability, or other logistical issues you may run into. You and the director may be able to handle those duties, but if you are already too busy, you need to bring on a location scout. This person needs to have a list of the locations from the script (provided by the line producer) and will find location options to match each of them.

Legal Counsel

We've talked a lot about legal counsel already, and if you can't tell, we think it's a really good idea to get advice from them whenever possible. If you can't afford to have them working with you full time, be sure that you have enough money to hire them to create the contracts and agreements needed when hiring the other team members as well as all the paperwork needed for the story rights.

Every agreement and contract with each team member should be in writing so that everyone knows what is expected of them, and what they will get in return. Large problems can occur if there is a difference between what people expect from you and what they receive. If you have everything spelled out in the contract, it's harder for there to be misunderstandings later.

Along with the contracts and agreements, there are a number of core documents and legal areas that need to be addressed even in the most basic film production. Depending on the complexity of the production, the producer may need even more legal counsel than what we've listed here. It is for this reason that we recommend hiring legal counsel early so that they can help you prepare for any legal issue that may arise. In addition, hiring legal counsel with a "flat fee scope of service deal" will likely save you money in the end. If your legal counsel agrees to a flat fee for their services, be sure that they have the following list of legal requirements included.

Legal Paperwork Needed

1. Clear Chain of Title

The producer's lawyer will need to draft agreements with the writer or owner of the material and draft or finalize all contracts for hiring writers, acquiring rights, and all other story-related contracts. If the agreements have already been created, the legal advisor will need to review those contracts.

2. Agreements with Investors

This includes any business plan or fundraising vehicle. Make sure you have proper legal disclaimers on any document discussing fundraising and get clarity from your legal team as to any government regulations on fundraising. Depending on how you are financing it, you may also need an operating agreement between you and your investors.

3. Directors Agreement

This will define the director's duties and time frames for those duties. This includes pre-production preparation, production schedule, and the director's cut of the film. It also includes the director's fees, any profit participation, payment schedule, and the credit they get in the film.

4. Producing Partner Agreements

When choosing a producing partner, it's a good idea to choose someone you know well or have worked with before. You are going to be working closely with them for several years, and you need to have a good understanding of this person's temperament as well as have the same vision for the film. Since problems can sometime arise in partnerships, you'll need to have a legal contract with all of your partners that clearly reflects the level of contribution, and the level of ownership or payment for each partner. If the partnership breaks up, you don't want the other partners to have a legal claim that can stop you from moving forward with the film. To avoid this, have a clear exit strategy for any partner who no longer wants to be a part of the film, or whom you may need to sever your relationship with. Your lawyer should lay out the exact wording of this, but be sure that it allows you to retain the rights to the film and the ability to continue to pursue production and distribution.

Partner agreement should also contain profit participation. Profit participation of a film usually involves a point system where each point relates to a percentage of the profits. While each deal is different, points in relation to producer profit share can be traditionally divided between profit participants, production company, producers, director, and any cast and crew who are participating in profits. For example, in a case where the investors and producers split profit return equally e.g.: 50 percent each and an actor is given five points of producers' profit, the actor would get 2.5 percent of the total profit return.

5. Set up your LLC. (Limited Liability Corporation).
This entity is used to make and own the film. Normally each film is owned by a separate legal entity mainly for the purposes of liability protection

6. Provide a Clearance Report on the Script
A clearance report looks at everything in the script to see if names, locations, or products that are to be used need to be cleared. Permits or a clearance release need to be obtained before they are used in your film.

7. Prepare and Negotiate Principle Talent Agreement
These define the talents payment, credit, and any other specific details relating to their deal.

8. Help with Union Paperwork
You may have chosen to use union members for cast and or crew, which needs to be documented and agreed upon with the relevant unions.

9. Contracts for Heads of Departments
This normally includes anyone head of a department such as production designer, director of photography, costume designer, and editor that you are giving an above-the- line billing.

10. Contract for Other Crew Members, Supporting, and Day Player Cast Members
These are normally in the form of standard templates.

11. Composer Agreement and Synchronization Licenses
This is in relation to any score or songs created for the film and any prerecorded music or songs licensed for the film.

12. Live Performance Agreements

This is in relation to any live music used in the film or dance numbers or live performances.

13. Copyright Registration

This normally covers script and title.

14. Distribution Agreements

Your film needs to be distributed through a variety of sources, including foreign and domestic. These agreements cover the terms of distribution with a foreign sales agency and domestic distributer.

15. Waterfall Agreement

The waterfall agreement shows who gets paid first as your film begins to collect money from the distribution company by using your contracts with investors, production companies, bank loans, deferments, or anyone else who is due money from the film's revenue.

16. Collection Agency Agreement (A.K.A. CAM Agreement)

To help make sure that the revenue of a film is paid back properly, a producer often needs to work with a third party company like a collection agency to handle the revenue and profits. For this they would need a collection agency agreement. This third party helps implement the waterfall agreement by receiving payment from the distribution company and then paying out each payment according to the waterfall agreement.

17. Template Clearance Agreements

Mostly used for clearance purposes, such as location releases, vehicle usage, and brand use.

18. Contractual Restriction Statement

When the film is released or sold for distribution, certain contractual restrictions normally apply and need to be disclosed and adhered to. These commonly include paid ads (essentially actor priority billing or commitments) and/or any restrictions on use (e.g. dubbing or permissions to use behind-the-scenes footage).

19. Insurance Agreements

You may want help acquiring E and O (Errors and Omissions) insurance if your distributors don't provide it.

Distribution Plan

The final stage of packaging your film is to determine your distribution plan. Do you use a classic approach and partner with a distribution company, or do you try self-distribution? Do you approach a distribution company while you are in development, or do you wait until the film is finished?

What Are Your Choices?

Distribution has changed a lot in recent years. Where there used to be few outlets for self-distribution, there are now dozens if not hundreds of digital outlets where any filmmaker can post their project for people to see the film for free or pay to see the film. Services like *Amazon*, *Indieflix*, *Yekra* or aggregators like *Juice*, *bitMAX*, and dozens of other small self-distribution options have popped up all over the web. For small-budget films, these may be viable resources; however, for any larger scale budget, you are still probably better off going through a proven distribution company to see a sizable return on your investment.

Self-distribution

Self-distribution can be appropriate for lower budget films. To successfully recoup your investment, you need to determine how many people need to buy your film before you make a profit. If your film's budget was $100,000 and you are selling your film on Amazon for $9.99 and Amazon keeps half, you have to sell 20,000 copies just to break even. But to sell 20,000, copies you are going to have to spend a lot of money in advertising and an extensive amount of time marketing your film, which would again add to the total cost of your film and the amount needed to recoup.

you are successful in building a large social media campaign, you may be able to build an audience large enough to make your sales numbers. If you only have 1,000 to 2,000 friends on social media, don't count on the campaign working. But if you have 100,000 friends or more, then it may be possible to recoup.

A possible solution for lower budget films is a hybrid service of the distribution model. A low-cost digital service like *Go Digital* may be able to get your film into the VOD market (video on demand), *Red Box*, *Netflix*, *Amazon*, and *iTunes*. This does not relieve you of the duty of advertising, as none of these companies advertise for you. In addition, as the market becomes increasingly saturated, companies like *Amazon* and *iTunes* require that your film have a limited theatrical release before they post it as one of their "featured" films. This featured section can be a boost to your sales as without it, your film can get lost in the thousands of yearly releases. (A limited theatrical release usually means four or more major market cities. At the time of printing, VOD requires a 15-city release before they will promote the film.)

If you plan to sell to the domestic TV market or to a foreign company, you need to know that buyers will rarely, if ever, work with an unproven producer directly. They prefer to only work with a known distribution company that has proven that they can deliver films properly. To get a TV sale or foreign sale (which may account for much of the profits on a film), you usually have to work through a reputable distribution company.

Sales Agent

It may be that you decide to wait until your film is finished before you send it out to distribution companies. If this is the path you take, you may consider working with a sales agent who will put the film in front of distribution companies and foreign buyers. This can be a good place to start if you don't yet have a relationship with a distribution company. Some sales agents sell to both the U.S. and foreign markets, and some just focus on foreign. They take a percentage of the sales and a marketing fee as well as the cost for any additional items needed to complete the delivery that were not provided by the producer as part of the initial delivery agreement. Foreign sales agents also charge a marketing fee to cover their costs of

attending the film markets, where they sell the film, as well as th
any marketing materials they create.

Distribution Company

Partnering with a distribution company can be the best way to ensure a
return on the investment. In addition, working with a distribution company
from the beginning of your film can assist you in making choices that will
help sell your film later in the market place. Good distribution companies
know the market and can tell you which genres are selling, which actors will
help sell the film in foreign territories, and which ones won't help at all.

A great way to start looking for a distribution partner is to check out
their company's website to see what type of movies they have made or are
selling and then look up how well that film did for them. Many distribution
companies focus on certain genres. Some are interested in horror films,
others are only interested in dramas, action, or comedies. It is important to
partner with a company that has a track record of distributing your genre of
film. If not, they may not be interested in or have the right connections to
sell your film.

Also, for U.S. distribution, look for a company that has a relationship
with wide outlets like *Target*, *Wal-Mart*, *iTunes*, etc. or relationships with a
company like *E1* (the largest distributors of DVDs in North America).
Without these connections, the distribution company may not be able to
get the sales needed for your film or they will have to outsource to another
distribution company, which will mean even more commissions will be
taken out of the profits.

If you decide to work with a smaller distribution company, be
prepared to help them market your film. In today's market, very few small
distribution companies have the funds to promote a film themselves. Set
aside some of your budget for marketing and even four-walling your film
(paying to take it out theatrically). Doing a limited theatrical release is vital
to get any press for your film as critics in major markets will not review
your film unless it can be seen by the general audience in a local theater.

Distribution deals are usually structured in two ways: either they pay
you an advance and then pay a lower share of the subsequent revenue, or

JULIA VERDIN and MATT DEAN

they give you no advanced payment but a higher percentage of the revenue. In both cases, the distribution agreement has clauses enabling the distribution company to recoup its expenses in marketing and distributing your film. How you handle your distribution agreement may be driven by how confident you are in the film as well as general conditions in the overall film market at the time. The less risky approach is to take the advance offered by the distribution company thereby ensuring you cover a large part of your production expenses and payback the investors but forfeit some of the revenue flow above the advance. If you are confident in your film, you may choose little to no advance to get a higher proportion of the film's sales. In a perfect world, you would get both.

Before signing with a company, take time to call other producers who are currently with that company to find out if the management and sales reps have been forthcoming and honest. Having run into many distribution issues on several films, we can't stress enough how important it is to learn everything you can about a company before signing away the rights to your film. The first couple of years of distribution are the most important, and you won't get a second chance to release the film for the first time.

"If I were ever stranded on a desert island
there would be three things I'd need:
food, shelter and a grip."

– George C. Scott

Chapter 10

Crew and Department Definitions and Duties

What's coming up in this chapter is a giant list - and lists aren't sexy, but knowing the title and role of each crew member is extremely important as a producer. From building the budget, to proper management, the producer needs to know what everyone on their team does and why they do it. If you are a more experienced producer and already know the functions of each crew member, you may be able to skip to the next chapter.

The Crew

We aren't going to lay out every single individual who may work for you on the film, but you need to know the main positions and what their duties are. On a small crew, people will take on more than one role and it's important to know what positions are vital to having a smooth running production. If you don't have the budget to hire someone to fill a position, chances are, you or one of your producing partners will take that role.

There is no hard and fast rule about how many people are needed on set, but looking at the script, you can usually tell what the minimum crew is likely to be. If your story is a drama set in one location with a cast of four actors, you can get away with a small, less expensive crew compared to filming a larger story involving a big cast, action sequences, many locations, and lots of extras. If you are setting out to accomplish an ambitious film on a lower budget, take note that special effects, stunts, and large sets all add to the size of crew needed and the cost of the picture. The best way to handle a lower-than-desired budget is to start with the basic items needed to accomplish your film and add onto it as the budget allows. This way, you may find that you are able to produce your film for a lower budget than you originally thought. Meanwhile, if the budget grows too large, you can cut back on the additional items without getting rid of the basics needed to complete your project.

A Simplified Crew for a Lower Budget.

The basic pieces that are needed for an ultra-low budget short film are the same pieces you need on a larger film. These are: (1) a story to film, (2) someone to film it, (3) someone in front of the camera, (4) someone to edit the film, and (5) someone to get it out to the public. Almost every job on a feature film branches out from those basic needs, and those jobs expand into more and more roles as the script or the budget for that script grows. On the smallest of sets, this may include only you and a camera on a tripod, or it may be a minimal cast and crew where you use available lighting, film in available locations using available props, having actors bring their own wardrobe and do their own makeup, hiring a DP who owns their own camera, an editor with their own edit system, and when finished, you release the film yourself online for everyone in the world to see.

With a small enough crew, or enough favors from friends, it is possible to create a film for little to no budget. If, however, you are going to make an ultra-low budget film by "borrowing" time and effort from people, make sure you take care of basic needs. Food, water, shelter, and toilets should never be left out of your planning. As you build your film, keep in mind the basic elements of what will be needed and find creative ways to fill those needs with the budget you have.

Crew Members and Budget Formatting

We mentioned in chapter 6 that you need to look ahead to the crew list to know who you will need - and this is that list. To construct your production budget, you need to know the positions of all the participants traditionally involved in the production of the film. We've broken this list down into a format similar to what you will find in an industry-standard line-item production budget, which can be found in budgeting software like *Movie Magic Budgeting*. This includes what is called "above the line" and "below the line." Normally above the line are some of the key team members we discussed in the last chapter, including your writer(s), producer(s), director, casting director, and name talent. Line producers and location scouts normally sit below the line along with the supporting actors, and all of your crew, such as the director of photography, camera operator, makeup and hair, extras, as well as the post production team including the editor, composer, visual effects, sound mixer, colorist, etc. As we have already given definitions for a number of these positions, we will only give details on ones not already discussed.

Above the Line

1. Writer

This is the person from whom you have optioned a script, are paying to write a script for you, or are paying to complete rewrites on a script.

2. Producer

This includes the executive producer, producer, and co-producer.

3. Director

In the budget, this category includes your director and if you have one, a choreographer and casting director.

4. Actors

This includes your leads actors playing the lead roles.

5. Casting Director

Helps find and hire the cast.

Below-the-Line

Production

1. Production staff

A. Line Producer

This person hires and organizes the department heads, the crew, and along with the production coordinator, runs the day-to-day operations.

B. Unit Production Manager (UPM)

This person works with the line producer to organize the below-the-line production needs and coordinates all equipment as it is needed on set. On a smaller budget film, the line producer may do this job as well.

C. First Assistant Director (1st AD)

The 1st AD creates the schedule so that all cast and crew know where they need to be and when. They work closely with the director to achieve the director's shot list, and then they keep track of any shots that are missed that day so they can be added to another day. Additional duties include giving out instructions and safety guidelines to the cast and crew, as well as helping the director with blocking scenes and coordinating extras. As the day moves forward, the 1st AD keeps track of the time, and how many more shots need to be accomplished. If the production is running behind, they will let the director know so the director can decide how to continue with the remainder of the day.

When hiring a 1st AD, it's a good idea to make sure they understand their role in keeping the set moving. A good AD takes much of the pressure off of the director by being the one who hurries cast and crew along and keeps the pace of the day foremost on their mind. The 1st AD needs to be your director's right hand, but also needs to hold a strong whip pushing even the director forward when needed. Sometimes a director may want to spend too much time on one shot, not realizing they are losing the rest of their day. The 1st AD needs to be able to give them the option of continuing with the shot while risking the remaining shots for the day, or moving on to the rest of the schedule.

D. Second Assistant Director (2nd AD)

The 2nd AD executes and adjusts the schedule as filming begins. They continually work on the schedule for the following days as things often change when on set. If you don't have a 2nd AD, then the 1st AD will have to attend to the schedule after that day of filming.

E. Third Assistant Director (3rd AD)

This person helps co-ordinate the actors moving from their trailer or dressing rooms to the set. They also help keep unnecessary people off of the set. On a lower budget film that is not a director's Guild of America (DGA) signatory, this role may be taken on by the 1st or 2nd AD. To keep things running smoothly, however, you are better off using a production assistant to take on this role so as to not overwhelm the 1st AD.

F. Set Production Assistant (PAs)

Set PAs are the on-set assistants and report to the ADs. They generally help out with anything needed on set from getting actors drinks, to helping with crowd control.

G. Script Supervisor

This is one of the most important record-keeping jobs on set. This person keeps track of what is being shot and the details within each shot. They make note of the camera angle, any dialogue changes, actors' movement and eye lines, the continuity of how actors use props, costumes adjustments during the scene, and any other item on set. They watch the details of the continuity to help the director and the actors stay consistent from one take to another.

When a director likes a take, the script supervisor circles that take in their script notes (thus the term, "circle takes"). At the end of each day of filming, the script supervisor hands over copies of their notes for the day (which will be combined into what some people call a continuity script) and that script will be used by the editor to determine what shots they have to work with in cutting the film. If the script supervisor does their job properly, it's easier to tell if you need additional shots before wrapping that particular set up. Their notes are vital when it comes to marking each shot properly on the clap board and even more vital in the edit suite when you are looking for a particular shot.

H. Location Scout

The location scout finds and secures locations for the shoot during pre-production. They bring back photos of the area for the production team to look over and assist the line producer with information about the location needed to secure the location for the shoot.

I. Location Manager

The location manager prepares the location prior to filming. They make sure that permits are in place, neighbors have been notified, doors unlocked, and that any production needs are looked after including: space for an on location office, dressing rooms or greenroom for cast, space for catering, and bathrooms. They know where the nearest hospital is, where base camp should be set up, where catering should set up, and weather reports for the area. On smaller budget films, the location scout and location manager may be the same person.

J. Production Co-coordinator

The production co-coordinator runs the production office. They work with the line producer to insure that everything and everyone is where they are supposed to be, when they are needed. They oversee the office equipment, office staff, and anything else needed for day-to-day operations. You want to hire a very organized person as your production coordinator. If your budget will not allow you to hire both a UPM and a line producer, the production coordinator may help take some of the load from the line producer by organizing rental equipment in addition to their normal duties. They are in charge of the office and the office paperwork, including contact information sheets, circulating script revisions, setting up production meetings, organizing locations scouts, read throughs, rehearsals, and travel accommodations.

K. Accountant

The accountant works with the line producer to keep track of the money spent on the production. They check the numbers they receive from the line producer with the numbers laid out in the budget to help make sure money is spent where it is supposed to be and that the production is not going over budget. They would normally be expected to produce a weekly cost report so you can keep track of where you are in the budget.

2. Art Department
A. Production Designer

The production designer is the head of the art department and is in charge of the overall look of the picture. They report to the director and help the director achieve the desired vision for the film. This person traditionally works with the costume and hair and makeup department, to communicate the director's ideas and desires. If the film is complicated with a lot of design, costumes, and sets (e.g. a sci-fi film or a period film), this person needs to be added to the leadership team before the line producer can finalize the budget.

B. Art Director

The art director works with the production designer to create the look of the world that you are filming.

C. Set Designer

The set designer designs the look of the set. This can be on location or on a stage at a studio. They build all set pieces that are not handled by the actor. A set piece is something in the scene but is not used by the actor, where a prop is an item the actor uses in the scene.

3. Set Construction

A team that builds any set that is required .

4. Set Operations

These people help with the basic work of the day-to-day operations.

A. Grips

Grips help with the camera crew. They help move the camera and other technical equipment around on the set as needed.

B. Rigging Crew

These people are used on larger lighting days when you need to put up special equipment or black out a set.

C. Craft Services

Craft services are any food and drinks supplied on location, with easy access for the cast and crew. This is separate from the catering service for main meals.

5. Stunts

A. Stunt Co-Coordinator

This person prepares the actor and stunt people for any stunt work in a film. This can be anything as small as tripping on a sidewalk, to being thrown from the top of a building. They work with the director prior to production to see how many people they need, and what stunts are needed. These stunts are prepared ahead of time and can take days, weeks, or even months to set up, depending on how complicated they are. They also work with your actors to insure they are trained properly for any stunt work they will be doing themselves. On a small-budget film, this person may also act as the action director and fight choreographer.

B. Action Director/Stunt Director

If you are producing an action film with a large number of action sequences, you may need an action director to work closely with the director and the stunt department to create an action style for the film.

C. Fight Choreographer

These specialists are needed on fight-heavy films like martial arts movies. They work closely with the stunt coordinator, and/or action director, to create a particular fight style for an action film.

D. Stunt Performers

When there are fight scenes or stunts too dangerous for your lead actors or any other cast member to perform, a stunt performer will double your actor. On a smaller budget film, if you can find a stunt performer who can also act, you might consider casting them for one line or non-speaking roles involving stunts. Stunt doubles should be hired after you know who your lead actors are so you can cast the doubles with a similar body build to your actors.

Stunts can include everything from a car crash to falling off a chair. If you are a SAG signatory film, then the stunt department falls under the SAG contract. If you are a non-union film, then you may not be able to use SAG performers without risking their standing with the union. All union fees apply, including stunt adjustments, which are special fees for particular types of stunts.

6. Special Effects

This department handles the in-camera effects on set. This

includes any and all fire, smoke, water, explosives, squibs (a bullet hit on an object or a person), or other in- camera effects. This can include any effect attached to an actor or any makeup effects. For safety reasons, this department usually consists of at least two people.

7. Set Dressing

The set dresser works with the art department to place appropriate objects on the set to complete the desired look. These may include pictures, curtains, chairs, lamps, or any other objects seen by the camera, but these are not objects handled by the actors. Objects that actors handle are props. On a bigger budget film with a lot of set dressing, an assistant may be necessary.

8. Property Department
A. Prop Master

A prop master acquires and keeps track of all props including fake weapons used by the cast during production. This person helps find or build all props that will be handled by the actors. When using fake weapons on set, the prop master or a responsible designee of the production needs to be fully responsible and keep the fake weapon in their possession at all times when they are not being used on set. Large casts often require the prop master to have a prop assistant.

B. Gun Handler

When using any real fire arms on set you need, by law, to hire a licensed gun handler with a license from the state you are filming in to be responsible for the firearms. If the gun handler feels that the safety of cast and crew are being jeopardized, they have the right to stop filming and take the guns off set until the film can proceed safely.

C. Weapons Specialist

The weapons specialist keeps track of all weapons on set. This includes any item being used as a weapon at any time (e.g.: guns, knives, sticks, rocks). The weapons specialist also teaches weapons safety to cast and crew.

9. Wardrobe
A. Costume Designer
Creates or purchases all costumes and wardrobe worn by the cast. If you have a large cast, you may need several assistants for this department.

B. Wardrobe Manager
Signs out and checks in all wardrobe worn by the cast. They also handle any costume repairs or cleaning. For a very big cast, you may need an additional assistant.

If on a smaller budget film you ask actors to wear their own clothes, discuss with them ahead of time the colors and tones required to fit the scene. Left to their own guesswork, they may or may not pick out something that is appropriate for the scene or the style of the film. Actors should not use their own clothes for any scenes in which clothes could possibly get damaged as you will need to have two sets of wardrobe for those scenes to avoid future problems with continuity. It is safer to buy cheap wardrobe to avoid this.

10. Makeup/Hair
A. Makeup and Hair Supervisor
This person works with the director to get the look needed for each actor. This can be as simple as some base make-up and as complicated as prosthetics.

B. Makeup Artist
In charge of prepping the actors' makeup for camera.

C. Hair Stylist
In charge of prepping the actors' hair for camera.

When working on your schedule for filming, you need to know that in normal filming conditions, women need around an hour in the makeup/hair department, and men about half of that. If you only have one make-up artist and 10 actors, you may need five or more hours to get everyone through. In that case, it's better to hire additional makeup artists and hair stylists. If you only have a couple of big days of filming, you could just hire additional help for those days. When working a large set, you need to have a crew that can handle the number of actors coming through without slowing down production.

On a low-budget film, you may ask the actors to take care of the makeup themselves. If the actors do their own makeup, make sure the director checks it to be sure they didn't use to little or too much.

11. Picture Vehicles
A. Picture Vehicle

Any vehicle used on camera. This can be any mode of transportation used on screen. These are hired by the line producer and managed by the production manager. Any picture vehicle required to have a license plate, should be outfitted with one specially acquired for filming and not a privately owned plate.

B. Stunt or Precision Drivers

These individuals drive any vehicle where the camera does not see the actor's face and any of the background vehicles. These are often skilled positions and may be part of the stunt team.

12. Animals
A. Animal Wrangler

Takes care of any animals used on set and helps with the animal performance.

B. Animal Performers

This includes any animal performing on camera. For your film to be certified by the humane society and to insure the safety of your animal and the crew, animal performances should be reported to and monitored by the humane society. Depending on your filming location, the animal may also need to be licensed by the local state or county.

13. Camera Department

A. Director of Photography (DP)

Works with the director to create the overall look of the picture. Directly oversees the lighting department. Next to the director, the DP is one of the most important artistic members of the crew, and we have included a lengthy section on the DP in chapter 11.

B. Camera Operator

Works with the DP in the movement and operation of the camera.

C. Focus Puller

Adjusts the focus during a shot to be sure that the desired object or individual is in sharp focus.

D. Data Management Technician (DMT)

When digitally capturing a film, the DMT is responsible for taking the data from the camera operator, backing up that data, and passing it off to the editorial department or the production company handling the storage of that data.

E. Digital Imaging Technician (DIT)

The DIT is a camera engineer responsible for working with the director of photography and the camera operator to set the color specifications of the camera. On a smaller film set, they may also work as the DMT.

14. Lighting

A. Gaffer

Head of the lighting department and helps the DP by helping plan and execute all lighting for the set.

B. Best Boy

Assistant to the gaffer.

15. Electrical

A. Electrician

Runs electrical lines (AKA: stingers) for the lighting department and any other electrical needs on set. This includes power for the trailers, catering, and any other department. Depending on how big your set is and your lighting set ups are, you may need several electricians.

B. Generator Operator

Operates the generator when on location and there are no power sources strong enough for the lights.

16. Grips

A. Key Grip

In charge of all the grips.

B. Grip

Grips can be assigned to different departments. Some work for the key grip, others for the electrical department, lighting department, or the camera department. These roles are essential to a smooth-running set as grips help move and adjust all of the equipment on set, including lighting, dolly tracks, the video village, and camera equipment.

17. Production Sound Department

A. Production Sound Mixer (AKA: Field Mixer)

The production sound mixer is in charge of all sound recording on set. They place microphones in key locations to record the best possible sound, without getting in the way of the camera. They mix all levels of incoming sound to insure a quality recording.

B. Boom Operator

Assists the field mixer by using a boom microphone to capture sound.

It's important that the producer be aware of who they are hiring as the location sound mixer. Sound is too often left as an afterthought on smaller budget films. Sound is, however, just as important as picture, and a good sound mixer can save you, or cost you, a lot of time and money. Bad audio can cost you thousands of dollars in post-production if you have to do a lot of additional dialogue recording (ADR - or some call it automated dialog recording) with your cast. Like your script supervisor, a good sound mixer picks up actors fumbling lines, sound interruptions, and other issues and tells the director that you need another take as well as keeps good records for post. It is usually inevitable that some ADR are necessary due to wind or elements that you can't control, but with a good sound mixer, this should be minimal. An audience can forgive a bad picture (e.g. every found-footage movie EVER), but they cannot forgive bad sound. (Even in found-footage movies, you can clearly hear the dialog.)

18. Transportation
A. Transport Coordinator
This person is responsible for coordinating who drives the various trailers for the cast, production vehicles, and cast members, to the set.
B. Driver(s)
Hired by the transport department to drive the trailers, portable toilets, cast members, and production vehicles.

19. Location
The location department encompasses a number of different items that help in the smooth running of the set.
A. Catering
Provides the main meals for cast and crew.

Catering should be aware of any food allergies and special diet needs. You need to find a good catering company to provide your meals and a craft-service person to organize your snacks and snack table. Feeding your cast and crew well is very important on films. No set can operate well without snacks, coffee, tea, water, and an assortment of soft drinks. A hot meal should be served every six hours and include healthy food rather than fried foods and carbs, as that will affect your team's energy levels. You want to keep them well fed and hydrated so people stay happy and motivated through the last shot of the day.

B. Toilets

If bathrooms are not available on set, it's the responsibility of the line producer to arrange portable toilets brought for cast and crew, and the responsibility of the location manager to be sure they are operational.

C. Housing

If the cast and/or crew are filming more than an hour from home, it's a good idea to arrange housing so that you don't waste two hours or more on people driving to set every day. Housing is arranged by the line producer and managed by the production coordinator.

D. Security

If you are filming in a location that is open to the public, security is important both for the safety of the cast and crew and also guarding expensive equipment. To obtain permitting at some locations, you may be required to hire police for public safety.

E. Medic

Even if you are not performing stunts, it's important to have a medic on set for any medical emergencies. In some states, it may be a legal or union requirement that a medic be on set. Check with legal counsel to be sure that your set operates within the federal and state guidelines or you may face steep fines or penalties.

20. Second Unit

This department includes a second unit director, camera operator, and any other staff needed to film shots that do not need to be supervised by the director.

21. Extras Casting Director

Extras casting done well can add value to a film. You need someone to pick out the right types and particular faces for the extras in scenes as they add to the atmosphere and overall look of the production.

Below-the-Line

Post-Production

1. Editorial
A. Post-Production Supervisor

The post-production supervisor oversees all of post-production through to delivery including the type of edit system, the editors, color correction, visual effects, music and audio mix, booking the actors for ADR sessions, and the main and end titles. They work with the line producer to ensure there are clearances for everything in the film, and then put together the delivery paperwork for the distribution company.

The post supervisor works closely with the DP to determine the best capturing format, then, depending on what camera you are using, they will work with the DMT to prepare any digital files to make sure the material is copied and a copy taken to the editor. They work with the director to choose an edit system, coordinate with the audio mixer to make sure of proper audio recording and recombining the audio with the video or film, oversee the editing, storage of data, visual effects, sound, music, color correction, and all delivery items. If any of these items are not handled properly during production, it will be too late to make corrections by the time you get into post-production.

B. Editor

Works with the director to edit the film. (We've included more detail on the editorial team in the chapter on post-production.)

C. Assistant Editor

Preps the video and audio so that it is ready for the editor to work with.

C. Colorist

Works with the director and the DP to create the intended look of the film.

D. Online Editor

Takes the completed picture from the colorist and the completed sound from the mixer and puts the two together to deliver the master of the film.

2. Visual Effects

A. Effects Supervisor

Oversees all the visual effects in the film. They help set up composite shots, green screens, and background plates where effects will be added in post-production.

B. Visual Effects Artist(s), (VFX)

These people perform the detailed work of completing visual effects and include the compositor, modeler, animator, matte painter, etc.

3. Music

A. Composer

Composes original music for the film.

B. Music Supervisor

Finds pre-recorded music for the film, including library music and music from other artists or bands.

4. Post-Sound

A. Sound Designer

Creates the original sound of the film. The sound designer often gathers sound effects in the field or creates them from scratch.

B. Foley Artist(s)

Fills in the movements from the actors where sound recording from set is not complete.

C. Dialog Editor

Cleans and preps the dialog for the mixer.

D. Mixer

Mixes and masters the final audio.

Below-the-Line

Other

In most budgets, the last section of below-the-line departments deals with the publicity and general expenses of the picture.

1. Publicist
The publicist often handles media relations, the electronic press kit (EPK), festival entry, and awards submission.

2. EPK (Electronic Press Kit) Camera Crew
For promotion and advertising the film, an additional camera crew is needed to film behind-the-scenes footage, cast and crew interviews, and any other promotional material.

3. Still Photographer
Shoots the production and behind-the-scenes still images.

There are many positions to remember. As you refine your budget and schedule, keep looking back at this list to determine who you need on your team.

PART III
SETTING THE STAGE

"In all things success depends on previous preparation,
and without such previous preparation there is sure to be failure."

— Confucius

"If you aren't in over your head,
how do you know how tall you are?"

– T.S.. Eliot

Chapter 11

Pre-production Part 1
Setting Up

As you complete funding for your project, you enter the stage called pre-production. This is where you establish your office, start hiring your crew, scout locations, finalize cast, and rehearse with the actors.

You have noticed by this point that the majority of this book is dedicated to development and pre-production. That is because your film will only be as good as your preparation. The first part of preparation gave you the script, the core team, and the budget. Now you get to work with that team to prepare to start filming. You first have to arrange a few more business items, but then you get to start working with the heads of departments on things like collecting props, costumes, and all the other production details that make this line of work fun.

The process of pre-production can be very fluid. Schedules for cast, location problems due to weather, and other issues can force you to make changes to your schedule on a continual basis. This should not mean that you don't try to lock down every detail you possibly can prior to production. The more you have ready, the more prepared you'll be for problems that arise.

Office Space

The first thing you want to do is set up a production office. This is where you will base your operations. For those of you doing ultra-low budget films who can't afford an office, you may be able to stage an office from home. No matter where you set up your office, you need enough space for multiple rooms for key positions (e.g. the line producer, who needs to make phone calls, have private conversations with workers, and discuss rates and confidential production deals).

In the office, you need to set up a phone and Internet line (preferably wireless), and if available, a wireless printer that the staff can connect to. It is important to have someone designated to answer the production company phones, or if you are using cellular phones for the production company, have one as a dedicated line. This is a great job for an intern and can give them the experience of working in a production office. You need a copy machine, enough outlets for staff to plug in their computers, Internet service, and a conference room or a large table for table reads and production meetings. Have a contact list with phone extensions, cell phone numbers, and the Internet password with easy access for everyone who works in the office. In addition, you need storage space for wardrobe and art department to house their materials as well as private areas for costume fittings.

Interns

Since we mentioned interns, we should note that if you bring in an intern, you need to check with your government regulations regarding the hiring of unpaid workers. If they are coming from a school, that school will have requirements for the student to receive school credits for working with you. Wherever they come from, there are restrictions on number of working hours and work conditions. In recent years, there have been a number of lawsuits concerning interns at production companies, so make sure you are working within legal guidelines.

Payroll

Next, you need to decide if you are going to use a payroll company or your accountant to handle payroll. If you have a very small crew and cast, the accountant (or you) may be able to handle payroll. The benefit of having a payroll company is that they take care of all the state-required paperwork, pay all checks sent to the cast and crew, and take out (and keep track of) the taxes for each person. The payroll company charges a percentage of the payroll for their service, but it takes a large load off your accountant or yourself if you have to keep track of more than a dozen people. At the end of each week of production, the payroll company supplies you with a weekly payroll report showing who has been paid and how much from the week prior. Most payroll companies need a few days after the work week is completed to run through all the paperwork and distribute checks.

A payroll service also works with union-required fringe payments. To take care of this properly, they need a list of who is in a union, and what the union fringe payment requirements are. The fringe payments are what are paid into the union members' pension and welfare fund, and each union has different requirements. Some payroll companies may also offer workers compensation coverage as part of their service. You should let all cast and crew know when they will get paid. Always be sure you have enough money in your account to pay everyone, and don't go more than a week without handing out paychecks. Much of your crew are blue collar workers who rely on the fees they are getting from your film. It's important for your reputation as a producer to pay the workers on time.

Known actors' representatives may ask for the actor's fee to be paid up front or escrowed. With union cast and crew, you have to abide by the union rules in regard to payment schedules. For non-union cast and crew, you need to pay attention to local labor laws to be sure you are at or above minimum wage.

Some of the department heads (e.g. the DP) may ask for or require a portion of their total fee upfront as a deposit to book their service. This deposit is often required by professionals who cannot afford to book work and then have that work cancel at the last minute. This fee is often non-refundable, so try to negotiate a reasonable deposit fee that will not endanger the production if you need to reschedule.

Other service contracts like rental houses for cameras, lights, etc., may also ask for part or all of their fees upfront as a deposit. In addition, some require a credit check or ask to hold a credit card number from the production company until equipment is safely returned.

Though the producer may need to pay some of these deposit fees up front, we recommend avoiding paying the entire fee upfront if possible. (e.g. If camera rental is $200 per day, and you are renting for 10 days, the total fee is $2,000 and you may see a deposit fee of 50 percent. Try to avoid paying the entire $2,000 upfront in case there are problems with the equipment that the rental house is responsible for.)

The payroll department needs a copy of the SAG exhibit G's (if you are using SAG actors), W9s, I9s, and time sheets to calculate payroll properly. Send them a copy of the time sheets each day or if you are not able to have them worked on each day, send them at the end of the week.

Production Insurance

Before you are able to secure locations, permits, rent gear or studio space, the production needs production insurance. This is usually handled by the line producer. The cost of insurance can vary depending on the amount of time you film, rental gear insurance requirement minimums, stunts, and special effects. Not all insurance companies provide production insurance, so you may need to consult a production guide or call around to see who does in your area. If you have trouble finding affordable insurance, you may be able to cover it through a co-production deal with a company that has its own production insurance policy. Many larger production companies carry their own insurance all year long, which extends to any filming they do. If you make a deal with a production company, you may be able to use their insurance to help lower your cost, though you may still need some additional coverage for special effects and stunts.

Insurance for stunts for small-budget films can be problematic as the producer may not be able to acquire stunt insurance on their own. In this case, the producer may be able to get insurance through another production company. We do not recommend performing stunts or starting any production without proper production insurance as you risk the inability to cover the costs of any injuries on set as well as leave yourself open for lawsuits. Many stunt performers will not work on a set where stunt insurance is not provided.

Here is a list of typical items your production insurance needs to cover:

1. All rentals, including gear, props, sets, and wardrobe.

2. Your production office and its contents.

3. Any property that could be damaged or destroyed on location by a third party.

4. Any equipment that could be damaged on set.

5. Any equipment that you own and are lending or renting to the production.

6. Any expenses you may incur if your location gets damaged and you have to move at extra cost to the production.

7. Protection for loss or damage to your film stock, negative, tape, sound, or digital image.

8. General liability insurance (for coverage if the production inadvertently caused damage to a member of the general public).

9. Automobile insurance to cover rental cars, cars under the production's control, or individuals' cars used for the production.

10. Workers compensation for cast, crew, and volunteers for injuries sustained on set while employed. (If using a payroll company, check to see if they cover this area already.)

11. Cast insurance is always necessary if you are using a completion bond for what the bond company calls "essential elements" including your director, DP, and key cast members. All individuals considered essential elements need to have a medical exam prior to filming to determine their current health so that they can be cleared for the production by the health insurance company.

12. Special effects involving any possible danger to the cast or crew need to be covered. This includes anything from smoke and fire to special gimbals created to move set pieces or rigging used on or near the cast and crew.

13. Stunts of any magnitude, including anything from a simple fall out of a chair to elaborate stunt sequences, need to be insured.

14. Special circumstances including water scenes and other high-risk scenes where cast and crew may be in increased danger.

15. Helicopters or other aircraft all need to be insured.

The basic rule is that the more risk you take in the script, the higher your production insurance is likely to be. If your film is a drama and mostly takes place on one location, your production insurance will be very reasonable. If you are shooting a stunt-heavy action film, with a lot of expensive locations and risky activities, expect to budget more for your production insurance.

Petty Cash

If you have an accountant, you need to let them know the petty cash requirements for each day of filming. Petty cash should be accounted for in your budget and set aside for parking, additional craft service needs, or any emergencies that arise.

Script Breakdown

Unlike the rough breakdown of the script that you did for the business plan, the line producer now needs to have a full breakdown of the script from the first AD. Each of the department heads needs a copy of the breakdown so that they have a full list of everything that is needed for filming and when it is needed. From this detailed breakdown, a final budget can be completed using numbers the line producer plugs in from all the production deals they arrange. From lights, cameras, food, locations, etc., the line producer gives each department the budget they will have to work with, and it is up to each department head to stay within that budget.

Tentative Schedule

From the final breakdown, the first AD then looks at actors' availability and location availability to create a tentative schedule. This is likely to be somewhat fluid as you move closer to production, but a final schedule needs to be completed once all the locations have been secured.

Hiring Department Heads

Now that you know what you need for your film, you can begin to hire any additional department heads that are not yet on the team. Each department head should be allowed to bring on team members they like to work with, as long as it fits within the budget allocated by the line producer. The size of each department depends on what the budget allows and what is needed to effectively run a smooth shoot. Each department head knows which members of their team are necessary during pre-production and who they can wait to hire until production. Anyone hired before they are needed will be a drain on your limited resources.

When it comes time to hire each member of the crew, you need a written agreement for their work. This includes all producers, the director, the DP, and each crew member down to the production assistants and interns. This can be called a "deal memo," "contract," or an "agreement." Whatever you chose to call it, its purpose is to lay out the full terms of the deal for employment, including when employment begins and ends, what their pay is, and if they have any claims to ownership on the film or participation in the profits. No one should start work without an agreement, and you should keep copies of all agreements to be included in your delivery book for the delivery of the film.

What to Look for in a Director of Photography

Your director will most likely have thoughts about a director of photography (DP) that they like to work with. This position is an important partnership with the director to help create the look of the film. If you have a director who is new to directing, it would be prudent to hire an experienced DP. An inexperienced DP may slow down the shooting process and could be unreliable in the quality of footage and coverage they capture.

If your director does not have a DP they regularly work with, or one who you feel is up to the job, take time to look at demos from skilled DPs. Look for someone who is great at lighting, understands camera angles, the basics of camera placement and camera movement, and can make decisive moves quickly. A slow DP can destroy timing on set and can lead to overly long days and budget overages.

If you aren't sure what to look for in a DP, it's a good idea to educate yourself on the basics of cinematography. Books like *The Five C's of Cinematography* by Joseph Mascelli, will give you a good basic understanding of camera angles, continuity, and composition so that you can be an informed producer.

The DP needs to be able to capture the vision of the film through the type of camera, lighting, and angles. In addition to the look of the film, they need to be able to watch out for the things that an inexperienced director may miss. Proper coverage (a sufficient number of shots from different angles) of your scene is needed to be able to edit your film. An inexperienced director may not understand all the coverage needed, which is where an experienced DP (and a good script supervisor) can help make sure you have every shot you need to tell the story and not have problems later in the editing room.

The DP should be consulted as to the type of camera they would like to use and should be familiar with that camera. They should understand the work flow of what it takes to get the footage from that camera into the post process and should work with the post supervisor to coordinate. Each camera is set up differently in regards to how it records an image and what color and contrast range it has. (How much range does it record from white to black, which gives you the latitude or "stops" of the camera. In other words - how dark can it be and how light can it be before you lose image quality.)

You may even be able to find a DP who owns a camera that you want to use on the film; however, do not make this a deciding factor of the type of camera you are going to use. Hire the DP because they are highly skilled and have the ability to capture the style and vision the director has for the film and not just because they have a camera. Rental of a good camera should not be out of range for most low-budget productions. Find rental house that will give you a good deal on a higher end camera and lens package, and when renting keep in mind that using a smaller format camera can jeopardize your ability to sell the film to broadcast TV and/or to get it accepted at the major festivals.

On a small budget film it can be very useful as well as help save money if the DP is able to operate the camera. Complicated camera moves may require a focus puller, dolly grip, or other key team members, but each of these should be weighed against the needs of the budget and the desire of the director for that shooting style. Traditionally, the key team members for the DP's department are the camera operator, focus puller, key grip, and best boy.

A second unit camera team may also be needed to film shots that do not involve the main actors. Using the scene breakdowns, the DP is able to tell if there are any shots (like establishing shots, scenic shots, or action sequences with stunt doubles) that can be filmed with a second unit.

Check the references of the DP with producers and directors of previous work. How quick were they able to set up shots, and how good did those shots look? Were they properly exposed? Did the director get the look they wanted easily? Some DPs can be perfectionists, which may work if you have a long shoot schedule budgeted. However, on a smaller budget film, you need someone who can work quickly, while getting the best image in the time allowed. If you are filming a "found footage" movie or "natural light" movie, experienced reality TV videographers and news photographers can be great at this style of filming and may be more affordable as they may want to break into features.

Creating the Look of the Film with the Production Designer

When hiring a production designer, look for samples of their work in previous films with budgets similar to your film. In our experience, the art department has a tendency to go over budget, so it's important to get references and ask previous employers about both the production designer's quality of work and if they stayed within their allotted budget. For a lower budget film, an affordable solution would be to find an art director who has had experience working with high-quality production designers and is ready to move up to the position of production designer.

Some of the departments the production designer will want to bring in during pre-production are:

Prop Master

A great prop master has connections for anything needed for the film. They can either find an object or have one made.

Costume Designer

On a larger budget film, the costume designer is hired during pre-production to begin designing and making the costumes. However on a lower budget film, the producer will likely buy pre-made wardrobe or have the actors bring their own clothes. On a small- budget film, the costume designer may not be needed until all of the cast has been hired and they are ready to do fittings on the actors so each item of wardrobe can be tailored to fit.

Makeup and Hair Supervisor

On films with extensive stylings, prosthetics, or high fashion, the hair and makeup team may be brought in early to help the production designer create a special look. For most low-budget films, the hair and makeup department is brought in a few days before filming. It's important to know that the hair and makeup department is able to work quickly as any delays here will set back the production while filming. Check their references with former employers to make sure they can stay on schedule.

Special Effects Supervisor

If the film involves any special effects, the production designer will bring in the special effects supervisor to oversee the design and execution of these effects. Depending on how elaborate, these may take a few hours or a few months to set up.

Preparing for Any Stunts with the Stunt Coordinator

If your film has stunts, it is important that those stunts are worked out well in advance of the day of filming. A stunt coordinator is able to tell you how long they need to set up any particular stunt and how many people they need to perform that stunt safely.

Prepare Early for Post with the Post-Production Supervisor

It's important to hire the post supervisor in preproduction as they will help set up the post process for the film. By hiring them early, you save yourself the trouble of having to fix mistakes in post-production, which could have been caught earlier, thus saving money and time.

Script Read Through with Department Heads

Before each of the departments begin working on the film, it's important to sit down with all the department heads and read through the script out loud. (This is called simply - a read through). Each department can mark areas of the script that may need clarification. Questions about VFX, staging scenes, issues with large crowds, animals, costumes, or even timing for hair and makeup can all be addressed at this stage with the group, and then on an individual basis as needed.

Locking Down Locations

You should already have locations in mind for the production, and now is time to start locking them down. If you don't know where you are filming, you won't have accurate costs, and the rest of the team won't be able to do their jobs as they won't know what production design, lighting, etc., is needed for that location.

Locking down the locations is the job of your line producer who may need to hire a location scout and a location manager. While still hunting for locations, you will rely on the location scout to come up with options and solutions. Once each location is locked, it will be the job of the location manager to make sure that each detail is handled so that the location is ready for filming. They will also need to be aware of all rules and any safety issues, notifying any neighbors, keeping location clean, and obtain any necessary permits and location releases. On smaller budget films, these roles may be taken on by the same person.

Before you send out your location scout, have them sit down with you and the director to go over the creative needs and desires for each of the locations. Have the director prepare a list of photos of similar locations or looks that they would like to see for the film. In larger cities like Los Angeles and London, studios have prebuilt sets that you can rent. Have the location scout check any studios for matching prebuilt locations on sound stages or backlots. The advantage to using studios is the controlled environment and ease of use.

When locking down the locations, the local film commission is an invaluable tool to help you with any information you need about filming at that location. You need to look into any local laws for filming in that area, including permits, hours available for working, lights at night, noise level restrictions, and restrictions for special effects or action sequences. You also need to find the nearest hospital, find out if the city or county requires a police officer on set if you are filming in a public place, and find out where your team can park trailers, catering, portable toilets, and personal vehicles.

If you plan to film in a certain country or state to take advantage of any tax breaks or rebates, keep in mind that certain costs of filming may offset those tax breaks. For instance, if you receive $1 million in tax breaks from a particular state but the locations, cast, and crew travel and accommodations, equipment rental, or shipping cost more than $1 million dollars, it may not make financial sense to move the crew to film in that state. Clarify and compare the amount of tax break and any additional costs of filming before locking down that location. Government regulations may require you to hire a certain number of police, or have specific permits for different types of filming (shooting at night, special effects, etc.). In addition, be sure that a highly trained crew is available in the state or country you want to film in or you will have to fly that crew in from elsewhere. Also, make sure that equipment rental houses have the equipment you need; otherwise you'll have to ship in equipment once again raising your costs.

Many local film offices have listings of properties that are friendly to film productions. A good location scout knows of or has relationships with these people and places and is able to access photos of those locations. The location scout should be someone with connections to local studios and should know how to work with the local film commission. They should also know the advantages and disadvantages of filming at each of the locations.

If you are on a low budget and have to scout for the locations yourself, contact the local or regional film offices in an area you are interested. You will need to send them your script and a list of location needs and ask them to send you photos of locations that fit your criteria as well as property owner contact details. Prior to spending time and money to go and look at the property, call the owner and get prices and availability by phone.

Once you or your location scout have options for the necessary locations, your director, DP, and production designer, need to visit and finalize the approval of the location. If time and budget allow, it would be advantageous for the producer and line producer to attend as well. While visiting locations, pictures and video should be taken for reference so you have something to show other departments.

As you scout locations, check the breakdown for each scene at that location and make sure that you are able to film everything that is needed.

Additional things to look for when you scout each location:

1. Is there electrical power available or will you need a generator? If so, how will you get it into the location?

2. Is there parking for crew, equipment trucks, and trailers away from where the camera will see them?

3. Is there a place for cast to change and wardrobe and makeup to be housed? If not, is there a place to park your trucks and honey wagons? (Honey wagons are the portable toilets.)

4. Is there a space for catering, meals, and space for the cast and crew to rest away from the weather?

5. Where is the nearest hospital?

6. If you plan to film in a public area or block streets, what are the regulations for hiring fire safety or police officers?

7. Are there any safety issues for cast, crew, or general public either from the location or by the film crew setting up at that location?

8. Are there neighbors who need to be notified about the production?

9. What is the cost of permits, and how long do they take to process?

10. Are there hours of shooting restrictions, noise, or other restrictions that might make it difficult or impossible to film there?

11. Are you able to use special effects, stunts, or weapons in the area if needed?

12. Can you move the camera in a practical way?

13. How much set dressing will be required?

14. Will you need to put up signs, paint buildings, obstruct walkways?

15. Do you need to protect the location by putting down padding or removing breakable items?

16. If you are filming a period piece, can you film without needing to remove lampposts or telephone poles? (Can your visual effects department digitally remove them later and at what cost?)

17. Will cellular phones work in the area?

18. Are the Internet maps to the area correct or do they need to be adjusted or corrected?

You also need to set aside an area on each set for the cast and crew to sit and eat. If you are on a tight budget, buying folding chairs from a clearance sale and keeping them in a truck so they move with you might be cheaper than renting them for the shoot. You might also be able to save money through a co-production deal with a company that has tables, chairs, tents, heaters, and other items needed for production. Larger cities have production companies with services like this, and in smaller towns, you can contact catering service or party rental service companies that will all have items like this.

In addition to the script needs for the location, it is helpful to identify areas that will help lower the budget while filming there. Are there local crews available? Is there a talent pool for additional actors? Are there production resources to cut down on shipping costs for cameras, lights, etc.?

If you are working from a very limited budget, another way to save time and money can be to find a location that is already dressed. Some studios have sets that come ready to shoot or you may be able to use a privately owned home. Some of the issues that come with using a private residence include ease of use, amount of space for cast and crew, insurance for damages, adequate power for lights, adequate toilets, home owner's access to living spaces, and the ability to use or replace copyrighted images or artwork.

Another tip is to try to find locations that are reasonably close together so that you can save on time moving from one location to another. Even a small move can take a half day or more and will affect your schedule as each move will cost the production valuable shooting hours.

As you lock down each location, have your legal team draw up contracts for the use of that location. You also need to photograph each location and send those photos to the legal department so the area can be cleared of any copyright issues. You may want to shoot in locations where there are paintings, pictures, signs, or landmarks that fall under copyright laws. You need to have each item cleared with the legal department or find a way to remove or cover them before you film there or find out if those items fall under fair use laws. Upon confirming the location, the location manager should photograph the area for any existing damage so that it cannot be blamed on the production. Once you have finished filming and after the location has been cleaned up, new photos and video should be taken so you have a record as to how you left the location in the event that there should be any damage claims later.

Final Schedule and Budget

With the locations locked down, the line producer can finalize and distribute the official production budget and work with the First AD to finalize the official schedule.

Clearance Reports and Copyright Laws

Having a clearance report for your script will save you much time and headaches later in production. It's simple to do and isn't very expensive, even for a low-budget production. You can usually find a clearance company that will go through your script for around $1,000 - $1,500. The reason for having a clearance report is to be sure that nothing in the script will cause any lawsuits later. This report lists every character name, location, and item and tells you whether or not you need to obtain a clearance for it to avoid copyright infringement issues.

These items can be alcohol bottles with labels on them, cars with logos, large signs on the street, character names referenced in the dialog, trademarked names or anything else that may be covered under copyright law. If you have permission to use that item, logo, or name, that permission paperwork should go through your legal team and be included in your delivery paperwork. If you do not have permission, your lawyer will need to check to see if it falls under fair use laws. The clearance report also usually lists alternative cleared names that you can use for characters.

Some amount of common sense applies to script clearances, and there are many areas that are covered under fair use laws. Rather than guessing whether or not you are going to have any problems, it's safer and less expensive to have the script checked early so that any changes can be made before it's too late.

Upon completion, the clearance report should be handed out to all the department heads so that everyone knows what has cleared and what has not. If you want to use items that are copyrighted in the film, you need to contact the owners of the item and get permission. You may also be required to pay a fee to use that item.

If there are logos, labels, or other distinguishing marks on items used on set, the art department needs to work to cover anything that does not pass the clearance report. If there are references to specific names or trademarked items in the dialog that need a clearance or permission to use, you want to change that dialog prior to filming unless you know you can get clearance. If there are vehicles with brand logos, you need to have them removed or covered up prior to filming. Also the costume department needs to be aware that clothing should not have any logos on them. This includes T-shirts, jackets, or any other item where a logo might be seen by the camera.

Failure to gain permission for any copyrighted item in your film can lead to additional cost to remove the item in post or may cause you trouble when selling the film. If there is artwork by an artist that would be seen prominently in the film and is not in public domain, you need to get permission from that artist and a clearance or replace it with artwork by an artist who you know is willing to give you a clearance at no cost.

Legal Requirements When Hiring

As an employer (which every film producer is), the producer is responsible for the health, safety, and proper payment of everyone in their employ. This is not a duty that should be taken lightly, and it should be noted that producers have been legally responsible for non-payment of wages, workplace violations, injury, and even death on the film set. Every producer should be aware of the legal requirements both federal and local and make sure that the film production operates within these guidelines. These guidelines include areas such as: wages; employees vs. contractors; volunteers and interns; minors (i.e. working with children); OSHA (Occupational Safety and Health Administration) safety laws; unemployment and workers comp; discrimination and harassment; and union requirements.

To be sure that the film is following all legal requirements, the producer should check with their legal counsel. If you are running a low-budget film and cannot afford legal counsel, make sure you have read very carefully all of the state and federal requirements. In California, the producer is required to hold a safety meeting prior to filming. This is, of course, a good idea no matter where you are filming and is especially important to include on days where you are filming stunts or filming in a risky environment.

"As one goes through life one learns that
if you don't paddle your own canoe,
you don't move."

– Katharine Hepburn

Chapter 11

Pre-production Part 2
Casting

How Casting Works

The choices made in casting have a profound effect on your film. Great casting can elevate a mediocre script, but bad casting can turn an amazing script into a terrible movie. Bringing your characters to life by creating the right balance and energies with the different actors you cast is a real art.

Though there are numerous ways to find your cast, your best option is to hire a casting director. A casting director's expertise can help the producer streamline the casting process by helping find great talent without the producer taking hours and days of time searching through thousands of submissions. Plus, a good casting director may have access to talent that a novice producer will not.

Experienced casting directors often have a trained eye to spot talent with potential and know if an actor has the range to deliver what you are looking for. In addition, they usually have great relationships that have been established over the years with talent, talent agents, and managers. They will also be aware of which name talent is open to working on an independent movie and what those actors' indie quotes (i.e. their cost) are currently set at.

If you are producing an ultra-low-budget film, you may still be able to afford a casting director. The first step is to approach an experienced casting director with your material. If they like it, ask if they would be willing to work with you for a deferred payment or a lower-than-normal rate along with a production bonus or profit participation (meaning they would receive additional payment after the film is funded or after it sells). You might also find a casting associate (the assistant to a casting director) who wants to make the step up to casting director by using their knowledge and relationships to help attach the right cast to your film. Often, casting directors know of actors who are looking for projects like yours, and adding those actors to your cast may help you increase the budget. (Which would in turn allow you to pay the casting director.)

Working with a Casting Director

To begin casting, your casting director goes through the script and, with input from you and your director, creates a cast breakdown, which consists of a detailed description of each role. They will then submit the breakdown to *Breakdown Services* - the main industry-casting service that all the agents and managers use to submit their talent for projects. Using their personal contacts, the casting director then talks to various managers and tries to sell your project and director to attach that manager/agent's talent. After contacting agents and managers, the casting director contacts each of the major agencies and finds what is called a "covering agent." The covering agent's job is to pitch talent (i.e. actors) to the casting director from that agency who are both available and budget appropriate for your film.

After pulling out the best submissions they received for each role, the casting director gives the producer their suggestions as well as a web link to the cast submissions so that the producer and the director can see all of them and pick out any additional actors they would like to audition.

Casting on Your Own

If you don't have the budget to hire a casting director, paying attention to detail and taking time to make good choices with your casting is key. To prepare for casting, you need to create a casting breakdown of all your characters. Write up a detailed description of each character, noting the age range, sex, and whether you want a certain body type and hair color. Also note if the character is a lead, supporting role, or a day player (just a few lines). If you only want star name actors submitted for certain roles, note that as well. The more detailed you are about what you are looking for, the easier it will be for agents and managers to submit specifically.

How to Use Casting Services

Breakdown Services is the main online casting service used by the industry. Other online services include: *Casting Networks (including LA casting and New York Casting), Now Casting, backstage.com, Everyday Actors,* and *SAG-AFTRA* who also have a website for union jobs. If you need professional background actors, you might want to contact an extras casting service. These services often supply you with an extras wrangler who organizes and books all the extras based on your notes as to what type of look and age that you need each day, and sign them in and out for you at either a flat rate or a percentage of what you are paying all the hired extras.

The benefit to casting services like *Breakdown Services* is that agents and managers have all of their clients' headshots, resumes, and demo reels (if the actor has one) on the website. In addition, each actor's profile section has details on their height, eye color, and skills. Actors without a manager or agent will also be able to view and submit to your casting call if you request that the breakdown also be placed onto *Actors Access* (also in *Breakdown Services*).

To use *Breakdown Services*, you have to sign up as a registered producer for the site. They will want information on your project, including: names of the producer(s), director, writer, filming location and start date, short synopsis and your script and a character breakdown. If you don't have a character breakdown, you can pay a fee to have them do one for you. They will also want to know if the film is union or non-union and if union, what level SAG contract you are on. They will check your signatory status to verify that you have become a signatory and your project will be listed accordingly.

Casting services are a great tool for finding talent; however, it can take a long time to sort through all the submissions yourself. To help reduce the number of submissions you receive, it's important to be as specific as possible about what you are looking for. Once you've received submissions, you need to organize them into your top choices for each character. By only looking at headshots, resumes, and demo reels, it may be difficult to tell if the actor has the skills needed for the role. You and the director will have selected actors submit video auditions or have actors come in for face-to-face auditions to determine their ability.

Additional Casting Sources

In addition to casting services, you may be able to find actors through social media actors groups or if you want more information on a particular actor, IMDB can be a good resource. If you live in a place like Los Angeles, sometimes you can get lucky and find an actor through an introduction from someone you know, a chance meeting at a coffee shop, or through social media.

Another time-consuming but possibly beneficial avenue for finding talent can be acting teachers and workshops in or near your area. Often, to showcase their talent, acting teachers hold special events, which you can attend to watch new actors perform on stage. These events can take several hours so don't make this your main source for finding your cast. The acting teachers may also have a list of their top students that they can send you if those students fit the casting breakdown.

Casting Calls/Auditions

If you are working with a production company or a studio, they may have a location for you to hold your casting call, or if your production offices are large enough, you can hold them there. If you have hired a casting director, they may have their own casting space. (Some casting directors require that you provide them with office space at your production office.) If not, you may need to pay for a location. There are specific casting spaces such as *Cazt* in LA that you can hire, but no matter where you are located, you can find a theater or hotel conference room that will work as a location for casting. If you don't have money for a casting location, a local theater group or acting school may let you use their space in exchange for considering their actors. You should also check with friends who may work at an office that has a conference room you might be able to use for free. In addition, some casting companies let you use their facilities for free as part of their casting deal with you.

Casting calls can be very time consuming both for the actors and for the producers, casting director, and director. The best use of your time is to have a casting director go through all cast submissions and do pre-screenings prior to a director/producer casting session. The casting director can sort through the actors that submitted for the roles and eliminate the ones who do not fit. After sorting through the submissions, they can call in the actors who have the right look and background for the role and record a taped audition to be viewed by you and the director. From those submissions, you and the director can choose who you want to see for a callback audition where you will both be present.

Before the actors come to the director audition, pick out one or two scenes of dialog from the script that best showcases each character and send them to the actors. These are called "sides" and will be used by the actor to prepare for the audition. You will also want to have a copy of theses sides available at the casting session.

Make sure to hold your casting in a clean, comfortable space with bathrooms and water to drink. If you are calling in a lot of people at once, have plenty of chairs and a good size waiting area. The best way to hold auditions is to assign people to a time so you don't have people waiting for several hours to read. This way, you'll get a better performance from them.

When the actors arrive at the casting location, have them sign a SAG sign-in sheet if you are doing film under SAG agreement. Even if the project is non-union, it's still a good idea to have a sign-in/out sheet so that you know who has been there. The sign-in sheet should include the time they arrived, the time they left, and their contact information or agent/manager's contact information. It's a good idea to tape your audition sessions so you can review all auditions again when making your final decision. If you plan to use this taping as part of your behind-the-scenes footage of the film, you should ask actors to sign a consent/release form, but be aware that some actors may not want their auditions used for this and won't sign a release.

Before you hold the casting session, print note sheets for yourself to make notes on each actor. Have a rating system as to how well they fit the part and how much you like their reading. If you need to have the actor read opposite another character in the scene, it's helpful to bring in a good actor to read the second part rather than you, the director, or the casting director. This way, the actor has someone to play off of, while you and the casting team focus on the actors' performance.

After comparing notes with the casting director and the director, decide on who you want to bring in for "call backs." You should bring in several actors at a time for roles that play opposite each other so that you can make sure they not only fit the role, but also look good on screen together and have some chemistry between them. To get a true feeling for the actor's performance capabilities, you should give yourself a little more time in call backs to work with the actors and have them read several scenes. If an actor you like cannot attend your casting because they live in another part of the world, have them put together an audition self-tape/video and either upload it or send it to you.

Lead Actors

Attaching the first named actor can be the most difficult, which is why having a great script and a talented director is important. A-list actors want A-list roles, and if your script is brilliant, you may be pleasantly surprised to find that the actor you want is actually willing to work on your film. We have found quite often that once we have a great script and a good director attached, the lead actors are not only willing to join the production, but they may also offer suggestions of other great actors they have worked with who they can contact and recommend that they join the project.

If a producer decides to use an unknown cast, it doesn't mean that the film will do poorly, just that it will be a lot more work convincing people to invest in the film. Hiring well-known actors benefits you both by their ability to help attract funding for the film, and in their many years of experience in bringing great roles to life. When you get a chance to work with new actors vs. well-seasoned actors, the differences can be staggering. If you cast an unknown as the lead, you may find it difficult to cast known actors to support them. If your goal is to have a known and sellable cast, go after the larger names on your list first. If the lead roles are spread out between multiple characters, having a line-up of B-list actors for an ensemble cast can also be helpful depending on the size of your budget. (B-list actors are actors who are known but on their own will not attract a large audience.)

A-list actors are approached constantly for film roles. If you want them to take the offer seriously, you'll need to either have a relationship with the actor you want to approach, hire a director who the actor wants to work with, or hire a casting director with the right relationships as well as have a "play-or-pay" fund set aside for casting. The role, the script, the director, and the budget must fit the actor you are looking to attach to your film. This can sometimes be a catch twenty-two. If you are trying to cast them during the development phase, you may not be able to realistically approach the actor you want. This is where a development fund and relationships help as you are able to give them a "play-or-pay" offer or convince them to work with you due to your ongoing relationship.

If your film is more of a genre project with an unknown director and no budget, keep your casting expectations realistic. A-list actors tend to either look to be paid what is called their "quote" (i.e.: the regular fee they have been getting on the last couple of movies) or they will want to do something with artistic merit and work with a director whose work they are familiar. If your budget doesn't allow for an actor to get paid their current rate, you are going to have to have something else of value. For instance, if the role you are offering gives them a chance to show a different side of their range beyond the typical characters they are currently cast as, they may be interested. Or if they have a production company and producing aspirations, you could see if they are interested in coming aboard as a producer. Some actors may be attracted to the project if you offer them a sizable profit participation, but don't count on this working for everyone. The actor and their manager will have to feel that your project has a strong chance of making a profit before they agree to a predominately profit-participation deal instead of their normal fees.

If you don't have the budget to hire known actors, make a strong effort to hire the best actors you can find through spending ample time casting. From time to time, a film breaks out without having a known director or known actors when the actors are matched well to the material. However, this is an exception and not the rule. Having no known director or actors can lessen the marketable value of the film, especially when you are only in the development stage trying to attract investors. Most (if not all), distribution companies respond to this type of film with a "wait and see" attitude, which means they'll let you finish the film before they decide to promise any returns or attach their company to the project, and this can make funding the film much more of a challenge.

Examine your final choices for the various roles, and ask if your choice for the lead has star potential and even if not a known entity yet, do they have breakout potential. The difference between the two is that the star potential is someone who is starting to get noticed but is not yet a star, and breakout potential is someone who is not yet known but is an amazing actor who is likely to get noticed soon. Look at who is representing them, and what films have they finished that may do well in the coming months. If the actor is not yet known but they are in a big studio film that is about to be released, or they are in a really interesting indie film that has great buzz about it, they are worth considering.

In hiring an actor, you also want to think about how you are going to promote your film once it's complete. Are your actors at a level that they can appear on talk shows and promote your film, or do they have a marketing hook that will have press interested in interviewing them? When they walk the red carpet, does someone want to talk with them, or do they go unnoticed? Any actor you hire, whether they are A-list, B-list, or unknown, should be working to increase their recognizably with the public through social media. Even a relatively unknown actor will be helpful in increasing the value of your film if they have the ability to access public awareness through interviews, blogs, Twitter, and other social media. When making your final decision on casting (after looking at the actor's ability to fit the role), consider the actor's capacity to reach their fan following and general audience through social media.

Bottom line, hire the best actor you can by having a brilliant script and a great director. Start at the top of your list and work your way down using first a casting director and then every connection you have. If you aren't able to get an A-list actor, at least hire someone who is a great actor and will work hard at bringing to life the script you've worked so hard to prepare for them.

Casting for Low-Budget Films

If you are on a tight budget, here are a few tips for finding a good or great unknown actor who may be much more open to reading scripts from new producers:

1. If you have a role for a young person, find an up-and-comer who has recently started doing TV work or has worked on other small films. As they are just starting their career, they are more likely to attach themselves to a project with an unproven producer and/or director. Even on a small-budget film, they may be willing to work with a new producer if the film has something to offer them like a great role or working with another actor who they've wanted to work with. These actors can be an asset. As they gain popularity, your film will also gain more attention.

2. TV actors are often interested in breaking away from TV to do films. Find a TV actor you like and who fits the part, and contact their agent with an offer. TV actors can lend their recognizability to a film and may help boost the audience numbers, especially if they are currently in a series that is being distributed worldwide.

3. There are hundreds upon thousands of amazing character actors from both film and TV whose faces are recognizable but who aren't offered many lead roles. You can often afford these wonderful actors for the union minimums or for a modest fee. These working actors will want to keep their name in the public, and if you can show that your film will have distribution and that the role is something they will enjoy, you may be able to get them to sign onto your film.

4. There are thousands of actors who are popular in foreign countries who are not yet known to the domestic market (North America), and want to get their foot in the door. If you are shooting a film in the United States, offering a part to a foreign actor can increase the film's market value in their native country. There are some additional steps you have to take to hire an actor from out of the U.S., but if the actor is well known in their country, the cost of travel, accommodation, and the work visa may be worth the value their presence adds to your film in the foreign market.

Agents

A project the agent thinks is worth considering may differ greatly from a project the actor thinks is worth considering. The actor often looks for a great role that challenges them, while the agent rarely looks to take any risks with the actor's career. Agents and managers tend to be very protective with their "name" talent. Their main job is to protect the actor's value in the market place and achieve a long-term career for them. If you are a first-time producer, the challenge for you is how to get an agent and or manager to have their client to read your script?

Agents are cautious. If they put one of their top clients in a project that fails, they can risk losing their client because of it. For this reason, they will go through all the elements and assess the potential risk very carefully before committing their client to the project. Is the budget too small? The director unknown? The producer unproven? The script too long? Agents push their clients to work in films with directors who make them look good, and those same agents hesitate if they think that your project will make it difficult to sell their actor as a serious contender in future projects. If your film fails to achieve box office success or gets bad reviews, it can damage their client's value and make it harder for the agent to place them in future work. The way to get around this is to have a relationship with the actor, their manager or agent, or have the right elements in your film that make it an attractive proposition for the actor and their representation team.

If you don't have a connection to the actor, you can best contact the correct agent through their contact info on IMDB pro or go through a casting director who will contact them for you. The chance of your script getting read depends on the person handing them the script. A known casting director, producer, or studio will get the script into the right hands. An unknown producer may have a hard time achieving this. This may seem like a road block, but don't be discouraged. Casting a name talent for indie movies can be a challenge, but if you are passionate about your project, don't be afraid to take risks. A good way to avoid the issue of the seemingly unapproachable actor is to research actors who are on the way up.

If your film is an idea or topic film, (e.g. *Milk*, or *Thank You for Smoking*) there may be some A-list actors who share the passion of that message and are willing to take a risk on your picture. Issues of gay rights, violence, endangered species, global climate change, or other topics may be important enough to the actor to get them to sign onto your film for a less-than-normal fee.

Prior to sending out your script, have your business plan ready so they can see that you are serious and that you have planned for: financing, scheduling, budgets, completion, and distribution. When you find an actor who you think is right for the role and if you are fortunate enough to get to spend a few minutes with their agent pitching the film, be ready to prove that you are capable of delivering the movie. Story boards, visuals, or a great short film can all be good selling tools to show people what you are capable of accomplishing.

Supporting Cast

Once you have your lead(s) in place, it's time to move on to any remaining supporting actors. It is not as important that you hire a known supporting cast; however (if your budget allows) the more known actors you can work with, the better your chances are of achieving good sales numbers later. In addition, known actors are often very good at their craft and can help raise the quality of your production by leaps and bounds.

Supporting actors are the ones who play a smaller part then the lead actors but are still an important part of the story. Whether you are hiring the lead or the supporting cast, be sure you hire competent actors who are best suited for that role. Hiring the director's girlfriend, boyfriend, or family members with no acting experience or other inexperienced actors in your lead and supporting roles can be detrimental to the integrity of your film.

Day Players/ Extras/ Background Actors

A "day player" is a role that normally has a couple of lines and just works for one day. We recommend you hire competent actors even in these smaller roles; however, if you need to make a place for a less experienced actor, day players are a good opportunity for someone to begin to get their acting experience.

Background actors are actors who have no dialog. If you are making a film with a lot of background actors, hire a casting company that specializes in hiring background actors.

Extras casting and wrangling is important to the look of your film as you want faces and body types with the look and build appropriate for the scene. When possible, hire a professional extras casting company that has a list of extras they like to work with. Professional extras know how to work on set and how to take direction. To save money, hire your extras locally so that you don't have to pay for boarding and transportation.

If you are on a small budget and have to use family and friends as extras, have the assistant director go over set protocol with them so they know how to follow direction, what parts of the set are off limits, and how to behave around the other actors. Unskilled extras may not understand that a working set is the same as any other work place and should be treated as such.

Working with SAG/AFTRA Actors

SAG is the Screen Actors Guild and AFTRA is the American Federation of Television and Radio Artists. These two guilds have joined forces in recent years to become the one union overseeing working actors in the U.S. If you have never worked with the unions on a film, don't worry. SAG/AFTRA can be very helpful and is happy to work with producers who want to hire their union members, even on low-budget projects. The union website offers various workshops you can attend where the union will discuss the various budgets and deals available.

To work with SAG-AFTRA (which we have abbreviated for the majority of this book as just SAG), you have to become what is called a "signatory." This means that your production company enters an agreement with the union. In exchange for working with union actors, you will follow union guidelines for the production. This means safety requirements, work hours, and agreeing to pay no less than minimum union rates for the actor services.

For those of you with a low-budget film, working with the union is still feasible. SAG has several levels of agreements, making it easy for low-budget films to still work with union actors. Low-budget minimums can range from $100 a day for an "experimental" level and "ultra-low budget" film, to $0 minimum for "new media." The new media contract covers any film that premiers on the web only (including Amazon or iTunes) and allows you to make an agreement with the actors for whatever they agree to be paid. Working under the SAG ultra low budget contract for theatrical and New Media contract for internet productions both allows the producer to hire both union and non-union actors and extras.

To become a SAG signatory, you need to present the union with the following paperwork. They require a copy of your LLC or corporate articles of incorporation, a copy of your operating agreement, and may ask for proof of funding if you are a larger budget film. You also have to sign a SAG assumption agreement. This means that you will assume responsibility for payment of SAG residuals that may become due. If you already have a distribution company or foreign sales agent on board, you may want to see if you can get them to assume this responsibility. You need to give the union a copy of your shooting script, schedule, and budget as well as a list of all the SAG actors you plan to use. On the new media agreement, you can sign as an individual or an LLC or corporation

Upon becoming a signatory, SAG assigns a union representative to your project who will answer any questions you have as you go through the process. The union also supplies you a SAG package with: a rule book, union daily and weekly contracts, Exhibit G (what the union calls the required on-set sign-in sheets), and any other paperwork you will need.

On any SAG signatory film, you pay into the actor's pension and welfare fund and you may be asked to pay the full estimated cast budget into a bond with SAG to ensure that the actors are paid on time. As this may be a considerable amount of the budget, you need to be sure that this amount won't set you back in post-production as it may take a few months for the union to confirm payments and release the bond funds back to the production. At the end of production, send the union a copy of all your union actors' contracts, exhibit G's, payroll report, final budget, and a list of all union and non-union actors.

Working with Kids

When casting roles under the age of 18, you need to be aware of child labor laws and adhere to the legal work hours for minors. If you use a child under 18 who is not emancipated, you need to have a tutor on set and a parental guardian. Educating yourself on the current regulations at your filming location is important as they will have an effect on your schedule and possibly your budget. Labor laws vary from state to state and country to country. According to some laws, you may only have access to the child for a few hours a day and will need to schedule your shoot around them. Filmmakers often look to cast 18 year olds to play younger in some instances because of these issues.

When auditioning an actor who is a minor, it is a good idea to also interview the parents as you will deal with them or the guardian of the child during your shoot. When preparing your schedule, note that working with child actors can sometimes take longer as they may not have the same level of experience as your older actors, and it may require more takes and more time to get the performance you need from them.

Stunt Players

It's highly recommended that you hire stunt coordinators and stunt performers for any stunts in your film. Even the smallest stunts like falling off a chair or taking a punch can injure an actor if not performed properly, and an injury could quickly end your production.

When casting stunt doubles, find individuals who are a similar size and build as the actors they are doubling. If the actors are performing stunts, those stunts need to be rehearsed through the stunt coordinator. The stunt coordinator can let you know how much rehearsal time he will need with each actor according to the difficulty of the stunt and the level of competency of the performer. If the stunt coordinator is not comfortable with the actor's ability or safety in performing a stunt, listen to them and hire a stunt performer.

On films with specific stunts in the script, you may need to hire stunt players with particular skills. The stunt community has specialized stunt drivers, high-fall artists, fire performers, weapons performers, and much more. Be sure to check the performers' credentials and get any video copies of previous stunts to be sure that they can perform the stunt you are requesting. A performer who has never performed a particular stunt may cause on-set delays or risk injury to themselves or others.

If your film is union, the stunt players all fall under your union contract with the same regulations as your other actors. Make sure to follow the same guidelines when hiring and log their time on set in the same way you do the other actors. To work with SAG performers on stunts, you need to show proof of insurance. As we mentioned earlier, small-budget films may find it difficult to insure their film when they have stunts as most insurance companies do not insure stunts for films under a certain budget range. If this is the case, you may need to limit your stunts, or find a production company that has a stunt insurance rider on their policy and work with them to get your film insured.

Use of Animals

From the smallest of rats, to dogs, to horses, the use of animals on set needs to be monitored by the *humane society* if you want to have the *humane society's* stamp of approval on the film. Though this may not be required for distribution, it is highly frowned upon to not have *humane society* oversight of all animal treatment.

Animals need a special wrangler who understands that animal and what it is capable of and what its limitations are. The wrangler needs to show you the action the animal is being hired to perform and that the animal is capable of performing that trick on cue. Animals that need to perform on cue may only be able to do so a few times. Your director needs to talk with the animal trainer to find out how the animal is likely to behave on camera and how many takes they think the animal will be able to handle.

Animals may not respond well to excess noise and commotion on set, so you need to talk with the trainer to find out the optimal performance conditions and what you need to prepare ahead of time. Animals can often increase the amount of time needed for filming on the day they are needed, so be sure the 1st AD takes this into consideration when preparing the schedule. You also need to consider safety for the animal, the cast, and the crew with additional security and medics on standby when working with larger or more dangerous animals.

It's important that any actors who have to work with animals are comfortable with what is happening in the scene and how they need to interact with the animal. In many cases, the visual effects department can use green screen effects to add digital animals to the scene later. For years, specialty glass dividers have been used to separate actors from dangerous animals while the two share a scene.

Other On-Camera Performers

If your script requires other types of on-camera performers such as dancers, musicians, or other specialized performers, check with your union representative to determine any regulations in hiring these performers. Like everyone else on camera, you need to have releases for their on-camera performance. If the performance is an original work like a dance or a piece of music, you also need a release to use that performance in the film. If the performance is not an original work created by them but is a copyrighted work by another artist, make sure you can get the rights to that work at an affordable price. These performances should be rehearsed prior to filming so that both the performers and the camera department know what to expect.

Screen Test

It is highly recommended that prior to hiring the actors, the producer and/or director run what is called a camera test on actors who will be performing together. If possible, dress the actors in appropriate wardrobe and have them run several scenes together. During this process the producer can tell who has the best chemistry before making the final decision on casting.

Hiring the Actor

Once you and the director have made your choices for each actor, you will send their agent or manager (or to them directly if they have neither) a deal memo. The deal memo should state the role, start date of services, weekly or daily payment rate, what type of billing they will receive, and any special provisions. For example, if you are shooting somewhere the actor does not reside, you might need to add to their deal memo that you will provide them with an airline ticket and accommodations, along with a "per diem" while filming. (Per diem is a daily payment for food when the actor is not eating on set. Union actors have a set per diem rate).

The actors you hire should also be given a long-form performance agreement. If you are asking for nudity, stunts, or other special performance, you want to have those specific requirements detailed in a "rider" (a one-page document outlining those requirements). This agreement also has to coincide with any union rules if they are a union actor. You can either get a template agreement from your production legal or a sample contract is included in our success in films resource guide. If you are SAG signatory, you have to fill out SAG-required paperwork for each of your talent and send or give them for signature.

Script Read Through

Before beginning rehearsal, it's a good idea to do a read through with the entire cast. The producer, director, and writer should all be there for this read through. Have someone (other than the producer, director, or writer) assigned to read the narration and scene descriptions so that you can listen without distraction. Here you will get an even better sense of chemistry between performers and a better feel for the script as a whole. Try not to stop the reading for breaks as it will disturb the flow and you may lose the feel of the story. Make notes about any character adjustments, performance choices, and script changes.

From this reading, you will be able to determine a couple of things:

1. Does your cast seem to complement each other well? (i.e.: Does each actor play well off the others or does anyone need to be recast?)

2. Are there areas of the script that don't seem to work as well now that you have a cast? (Things that seemed right on page may not work as well when spoken. These areas may need to be rewritten or eliminated.)

3. How is the timing? Is your script longer or shorter than what you thought it would be? Are there spaces that need to be trimmed or lengthened to help the story?

Rehearsal with Actors

As you move toward production, it is important for the director to spend time rehearsing with the performers. If the budget allows, this should be paid rehearsals for the actors as it is taking up their time. You are required to pay union actors for any rehearsal time. Check with your union rep to ensure that you are following union guidelines.

Rehearsal may cost you for cast time, but it is a lot less expensive than having the entire crew waiting on set while the actors go through a scene that could have been rehearsed in pre-production. During rehearsal, give your actors plenty of time to ask questions and work through details of their character so that they can give you their best performance when it comes time to roll the cameras. Character motivations, back story, and other areas that may not be covered in the script should be worked through during rehearsal time rather than waiting to do this on set with a full crew standing around.

When possible, hold your rehearsals at the shooting locations as this can help with the blocking of scenes. If you are able to have your rehearsals at the locations, try to have your DP attend the rehearsals so they can get an idea of how they will address the lighting needs.

Stunts Rehearsals

Prior to rehearsal, any elaborate stunt sequences should be worked on paper. Camera angles, crew placement, safety issues, and the stunt performance should all be coordinated. In this pre-rehearsal meeting, all safety procedures both for the performers and crew should be discussed as you look for any and all things that could go wrong.

Once the details have been worked out, all stunts should be rehearsed for the director and the DP. The DP needs to work with the stunt coordinator to determine the best placement for cameras to achieve the best angle for filming. Not all angles will help "sell" the stunt. Fight scenes shot from the wrong angle will look faked and damage the credibility of the scene. In setting up for the stunt, the DP may determine that the scene needs more than one camera to properly capture the event, especially if it can only be performed once. Prior to any stunt rehearsal or the filming of any stunt, the producer should hold a safety meeting for everyone involved in the shot so that everyone knows what to expect.

"I have a wonderful make-up crew.
They're the same people restoring the Statue of Liberty"

— Bob Hope

Chapter 13

Pre-production Part 3
Production and Art Department

The clock is ticking as you quickly approach the day you are supposed to start filming. Your office is set up, the budget, schedule, location, and cast are ready. Now it's time to visit the production department and look at the day-to-day operations of setting up to shoot the film. The producer needs to keep watch over each department to make sure everyone knows what they need to do. From locations, to food, to who is supposed to be where and when, the production team needs to keep all of it running smoothly.

Production Department Preparation

Checking In on the Line Producer

To create a final production schedule, the line producer works with the 1st AD to set a locked start date for principle photography and a corresponding shooting schedule. They need to make provisions for actors' schedules, weather issues, and for additional days of filming in case the film goes over schedule due to any problems. All departments should be given copies of the schedule as soon as it is locked so they clearly know what will be needed when.

Having completed the budget and schedule, the line producer now turns to making sure that the department heads know the limits of that budget and the planned schedule. They should work to get the best deals possible in all areas and keep an eye on each department and their spending so that your budget can stay on target. They will allocate resources to each department accordingly and decide how to handle any overages or adjustments. If a department needs additional funding, the line producer reviews their budget and their request. If they think the requested addition is an important expenditure for the film, they will try to find somewhere else in the budget to cut. If this decision makes a large impact on the film, it may need to be approved by you and if it affects his vision, the director as well.

It is not advisable to raid your contingency fund, (which should be 10 to 15 percent of your budget) for pre-production desires. Real emergencies may arise during the production where this will be needed. Make the departments stay within their allotted budget and ask them to be creative to find solutions for problems. If you don't stay on budget during pre-production, you risk not being able to finish the film when you get to post. Don't count on raising additional funds later. It may not happen.

If you are working on an extremely low budget, ask the line producer if they have connections to films schools that have students who may be interested in working on your film or if they have connections to young crew who are looking to get additional film credits. It may be tough to get a reliable crew with no budget, but there are people who need credits and experience before they will be trusted with a larger job, so they may be willing to help you at minimum cost.

Help from the Unit Production Manager

The line producer and UPM's duties can be interchangeable. On larger films where both are needed, the UPM works closely with the line producer to insure that departments stay within the budget and the schedule. As resources for filming come in, the UPM helps the line producer make sure that everything is going where it needs to. They help watch over each department and rent additional equipment, make sure that all needed paperwork and payments have been made to secure locations, equipment ordered, fire and safety officers booked, etc.

Setting Up Locations

The location manager is brought in a couple weeks before production to work with the line producer or UPM and help lock down and manage each location. Permits need to be arranged often several weeks in advance of filming, and deals need to be brokered and signed with property owners so that you have the location releases you need to be able to shoot at that location.

They need to contact the local film office or local government to check on any restrictions or local laws that need to be abided by. They will double check the permits, when police or fire department need to be hired, catering, shelter, bathrooms and work with property owners to be sure that the location is unlocked, cleaned, and ready for the production.

If anything is out of order, they report to the line producer or UPM with the problem and possible solutions. If you don't have a location manager, the line producer will need to take on these duties.

Tech Scout of Location

With the locations locked down, the line producer, director, production designer, DP, 1st AD, location manager and ideally the key grip and gaffer should go to each of the locations and walk through what will be shot there. They should make note of any special needs or problems they may have filming at that location. This way, solutions can be identified or if needed, new locations can be found prior to filming.

Office Management

The production coordinator should be brought in to help manage the office as soon as the office is opened. They are needed to run the day-to-day operations of the office, and the rest of the team relies on them to have working phones, Internet service, copy machine, and all other office necessities. They stay in the main office handling the daily office business during the entire production.

They arrange travel and accommodations for cast and crew on location, organize any cast and director medicals if needed for insurance, and coordinate rehearsals. In addition, they make sure all cast and crew have copies of the schedule and latest draft of the script. Any script changes need to be distributed with different colored pages so it is clear which version the team is working from. The WGA has a list of the color coding for each revision starting with unrevised - white pages, 1st revision - blue, 2nd revision - pink, 3rd revision - yellow, etc. (See the WGA website for the full list.) The coordinator also works with the line producer, UPM, and all heads of departments to ensure that information is passed to all who need it, coordinating any production meetings, and making contact lists for crew and cast involved in production.

Putting Together the Finalized Schedule

The 1st AD, and sometimes 2nd, are brought into the production department a couple of weeks prior to filming to work on the final detailed schedule for the cast and crew. Schedules often have to be moved around due to cast and location availability as well as weather, holidays, and other issues. On a smaller budget film, the 2nd AD would be hired a couple of days before shooting starts. They work with the UPM or line producer to go over the current schedule, then just prior to the first day of filming, they create what is called a "call sheet," which lays out a detailed report of everything and everyone that will be needed on set, where they will film, and what they will film.

As shooting progresses, the 1st AD is on set working with the director and the 2nd AD takes over running the call sheets and printing sides. With each day, the shooting schedule may be adjusted as scenes are extended, changed, or finished early. The 2nd AD confers with the 1st AD as to what was completed each day and what scenes, if any, need to be moved to a new day. They print out the call sheet and the sides for the next day and pass them out to all the cast and crew. On a lower budget film to save printing costs, cast and heads of the department get both the sides and the call sheet while other crew members only receive the call sheet. The 2nd AD is also responsible for sending out production reports at the end of every day to the bond company (if you are using one), producers, and any investors who require it. The production report states what was shot that day and any production problems encountered.

Call Sheets

The call sheet is the guide to each day of filming. Here is a list of what should be included: the production title, production company name, contact phone numbers date, day of filming and how many total days of filming, location of filming, weather report, location of nearest hospital, crew parking location, breakfast and lunch locations, scenes that are planned for filming, cast members needed for those scenes, times for cast to report to makeup and report to set, special props, special makeup, vehicles or stunts needed, crew needed and crew call times, and the heads of departments with their contact numbers.

If you are using union actors, you need to send your union rep a call sheet for each day of filming since the union reps have a right to visit the set if they want to. If animals are used on set, and if you are working with the *humane society*, you need to send a call sheet to them as they may want to send a monitor to set to check on the set conditions and treatment of the animal(s).

Sides

Sides are usually quarter-sheet-size versions of the script with only the scenes printed on it that are being filmed that day. Each day, the 2nd AD prepares the sides for the next day. They do not want to print out all the sides ahead of time for the entire shooting schedule as the schedule may change during production and the scenes may change order.

Preparing the Script with the Script Supervisor

The script supervisor is the person who makes notes on exactly what in the script has been shot and what still needs to be covered. They are brought in the week before filming or on a small budget a few days before filming to become familiar with the script and make notes on the shooting schedule. The majority of their work takes place on set where they will take meticulous notes on their copy of the script of what is happening in front of the camera. Their notes are essential in post-production during editing. Each of their note pages needs to be copied after filming and placed in your producer's book that will be duplicated and included in the producer's bible, which will be given to the distribution company. A trained script supervisor not only keeps track of what was shot, but also keeps an eye on costumes, props, details such as which hand an actor picks up a glass with, actors' eye lines so you have good continuity (the continued action from one shot to another) so in post, shots match and cut together.

Setting up Catering

Now that you have a more accurate count of cast and crew and the filming locations, you can begin planning how to feed everyone. To save on costs, it's best to plan meals several weeks in advance. For additional cost savings, look for local catering companies. If there are no official film catering companies nearby, a good option is to find a restaurant accustomed to serving buffets. They may be willing to cut you a per-person deal, and often buffet restaurants can aptly serve a variety of food to fit your crew. If the restaurant doesn't deliver, make an arrangement with them to send a production assistant each day at a certain time to pick up the meals.

One area to be extra careful of is allergies and dietary restrictions. As soon as cast and crew are hired, ask them for any food restrictions so you can work that into the catering needs. People don't work well when they are not fed properly, so this is not an area to sacrifice quality just to cut costs. It is always good to check your crew's preferences so you can feed people what they like to eat.

Craft Services

Craft services are the snacks and drinks available between meals for the cast and crew. This should be simple items like nuts, sweets, fruit, water, coffee, tea, bagels, cold cuts, chopped vegetables, chips, and Gatorade or other vitamin drinks. When possible, stay away from a lot of starches and large bowls of candy as those tend to slow people down.

One way to lower costs in craft services without sacrificing quality is to contact companies launching new products. It is often possible to get water, vitamin drinks, and snacks donated to film productions as companies want people to try out new products to create future consumers.

Picture Vehicles

During pre-production, your line producer, production manager, and production designer need to look into any vehicles needed in front of the camera. Rentals or purchases need to be made along with a plan for return or disposal. Cars should be outfitted by the art department with proper license plates that are cleared for film usage, have any brand names covered unless you have a release from the car manufacturer, and dressed as needed according to the script.

Organizing Transportation

Vehicles used to transport cast and crew as well as portable toilets, cast trailers, production trailers, and any other equipment trucks need to be arranged by the line producer and or the UPM. They assign a driver for each vehicle and set a schedule as to when and where a vehicle needs to be, along with any permits for parking. They also need to find where to dump waste water from the trailers if that is a service that is not provided by the trailer rental company. Most portable toilet companies have a service arrangement to drop off cleaned units and pick up full units when needed. Depending on your arrangement, you may need to provide a driver for portable toilet trucks between locations prior to them needing emptying.

The line producer, in conjunction with location manager, also needs to provide arrangements for cast and crew vehicle parking, either on location or at a separate location from where they will be driven to set. On a micro-budget film, cast and crew may drive themselves, and the line producer needs to check that there is free or low-cost available parking for all at your locations.

Power

Depending on where you film, you may need additional power. This should be determined when doing the tech scout of each location. You may be able to use the electricity supply if it is available at each location, but have the electrical department make sure that there is enough power for each department. In addition to the camera department, you need power for hair and makeup, catering, craft services (coffee pots), and many other departments. If you are filming on location in an area with no power, the line producer needs to check with each department to see what their power needs are.

If the camera department brings a generator, you may be able to work off of their power, but don't just assume this is true. Make sure the line producer checks to see if an additional generator is needed so that you don't run out of power for the camera department.

Contingency Plan

Be prepared for bad weather, injury, or camera problems. Things often go wrong, and you need to have a backup plan. When possible, have a second camera on set in case something happens to the main camera.

If you are filming outdoors, plan for uncooperative weather. Where possible, have alternative scenes that can be shot indoors while you wait for a break in the weather. In case of sudden weather issues, have tarps and rain gear standing by for cast, crew, and equipment. There should also be a tent or a building nearby that can keep cast, crew, and equipment out of the weather. Too much sun can be just as bad as a rain storm, plus, cast who spend the day out in the sun will become increasingly tanned, which may not help the consistency of your film.

For long nights of filming, have heaters available for cast and crew. If you don't have power for electric heaters, gas heaters like the ones used in many outdoor restaurants are perfect for keeping people warm on set. The makeup room or trailer should also be equipped with heaters as actors may have to sit for a long time getting ready, and you don't want them to get cold.

Cast or crew illness can also be a problem. While you may be able to replace some crew members, cast can be more difficult. If a cast member gets sick, work with the 1st AD to rearrange the shooting schedule to shoot around the cast member while they recover.

Art Department Preparation

During pre-production, your art department works closely with the director to create the vision they have for the film. On smaller films, the art department is often the one that suffers the most. When filming a modern-day picture on a low budget, art design may seem like a low priority; however, art design may be one of the key elements that sets your film apart.

If you are working on a low budget, try not to overlook this department just because you are scraping by. On a smaller budget film, you may be able to save costs by finding pre-existing locations that fit the mood you want for the film and just need some set dressing. You can also find inexpensive but creative wardrobe from thrift stores.

To achieve their vision, the director works closely with the art department creating several "pre-visualization" versions of the picture. This also helps you get an idea of where the director wants to go with the overall look and feel of the film. Even if you are filming a documentary-style film, it's still a good idea to layout the look of the picture with the art department. If you are filming a larger budget film or a picture with a lot of visual effects, these steps are a necessity so that each department knows what is expected.

The Production Designer's Assignment

The production designer works with the director during pre-production to oversee the creation and implementation of the director's vision for the film. They work closely with the director on the creation of pre-vis, storyboards, and sometimes pre-vis animations for the film. Once the overall vision of the film is discussed with the director, the production designer oversees the looks being created by the art director, wardrobe, set design, hair and makeup, and props to make sure all suits the overall required look of the film.

Setting the Look with the Art Director

Working closely with the production designer and the director, the art director helps create the look of the film. During pre-production, they first work with the production designer to find or create drawings, photos, and or models of the different looks and styles they want to create for the film. Each idea is passed through the director by the production designer before it is implemented. The art director works with the production designer in designing the look of each set, picking out vehicles, costumes, and the color, texture. and detail of each shot.

Once they've established a look for the film, the art director works with the set designer, wardrobe department, hair and makeup, and the props department to insure a unified look that matches the director's vision.

Pre-visualization

Pre-visualization is important to planning out each shot of the film in the effort to save time and money on set as well as plot out any stunts, special effects or visual effects that will be needed. This involves completing a simple storyboard and sometimes pre-visualization animations.

Storyboards

Storyboards are sketches or computer renders of each scene with the camera angle, the subject(s) of the scene, movement of the subject(s), and the movement of the camera. These are incredibly important especially on low-budget films. The more you plan what you are going to shoot, the better chance you have of shooting something spectacular. Planning each shot prior to production saves you set-up time when you get to set. Often, ideas you have in pre-production may have to change when you get to the location, but planning ahead of time will still put you at an advantage. When the director goes on the tech scout with the DP, have them bring the storyboards to look at each of the desired shots and note any adjustments.

Pre-visualization Animations

Created on the computer, pre-visualization animations is the process of shooting a complicated film in a virtual space, long before rolling on location. These are often used when there are complicated special or visual effects that need to be tested so that camera moves and VFX shots can be pre-planned.

Pre-vis animations are similar to motion comics or may even integrate video that your team has shot. Each scene of the film is acted out (usually just with voices and computer animated stand-ins), "shot" and edited like the real film. From this, the director can look at each intended camera angle and move, VFX, and pacing for the edit, then make changes as needed with minimal cost to the production. A good pre-vis gives you a good idea of what the film will be before you shoot a single frame. Since this process can be lengthy, it may be too much to do for a smaller film and may not be needed for all genres. However, for larger budget films or films with complicated action or VFX, pre-vis saves you a lot of time on set and a lot of money reshooting scenes that weren't properly shot.

Visual Effects (VFX)

Visual Effects are the effects created after the image is shot. Though these days on many larger budget VFX films, many VFX elements can be integrated into the actors' performance live on set. Often, today's VFX are a mixture of set pieces, green screen, and live actors' performances. To accomplish this, the VFX shots must be prepared ahead of time.

In the same way that pre-vis helps map out the camera movements, it also helps in preparing for any visual effects. If your film has VFX, you need to hire a visual effects supervisor who goes over the pre-vis with the director and talks about the effects shots. That person also works with the camera department to create any "plates" needed to complete the effects. (Plates are shots used to composite the visual effects in post-production.) If a green-screen is needed, or a matte painting, this also helps determine how much of the set needs to be built and how much will be created in VFX after the filming is completed.

Some VFX can be very expensive and should be planned according to your budget. However, there are a lot of great tricks that can keep these effects budgets down. Plotting out each effect with a VFX supervisor helps you see which effects are viable and cost effective and which ones are not. Depending on the type of shot, budget, and safety of the cast and crew, your shot may be better as a special effect (i.e., practical effect, which means it is shot on set) or it may be safer to add the shot in later.

Green/ Blue Screen

To replace the background, the visual effects department will often shoot against either a green or a blue screen. The color will depend on which the VFX supervisor thinks will work best for what your film needs. When using either of these methods, the screens should be properly lit and marked for tracking or you will have difficulty creating the proper effect in post production. Work closely with the VFX supervisor to insure the best results and test the methods you are going to use during pre-visualization to be sure everything will work as planned.

Special Effects (SFX)

Special effects are shot live on set, sometimes with the actors or the stunt performer. SFX involve water effects, fire, explosions, smoke, makeup, squibs - basically, any effect shot live on camera is a SFX. Special effects need to be worked out between several departments. The art department that monitors the look of the SFX, the AD who watches out for the actors performing with the SFX, the stunt team who may perform with the SFX department, the director, and any safety department, including the medic, fire, and or police.

Depending on the level of complication and danger, SFX and stunts should always be planned out and rehearsed prior to filming as well as rehearsed the day of filming.

Set Design and Construction

Now that you know your shots and your locations, you can determine if you need to build any sets. If sets are needed, the set designer will work with the art director to determine the look and the size of the set. They then work out the logistics of building a safe set that fits the creative needs of the production before hiring a construction coordinator and crew who they will oversee. If you are on a tight budget, building a set may not be an option. In this case, prebuilt sets can be found at several studios and can save you the cost of construction.

Set Dressing

The set dressing department works with the art director and the set designer to bring in additional elements to the set that help add to the scene. If the set has been built to look like a living room, the set dresser may bring in tables, chairs, a couch, a TV, curtains, paintings, etc. Any item that is not built into the set is part of the set dresser's job. If you are filming on location, the set dresser needs to look at what items need to be removed or covered and what further set dressing is needed. Each of these items needs to be planned out in pre-production so that they are on set the day of the shoot and they fit in with the production budget.

Property Department

The props department is usually brought in early in pre-production so they have time to find all the items listed in the break down. If your cast uses an item on camera, it is a prop and the prop master must find, rent, or buy each item. The props department works with the art director to insure continuity with the set and the look of the picture.

When your cast and the director begin to rehearse, they may decide they want additional props to help them with the scene. The props department needs to check in with the director to make sure that any of these additional needs are met.

Wardrobe/ Costumes

The wardrobe department is brought on fairly early in pre-production, especially if you are doing a period piece where the costumes are elaborate and need to be made by hand. The costumes and wardrobe are designed in collaboration with the production designer and the director, and each piece is measured and fit to each actor.

If you are on a lower budget and have the actors use their own clothes as wardrobe, make sure that their clothes are appropriate to the style of film. The director needs to view wardrobe choices and approve them prior to production so that any changes can be easily made. Having colors that clash visually or that are not in keeping with the style of film is avoidable if the wardrobe is approved ahead of production.

To keep track of each wardrobe item, even if it is brought from home by the actor, each item should be catalogued and stored by a wardrobe department. Items should be checked out at the beginning of the day and checked in at the end of the day. Each day of filming can lead to wear and tear on wardrobe, and it is a good idea to have a second set on hand at all times. An accidental tear or spill can lead to hours of shutting down the set if a second costume is not available.

It is particularly important to have doubles of clothing for stunts and SFX involving squibs, as you may need to do several takes. If a shirt is covered with blood from a squib or dirt from a fall, you cannot use it again that day. In addition, wardrobe worn by stunt players needs to hide pads or SFX items like squibs. Wardrobe choices for these types of scenes should also be discussed with the stunt coordinator to insure you can pull off the intended stunts in the chosen wardrobe.

If you are filming in cold weather, make sure the actors are warm in their wardrobe. This may mean you need to purchase thermal underwear for the cast. If it's not feasible for them to wear thermal underwear, an assistant should stand by with a blanket for the actor when they are between takes.

Make sure your wardrobe department watches out for brand name logos or tags that may show in the film. These items need to be cleared if you are going to use them.

Finally, keep track of all the wardrobe, even when you finish shooting. You may need reshoots, and if so, you will need that wardrobe again

Makeup and Hair

The extent of how elaborate your hair and makeup is determines the level of preparation you need. If the film is a modern-day piece with simple hair and makeup, you may only need to have a brief conversation with the team prior to filming. If, on the other hand, you are filming something more elaborate, or involving special makeup effects like a horror film, you should bring them in advance so they can discuss the look with the production designer.

For a monster, horror, or fantasy film, they may need to work with the special effects department and create Special Effects Makeup such as prosthetic faces, noses, ears, special wounds, and blood effects. If your film has a lot of makeup effects, make sure that your makeup department has those skills, and if you are only going to need SFX makeup for a couple of days, you might want to hire someone who specializes in that area for those specific days.

If there are a lot of effects in the picture, talk with the head of the makeup department to determine how long it will take to create each of these items. You also need to find out how long each person will take in makeup after arriving on set. This information needs to be relayed to the 1st and 2nd AD so they can schedule an actor in at the correct time for hair and makeup, prior to being needed on set.

If actors need to be fitted for special prosthetics, or if they need to have molds made, make sure you bring the actor in during pre-production with enough time to create the molds. Your effects department will let you know what they need and how long the process takes. When casting, check with the actor to be sure they are comfortable with prosthetics. If they are not, you may need to look at casting someone else in the role.

Talk with the makeup department to find out how long it will take to attach and remove the item each day. This also needs to be added to the schedule for the actors' work day. Keep in mind that union rules apply to when an actor has been called into makeup and not just when they are called onto set.

You also need to check with each actor to make sure they do not have an allergy to makeup or to prosthetics. Though there are some solutions for allergies, actors chosen for heavy prosthetics should be checked immediately for issues in case they need to be replaced.

"Anxiety is the handmaiden of creativity."

–T.S. Eliot

Chapter 14

Pre-production Part 4
Camera Department and Post-Production Preparation

One of the important decisions you make on your film is the type of camera you will shoot on. This is something you want to discuss with the director, the DP, and the post supervisor. Photography/videography starts with the camera department, which under the helm of the director of photography, works closely with the director to create a style of shooting for the film. From a slow-paced drama to a fast-paced action film, these choices affect much of the schedule and the budget so this decision needs to be carefully thought through and discussed with the line producer for any scheduling and budget implications.

Choosing a Filming Style

During pre-production, the director of photography (DP) works with the director to choose the type of camera, shooting style, camera angles, and lighting that best serve the story. They also work with the production designer and the art director to see how the lighting affects the artistic choices for the film. The DP may ask the art department for additions to the set or to set dressing if they want to adjust the look in the frame. For example, if upon inspecting the location or the set, the DP wants more foreground material to put in front of the lens, they will talk with the art department about what can be used to help augment the frame. Or if the set is too cluttered, they may ask to have things removed so that the actors are not overshadowed by the set around them.

The director should have an idea of the style and color of every scene, and these choices should be discussed from the beginning of pre-production as they will affect everything from the camera to the art department. In regards to filming style, be cautious about doing in camera effects and coloring as you will be stuck with them in post. If you are going to adjust the camera in a way that won't allow you to get that setting back to neutral, you want to be absolutely sure that what the DP and the director are getting the look they want. The only way to insure that is to run tests with the camera department prior to the initial film days. Many cameras can shoot in a "raw" format, which allows the DP to choose a particular look that is recorded in the meta-data (the information that is digitally included with the picture), without changing the raw information of the picture so that the image can be changed in post if necessary.

Choosing a Format

Pre-production for the camera department also affects preparation for the post-production department. To insure clarity, the director, the DP, the post supervisor and possibly the editor need to talk about the format for filming, how to transfer the material into the edit, and what the final delivery will be. To know the final delivery requirements, you need to know how you plan on releasing the film: theatrically or direct to video and 2k, 4k, 3D, or other. Requirements for some formats are easier to work with than others. Some take up a lot more hard drive space and take more time to manage the media and edit. Between the DP, director, and post sup, you should be able to come up with a good recommendation for the best format for the type of filming you are doing and the type of release you are aiming for.

If you want a theatrical release, it is likely you want to shoot on a high-end camera so that the image holds up to projection on a large screen. This means film, high-end tape, 4k digital or higher. Can you get away with less?

Perhaps, but with a degraded image. In addition, if you are working with a distribution company, they may require you shoot with a certain level of camera.

The style of camera and format also depends on the way your director plans on filming the picture. Certain filming styles require smaller cameras that can move quickly, while others require larger cameras that require heavy rigging. There are also different costs involved in different camera set-ups and formats.

Even if you are running a low-budget film and can't afford to bring on a post supervisor, you need to have someone oversee your post process. This can be your editor if they have an understanding of the post-production work flow. If the editor isn't sure how the format will affect what they are doing, have them consult with a post-production house so they can be better educated on this process. Without a clear understanding of formats and the positives and negatives of each type, you can run into larger problems when completing and releasing your film. You want to be aware of how the different camera and shooting costs will affect your post budget. Once the decisions is made, you will to deal with the post costs of the work flow that has been set up, and it will be too late to worry about budget overages.

If you aren't sure if you are going to do more than a video release, aim for the highest quality of camera your budget can afford. The better image quality, the more you can do with it in post and the better it is going to look to your audience. Quality is especially important in drams, but even "found footage" films are using higher end cameras and degrading the image in post-production if or when it is needed.

Higher-quality cameras react better in low-light situations and give you more latitude between dark and light. This way, when you are in post, you have room to lighten or darken the scene as needed. If you don't have the latitude, your white levels may be blown out or your darks too black. Once you've crossed into the extremes of those scales, you can't do anything about it in post. For the "found footage" film *Chronicle*, D.P. Matthew Jensen used the Arri Alexa, which, at the time, was one of the top HD cameras. This allowed them to adjust where needed and add in the visual effects without running into high grain levels, artifacting (a condition that occurs when you have a low pixel count), and bad video levels. They then added a "found footage" look in post- production.

If you are shooting on a small budget, look into finding a DP who owns a camera that is the quality you need to use. You should be able to make a deal with them for their fee and the fee for the camera less than a rental price from a rental company. The benefit is that they know their camera and will be fast at setting it up and operating it. The downside is if something goes wrong with the camera, you may not have a backup. If your DP does not have a second camera standing by, it's a good idea to have a second camera available from a local rental house. Even with the best cameras, something can go wrong.

Whatever camera you decide to use, talk to other filmmakers who have used the camera so you can be aware of any problems they may have encountered and recommended solutions.

Camera Tests

Different from the casting screen test, this is a test of the camera systems to see if they perform in the way that the director and DP expect them to. Any special filters in camera effects and special frame rates should be tested to be sure there are no surprises on the day of filming.

Lighting, Grips, Generators/ Special Equipment, and Gear Rental/Acquisitions

With the full breakdown of the script, the director and DP should go through every shot in the film, discussing angles, shot locations, movements, and anything special the director needs. From there, the DP can determine their grip, electrical, and gear rental needs. They may need to rent a crane for a large sweeping shot, a car-mounted rig for traveling shots, or special camera cars designed for chase scenes. They may also need special lighting for night scenes, a generator when the location has no power, or special camera mounts for whatever the director has dreamed up. When completed, all this information is given to the line producer so they can make sure the requested items fit within the budget. If the budget won't allow for expensive camera rigging, let the DP know so the camera department can come up with a creative solution or make some compromise.

To save money in this department, a producer should make a production deal with a production company that can loan out or give a discount for the camera, lighting, and grip gear. Another option is to find a DP who owns their own lighting, grip, and camera package that they can bring with them for a discount price.

Equipment Rental

For any equipment rentals, the production manager should arrange safe pickup and return of the item and a secure storage location while it is in use. They should also make sure that there is a list of all gear and that it has been checked at the rental facility before going to the location and checked in upon return to insure against any loss or damage. Many rental houses require a deposit, a credit card on hold, or a credit check for any production company wanting to rent gear.

Post-Production Preparation

Depending on how you are recording the image, you will have a different procedure for the post department during filming. If you use hard drives or flash cards, you will download the material every day and return the drives and cards to the camera department. The post supervisor works with the editor and DMT to insure that all the drives are copied and one copy is given to the producer, one is put into storage for safe keeping, and one is given to the editor to begin the rough cut/ string out. If you are shooting on tape, you need to have the post department take the tapes to the lab where they are transferred to hard drives and then brought back to set the following day to review as dailies and begin editing. If you are shooting on film, the exposed film is taken to the lab to be developed, scanned into the computer system to created dailies, and sent back to the editor and producer to be watched the following day.

The post sup also works with the team to make sure that the picture is ready for the chosen final distribution of the film. Preparations for a theatrical release are much more intensive than a release on the Internet, and the post-production team will want to know what the end goal is for the picture. In addition, the post sup is ultimately responsible for the paperwork collected by the line producer throughout the production. SAG paperwork, camera and audio reports, permits, script notes, and all contracts need to be collected by the post supervisor to hand over to the distribution company. To make less work at the end of production, the producer should be sure that the line producer has gather the required paperwork from each department and set it aside for the post supervisor to review before delivery. If the producer doesn't have a deal with a distribution company yet, they should get a copy of a standard delivery list from a domestic or foreign sales company so they know what is required.

Post-Budget Issues and Warnings

It is very important when reworking a budget after production has begun to be extremely careful about pulling money from post-production to put toward extra items in the production budget. Doing so can cause issues with completing the film the way it was planned. If the additional budget needs are not covered by the contingency that were put into the budget, the producer is better off taking additional production costs from another area of the production budget. It is also recommended not to spend more than half of the contingency fund in the production period, saving the other half for post, delivery, and marketing emergencies.

Hiring an Editor

We recommend hiring an editor or an assistant editor (AE) on the first day of production as editing while filming is a great way to know if the director has captured the coverage needed to tell the story and if the performances are coming across as intended.

The editor should not just be someone who knows their way around an edit system, but they should be someone with a good sense of storytelling and timing. The editor should have a strong technical background or they should have a good assistant who has that technical background as they will need to prep the video files for edit, prep and export shots and plates for the visual effects department, export audio files for mixing, and set up the EDL (Edit Decision List) for color correction. If the editor is also the online editor, they also need to be able to match back all master files to create the final master of the film. We'll get into the details of this in the chapter on post- production, but for now, just know that the editor position is one of both creative and technical expertise that should not be taken lightly.

If the director does not have an editor they normally work with, ask the post supervisor if they can recommend someone. As with other staff positions, check with producers and directors the editor has worked with in the past to be sure that they can keep up with the post supervisor's schedule.

"Many a small thing has been made large
by the right kind of advertising."

– Mark Twain

Chapter 15

Pre-production Part 5
Marketing and Publicity for the Film

Preparation for Marketing and Advertising

Marketing is the process of getting the word out about a film by any means necessary and should always begin when the producer is in pre-production. The more audience awareness and interest you can raise for the film early on, the better chance you'll have of gaining an audience and selling more copies of the film. Studios spend millions of dollars making sure that the potential audience knows about their film through pre-release posters, teaser trailers, and interviews with the cast and the director. Though that may not be an option for some producers, there are still plenty of other ways to let people know about a film without spending as much as the studios. This includes festivals, social media, press releases, blog sites, and special screenings for taste makers who will spread the word.

Whether the producer is selling through a distributor or distributing the film on their own, chances are they are going to need to do some or even all the marketing themselves. Smaller distribution companies are mainly set on selling to other buyers and not the general public. Unless the distribution company is planning at least limited theatrical releases, you may find that your distribution company can get your film into *iTunes*, *Amazon* and other VOD and Pay TV services but will not do any advertising for you.

Larger distribution companies may do advertising and marketing, but some of their success or failure is tied to how much marketing the producer has already done to begin gathering an audience for their film. In addition, the size of audience the producer has rallied around the film may be a deciding factor for a distribution company to agree to see the film.

When creating a post-production budget, we recommend that the producer set aside a portion of that budget for marketing. How much of that budget is set aside depends on how large of a reach the producer wants to have and how much of a return they expect for each marketing and advertising dollar that is spent. For example, if you are screening your film at several theaters in a major city and look for a large turnout, you may want to look at the costs of advertising through TV, print, and web. If you are going straight to digital sales, you may only want to look at the cost of web advertising and social media ads.

Publicist/ Public Relations (PR) Agent

To help with the advertising and marketing process, it's helpful to bring in a publicist early in the pre-production phase. They can work throughout the entire length of the production to oversee all of the marketing and promotion of the film, including the behind-the-scenes videos for the electronic press kit (EPK), arranging interviews of cast and crew on set, creating and sending out press releases, overseeing promotional photography, collecting cast and crew bios and headshots, and helping with social media outreach. A good publicist has contacts on the web, at newspapers and TV, and knows how to approach them in a way that will have them interested in your story. With the right person, you should be able to get press coverage, radio interviews, and even TV interviews. Really good publicists aren't cheap, but if you can afford to add them into your marketing budget, they can be well worth the extra money.

If you have a small budget and can't afford a publicist on staff the entire time, hire them at the beginning to get their advice on what you need to do during production as well as have them help set up your social media campaign. Then, hire them back when you have completed the film and help you promote the film's release.

If you can't afford one at all, you still need to create press releases, investigate who you should contact at the local newspaper, magazines, radio stations, TV stations, blog sites, and online media that cover film to see who may be interested in coming to set. This may be easier when you are filming away from Hollywood as newspapers and local TV stations in smaller towns may not have as much to report on for that day. Good days for inviting press are when there are larger crowd scenes with an interesting event happening, stunts, or when you have known actors on set. Prior to contacting the press, write a press release that not only sums up the film, but why the audience should care and why the reporters and websites will want to talk with you and your cast.

Items Needed for Promotion and Advertising

Press Release

Press releases should be changed regularly and sent out throughout the life of the film beginning as early as pre-production. The press release should include the one-line, the one paragraph summery, a paragraph on the cast, a paragraph on the director, and all the interesting facts about your picture so that journalists know what they can write about. Entertainment publications like *Variety*, *Hollywood Reporter*, and *Deadline* report on key casting for new films, while other publications like *LA Times*, *New York Times*, *Entertainment Weekly*, and *People Magazine* may want to wait to release an article about your film or delay publishing a cast interview until the film gets a release date. Small press publications (especially web news sources), however, love new and even speculative material, and they may print updates and press releases on your film during production. Adding your website and social media links to press releases is a good idea, too, as those who are interested can get their own updates and follow your progress. For easy access, press releases should be made available for download on your website.

Press Kit

During pre-production, you need to assemble the first version of your press kit. This includes the film title, a story synopsis, any current press releases, photos of the cast, bios on the cast and crew, and any other promotional material that has been created for the film. At this point, you are unlikely to have any video clips to show, but those can be included as they are completed during filming. Find aspects of the film story or about the filmmaking process to include in the press kit that will be interesting both to the audience and to the press. Any topic that gives you an advantage over other current film productions helps your film receive more attention.

As you begin filming, your publicist or one of the producers should interview the lead cast, the director, and the producer and have them answer questions about their roles, their experience making the film, and what the film means to them. These answers can be added to the press release, sent to publications, or if videotaped, they can be included in the electronic press kit.

Website

You should have set up the film's website in preproduction and begun building your social media around the film. This should ideally have links to all your other social media sites, the distribution company's site (if you have one), a blog space, and info on the producers, director, writer, lead actors, and key heads of departments. It should also have production stills, interesting information about the making of the film, press clippings, any good reviews of the film, and a trailer for the film once it's ready. To make information on the film easily accessible for the press, have a downloadable press kit available with any important marketing information included. To update the page regularly, hire a professional web designer or to save money, create a simple site where you or other team members can blog about the day's events and easily post photos.

IMDB Page

You are going to need your website and at least one of the following to request an IMDB page: A distribution company, film festival listing, and/or a legitimate web news report. IMDB requires an outside source confirming your film is real. This is one of the reasons it's important to do interviews and have news reports on your film while you are in production. If you are still struggling with getting the film up on IMDB, you can do your own press release and try to get it placed in industry trade press sites or publications like *Variety, Hollywood Reporter* or *Deadline Hollywood* to name a few.

Social Media Site

This is separate from your website. Social media sites such as Facebook, Twitter, Linked-in, or other sites can be used for updates, links to your site, promo teaser videos or trailers, and photos from the production. The more you post, the larger your audience will be, and the more you engage with your audience, the more support you are likely to have when you release the film.

Poster

This is the most important tool for selling your film and should be used in most (if not all) of the marketing you do for the film. As this is likely to be the first image that your potential buyer and your audience sees, it is vital that it captures their attention. It should be a high-quality image created to match the style, feel, and quality of the film, but most importantly, it should display the most sellable aspect of your film. This may be an iconic image, or your named cast, or both, but whatever you use, know that it could make the difference between the buyers purchasing or passing on your film.

If the distribution company is not creating one for you, or you have not secured a distribution company yet, it's a good idea to hire a graphic artist for this job. Depending on the quality of the artist, you may pay between $500 and $1,000 for a simple poster. The costs will be a lot higher if you hire an art firm in a major city.

To properly shoot the cast for the poster, you may have to hold a separate shoot after filming. To save money, however, it's a good idea to try to get the photos at or around the time of filming when your cast is all together. The photographer can shoot with the main cast during their down time on or off set. To make sure you have what you need when designing the poster, get both individual shots of the cast as well as group shots or staged shots on set.

You may be able to get away with still images from on set, but it's a bad idea to try to use frame grabs from the film as they may be too small to have proper clarity for a 40x27 inch poster. Cameras that delivery a 4-5k image may do better with this, but don't rely on having a good image to grab even if you have high resolution. Often, an actor's movement in frame looks great for the moving picture, but is not as good when frozen in a still frame.

Trailer/TV Advertisement

Next to the poster, this is the second most important tool for marketing your film. You should have a trailer that ranges between one and a half minutes to two and a half minutes long. You are only going to need a 30-second version if you do television advertising. This needs to be the best moments of your film. It should explain what the audience can expect to see, what the tone of the film is, and enough of the story so that they want to see the resolution of the drama.

As with the poster, it's a good idea to hire a professional to handle this. A great trailer editor can make the difference between the film selling or not. This is the first piece of the film that your audience sees, and it's your best chance of enticing them to spend money on your picture.

If you are using music from the film, make sure that you have in the contract of the music provider, stipulations that you can use the music for marketing purposes. If you are using music specifically for the trailer, make sure that it is licensed for international and domestic use and for the life of your film. If you don't you can run into copyright violation issues.

If you need to purchase ad time on television to run your 30 sec trailer, you can do this by contacting the TV station's sales department directly, or by going through an advertising agency. Check with both groups to see who can give you the best deal and can place the ad in the right time slot to hit your audience. An ad agency will be able to place your commercial with several stations on both local TV and paid TV, and may be able to get a better deal when buying in bulk than contacting each station individually.

Behind-the-Scenes, Scene, and Character Photos

Promotional photography is an extremely important part of your marketing campaign. The audience loves to see the antics behind the scenes. These photos are a wonderful tool to help drive the social media conversation about your film. In addition, you should also capture "hero" shots of each of the main characters. The hero shot is a single shot of the cast member in costume and posed properly for their character. You should have a set photographer get these photos on set or even prior to filming so that you can use them to promote the film while you are still in production.

While in pre-production, plan out the type of images you want to capture and what could work for posters, box cover art, web images, etc. You should plan which scenes are the most interesting to capture, which sets are most interesting, and what shots will most attract your audience.

If you are working on a lower budget film, you may not be able to have a photographer on set every day, so to keep costs low, plan which scenes are best for promoting the film and hire the photographer for those days.

When you start shooting, be sure the AD knows what days the photographer is scheduled to arrive and if those scenes are moved due to scheduling changes, make sure the photographer's schedule is changed as well. The 1st AD also needs to be sure that the behind-the-scenes photography won't interfere with the day's filming and that actors won't be released from the set before you have a chance to take the photos.

When shooting "scene" images (i.e. stills of the scenes as they happen in the film), the photographer should use the lighting setup by the DP to retain the artistic quality of the film. If they need to use a flash at any time, the photographer needs to call "flashing" before a flash goes off. The reason for this is that when lights blow out on set, they look a lot like a flash on a camera. Rather than give your DP and grips a heart attack, the photographer should call flashing before they begin taking pictures.

You are going to need high quality images from behind the scenes as well as posed images of the actors in costume for use in the posters and other promotional materials. Even if you can't bring in a professional every day of filming, it's a good idea to have a pro do your poster shots and then have someone else take behind the scene photos.

If you can't afford a professional photographer for even one day of filming, make sure that you have someone on set taking pictures. This can be a friend or another crew member, but behind the scenes photos will be requested by the distribution company as an expected delivery item. These images will be used on press releases, blogs, and your website.

When sending out photos, make sure that they have been approved by the cast who appear in them. Many cast contracts, especially with known actors who are conscious of their public image, require that the actor or their publicist approve all photos from the film before are released for publicity. Usually the contracts require that the actor approve at least 50 percent of the photos submitted to them and give that approval within three to five business days.

On larger studio films, many producers do not allow photos to be taken by cast and crew due to confidential plot points or character looks that they do not yet want released to the public. For this reason, many contracts include these stipulations so the producers (after standard approvals are given) can control what photos are released. Some actors may not want press on set at all, though this is a rare issue as marketing and press are vital to the success of the picture.

If you don't want cast or crew releasing on set photos or info, it is good to put a clear guide line about photography on your daily call sheets, letting the cast and crew know that no personal photography is allowed on set. If you have story lines or a plot surprise that you want to keep under wraps until the film is released, or you want to keep control as to what press is released, it is a good idea to have a confidentiality clause in all crew and cast contracts. This way you can make sure that only approved pictures and information is released when you want it released in a way that best represents the film.

Screen Shots

A screen shot is a freeze-frame or still image taken directly from the final mastered version of your film. They can be used on your website, social media site, and press releases.

Business Cards

You need business cards for yourself as you meet with distribution companies, but you may also want business cards for the film. These are only needed if you are going to be in places where you or your associates are personally meeting with the public. Conventions, screening, or other public events give you an opportunity to give out cards. Each card should have the name of the film, the lead actors, and the website. You should also include any programming devices like a quick response code (QR code), which can be read by portable devices and link directly to the website, a trailer, or a place to purchase the film.

Screeners

Distribution companies, critics, festivals, and bloggers will want to review your film. For this, you need to create a DVD or digital screener with a watermark. The watermark can say "This film is for screening purposes only" and have your logo or the distribution company's logo. The screener does not have to be at the highest quality bit rate, but should be good enough that they have an idea of the final quality of the film.

The digital screener should be used through an online monitoring service that knows who watched the film and when, with safeguards so the film cannot be downloaded. If possible, number the DVD screeners on the watermark and attach that number to a list of who you sent it to. This way, if it ever gets out, you know where the leak came from.

Leaks can be an issue for some films, and often screeners and festival submission can be the source. Don't send master copies of your film to anyone who wants to screen the film. Use locked DCPs when possible for theater screenings, and don't send masters to distribution companies until you've signed with them.

Electronic Press Kit/ Behind-the-Scenes Videos and Supplemental Material

The EPK is a collection of behind-the-scenes videos, interviews, and clips from the film. This can be a completed "behind-the-scenes" edited video and can also include individual interviews with the actors, director, producer(s), and writer(s) as well as clips from the film and extended behind-the-scenes clips.

Often, entertainment news shows use this material to run news stories about the film. They may take pieces of the video you edited, or they may take partial or complete interviews with the cast and crew along with clips from the behind-the-scenes videos. Most news organizations like to have a choice to run either a completed piece or individual segments, so it's a good idea to prepare more than just a completed video, but also include the interview segments from that video in a clean format without b-roll or music over them. (B-roll is a video source other than interviews.)

Behind-the-scenes videos and interviews are important for connecting to your audience, giving them something new and interesting to see about your film. The more material you can feed into promotions, the wider your audience will spread. A large number of productions are even releasing promotional short films with additional content that preludes or relates to the film (e.g. *Prometheus* did an entire campaign of short films).

The promotional videos are an important marketing tool and a delivery item your distribution company looks for. You may want to use certain clips on your website, social media sites, or to include in the DVD/Blu-ray bonus extras, and you should have full resolution clips ready for broadcast and cable TV, which means the promotional videos. Any clips meant for broadcast TV also need to pass quality control along with your film.

If you have a budget that allows, have a professional company shoot the behind- the-scenes videos. To best utilize cast time, have the video crew film them when they are not needed on set, and let the cast know ahead of time they will be interviewed. You may not have time to interview the director or producer(s) while they are on set, so you may need to set aside additional time for this on an off day or right after filming.

From makeup and hair, to VFX, to stunts, when possible, shoot each department at work. Each will have something interesting to add to the behind-the-scenes footage, plus, the more material you have, the longer you can keep sending out new clips and keep your audience interested in your film.

Along with having a good behind-the-scenes crew, it's a good idea to give small cameras to some members of the cast and crew and have them interview each other during filming (if they are willing). This can be a fun way to see the actors with their guard down. When conducting the interviews, be sure that the shooter has a good microphone and preferably a mic placed on the person they are filming. Bad sound on interviews means you won't be able to use those clips to promote the film and you'll have wasted the time, effort, and money.

Some things you may want to include in the videos are: showing how big scenes are filmed, how the special effects work, showing the producer, director, and department heads working on the film, and interviews with all the key players and the lead actors.

Promoting the Film

You don't have to wait for all the pieces to be ready before you begin marketing. However, you do want to maximize your efforts so you need to look at who your target audience is and you can reach them.

As the web has developed, there has been a fine tuning in the marketing model. No longer do you have to aim your advertising and marketing toward a wide group and hope that you reach them. Through social media, it's easier to target the exact audience who like things closely related to your film. If your film is a romantic comedy that takes place in a chocolate shop in Paris, you can target your film toward women who like chocolate and travel. If your film is a buddy cop movie with an older action star and a hip young comedian, you can find that the followers of both of those actors and market directly to their audience.

Whoever your audience may be, if your budget is limited, you can reach a more precise group through web advertising than through the broad and expensive reach of TV or print. This doesn't mean that you completely avoid TV, radio, or print media. If you are doing a theatrical release of your film, you should have a targeted marketing campaign in the cities you are screening the film. If it's a limited release, target the audience who likes indie films in your genre.

Enlist the Cast

Your cast should be heavily involved in helping promote the film. Actors with large followings who love to blog and stay in touch with their audience can be a great support to your project. For actors with a large following, you may want to encourage them to write about the production and send photos of themselves with cast and crew members as you are filming.

If some of the actors have any type of photo approval in their contracts for the photos that are to be released, don't allow any on-set photography except through your approved photographer. You can then give out approved stills for the cast to tweet, post on Facebook, or promote in other ways.

Blog Sites

In addition to your social media site and website, you should find bloggers who talk about things connected to your film and contact them. These do not have to be blog sites just about films. There are large communities online for everything from Sci-fi, to horror, to fan sites for actors, social topics, fan-sites for countries, etc. For example, if your film is an Irish comedy about fishermen staring Brendan Gleeson and James Nesbitt, then look for blog sites on Ireland, comedy, fishing, and fan sites for the actors.

There will be dozens of websites and blog sites that you can come up with that will be interested in your topic, the genre of film and the actors. All of these blog sites are looking for new information to post as they need to drive people to their site. The more exciting and topical you can make your press releases, the more these people will want to post info on your film. Here is where additional photos, interviews, a trailer and a constant stream of new information will be helpful.

Actors on Social Media

Most actors have social media accounts where they can quickly and easily reach out to their fans. Encourage your actors to tweet, blog to and otherwise contact their following as they are on set, or at a screening or when the film is released.

To help the actors know what to promote and when to promote it, it's a good idea to create a clear strategy on releasing info about your film so that it goes out in the way you want it to. Have clear guidelines that you can give to your cast as to what type of information can and cannot be put out about the film. With guidelines in place, you can help avoid accidental or purposeful releases about spoilers, surprise plot points, or any sensitive info.

Purchasing Views

There are marketing companies on the web that can help you accrue more views on YouTube, Facebook, Twitter, etc. If you decide to use one of these, look carefully to be sure that what they are selling you is achievable and that it follows the rules of the social media site. Some sites will take down your account if it is misused to gather additional followers. Most social media sites have advertising options that can help your posts get seen by more people.

What goes "viral"?

People love clips that are cute, funny, or involve celebrity mistakes and epic fails. Find interesting ways to post info and images from the production so that they have a better chance of going viral. If you are posting something that may make one of your actors look bad, be sure to ask them first and be sure it isn't going to do damage to them, or the credibility of your film. When you prepare these posts, ask yourself if someone would not only look at this, but resend it to their friends. Creating contests and competitions can help engage the audience. It is the audience involvement in reposting of your film's material that will help it go viral.

Posting Additional Clips

Some films have put together a marketing campaign that includes additional footage that is not in the film. These can be prerelease set-ups for the film, interviews with the cast, or extended clips from the finished film. Some studio film marketing plans use additional videos that are preludes to the film with added info on the characters, story line, or messages from fake companies set up for the film.

The Press

Even in the age of the web, TV and print press can still be a huge asset. But how do you get a critic in a major city to review your film? First of all, the film has to be playing where the general public can see it. If the film isn't going to be in theaters when the critic's review comes out, then critics in the larger cities won't review the film. This involves at least a limited theatrical release from the distribution company, or the producer(s) "four walling" the picture, (i.e., paying for the theater space). Online film reviewers may not require theatrical screening of your film however, they will usually require a release date for digital or DVD.

Getting the attention of the press depends on how known your actors and director are and how topical your picture is. If you have known actors, critics are more likely to watch and review the film. Even if you don't have big actors, you should still contact film reviewers around the country to see if any of them will screen your film. However, don't harass them. Send one email with a link to the trailer, a poster and summery of the film. Calling a critic over and over or deluging them with emails may cause them to ignore your film or give you a bad review. Many smaller cities and blog sites are happy for new entertainment news and may be open to reviewing your film.

Another great route for getting press on your film is through a well-known film festival. If you are able to get the film into a festival where press attends, then either your publicist or you need to get a list of the attending press agents and film reviewers as well as their contact information so that you can personally invite them to your screening.

Advertising

Advertising can be expensive so you should do a market analysis to see if the returns justify the cost. Larger studios often spend the same amount on advertising as they did on making the film. If you have a larger budget film, you are going to need to do more than just blogging to see a decent return. This is where it is important to have a good distribution company and a good plan to market the film. The cost of TV ads, print ads and billboards for a limited theatrical release can be prohibitive for the indie producer. If you are taking the film out on your own, you need to set aside a large budget for advertising, or go with free online marketing and word of mouth.

PART IV
PRODUCTION

"He who is best prepared
can best serve his moment of inspiration."
– Samuel Taylor Coleridge

"Pick up a camera. Shoot something. No matter how small, no matter how cheesy, no matter whether your friends and your sister star in it. Put your name on it as director. Now you're a director. Everything after that you're just negotiating your budget and your fee."

– James Cameron

Chapter 16

Outline of a Production Day

FINALLY! It's here – your first day of filming! To us, this can be the most exciting part of the production experience. Even screening the film before an audience for the first time is rarely as exciting as the actual filming. At the screening you are nervous that something may go wrong with the playback or the sound - or both. Being on set is a LOT more fun.

Your eyes shoot open as the alarm clock beside your bed rings. It may not even be light outside, but it's time to wake up and head to the set. Filming has begun. Everything is moving quickly and you need to be sure that everything and everyone are where they need to be. Whether it's $10,000 or $10 million on the line, you and everyone around you has poured everything they have into this moment. This is a day in the life of your production. First up:

Call Sheets and Sides

Every cast member and crew member should have a *call sheet* that they received the previous night to prepare them for what they need to do on that day. Along with the call sheet, the cast and heads of the department should also receive the *sides* for the day. Sides are quarter-sheet-size versions of the script containing only the scenes that are filming that day. (The associate directors should have extra copies of the sides on set in case people forget to print them.

What Needs To Be Prepped for the Day?

Now that you've looked over the call sheet, check to see what must be prepped for the day. Are there any stunts, props, or special effects? Check with each department to ensure they understand what scenes are being shot and determine if special situations may arise.

Arriving at Base Camp

Base camp should be prearranged prior to filming. If you are filming in a studio, back lot, or a location like someone's home, your base camp should be at or near that location. If the shooting location is large enough, you may have enough room to set up spaces for wardrobe, makeup, and hair; dressing rooms for the cast; bathrooms for the crew; and a place for craft service and catering. If you're shooting in tighter quarters, you may need to add tents, tables, and chairs. You also want to have enough bathrooms and/or portable toilets for your entire team and cast.

If you are filming in a location that does not have a provided space for cast and crew, you will have to set up a base camp. If the base camp cannot be where you are filming, you must arrange transportation between the base camp and the location. To minimize disruptions and down time, try to have a base camp as close as possible to your filming location. If your equipment trucks cannot park where you are filming, you'll need to find a way to transport gear to the set.

Set up the Craft Services Table

Whatever your budget level, good and healthy food is imperative on any film. Your craft service table (which is often the first thing people see), should be well organized. You need coffee, hot water, an assortment of teas, milk, and sugar. You also need bottled water, vitamin drinks and soft drinks. If you want to be eco-friendly and keep costs down, provide water bottles that the cast and crew can write their names on. On-set water coolers can minimize the clutter and waste of discarded and half-used water bottles.

Depending on your shooting schedule, you may not have to provide a full breakfast. However, you should provide healthy snacks from beginning to end of the shoot day. Bagels and fresh fruit, health bars, vegetables, sliced meats and bread for sandwiches, and packets of soup for cold days are good options. Stay away from donuts and other sugary foods as the sugar high will cause energy crashes later.

No one works well on an empty stomach and no crew works well without a constant flow of coffee. Do yourself a favor and have good coffee. It doesn't have to be the most expensive, but don't buy coffee that tastes like dirt. The crew will know the difference and appreciate it.

Check in on Set

If there is space, the AD department should set up a check-in table for all cast (including extras) and crew. If this is a union film, each actor must sign their SAG paperwork (known as SAG Exhibit G) each day when they check in prior to going into make-up. If the actors are non-union, they should sign non-union time sheets. On the first day of filming, the second AD should ensure that all cast and crew have completed all paperwork for the payroll company and for accounting. This includes any tax paperwork like W-4s, i9s, or any other paperwork required by your country or state's tax authority. All cast members should also sign their contracts and extras should sign their on-camera releases before anyone sets foot on set. This ensures you have all of the performance rights you need. After signing in, each crew member should check in with their department head to ensure they know what the director wants first.

Review the Shot List

The producer, director, DP, and AD should go over the day's planned shots. As a contingency, the director can tell the AD what shots are most important and should be scheduled first and what shots are less important in case the day goes long and shots must be moved or deleted.

Communication

If you are on a tight budget *and* have unlimited minutes on your cell phone plan, cell phones can be a great option for communication. However, cell phones are not always practical and cell-signal coverage can be spotty. When the AD checks in, he or she should go to the equipment truck and pick-up walkie-talkies. Key members of each department will need walkie-talkies with them all day so that they can easily communicate and locate cast or crew members who are needed on set. This is particularly important when you are on a big set or are away from base camp where your wardrobe and make-up departments are set up. Walkie-talkies are inexpensive and can keep you and the AD from having to run off set every five minutes to find someone or something.

Walk Through with Actors

Once the actors in the first scene have checked in, the director should have them do a quick walk through on set to ensure everyone knows what is happening in the scene. The actors will perform a quick rehearsal as the director finalizes blocking, camera angles, and lighting and makes any final adjustments for props or anything else on set.

Crew Set-Up

After the blocking walk-through, the crew will set up for the scene. They will pull any additional cables needed, set up lights, address anything that might be a safety issue for the cast or crew, set up the camera, dolly, or any other gear needed to get ready for filming.

Camera Set-Up

The camera set-up should be handled by the camera operator, the DP, or the camera assistants - *not* other members of the crew. The camera may need to be placed on a jib, dolly, tripod or stead-cam, depending on what the director needs. Be mindful of how long the camera department takes to set up and make sure they have enough time for each scene. If you begin to run behind schedule, find out if there are ways that any additional camera or lighting crew can begin to setup for the next shot while the first shot is still underway.

Lighting Adjustments with Stand-Ins

Stand-ins are important for the lighting on set. Actors will be in make-up and wardrobe, so you don't want to disturb them or waste their energy standing on set waiting for lighting adjustments. On a larger budget film, you'll have assigned stand-ins for each major actor. Each stand-in is chosen with a similar height and look to the actor so that any lighting and camera adjustments will match for the actor. On lower-budget films, you often ask assistants to help out. Stand-ins are important for the DP to see how the lighting will affect the actors once they are in place.

Permits and Releases Handy

Make sure your location manager has all the permits on hand and ready in case you get a visit from the local police. Occasionally, a film sets get visited to ensure that everything is in order. If you don't have permits accessible, the authorities can shut you down and you can lose thousands of dollars for one small mistake. Also, be sure that any union paperwork is handy, in case an SAG representative visits the set. And make certain that any working animals are well cared for, following best practices, so you are prepared if the Humane Society visits.

Actors are Prepped in Makeup and Wardrobe

When the actors are finished with the walk through, they should return to make-up and wardrobe to continue getting ready for filming. Be sure your first AD has discussed with the make-up team how long they will have with each actor. You want a clear plan for how much time they need to get ready. If you call them in too late, or you don't have enough makeup and hair people to handle the number of actors, you'll have an entire crew waiting.

Give yourself a little extra time the first day so that you can gauge exactly how much time will be needed. Makeup times usually get better with each day as the make-up team and the actor get used to their routines. If the makeup department takes longer then planned, have them find the cause of the issue and determine if you need more staff or a more experienced team.

Make sure each performer has enough time to get through make-up, hair, and wardrobe and can then spend time getting into character. Not all actors can treat each scene like they are turning on and off a switch. Actors often need time to transition into character and if they are rushed onto set without time to prepare, you may not get the performance you desire.

For a contemporary scene with simple makeup, each actor may only need 45 minutes to get ready. But if you are filming a movie with complicated prosthetics, SFX makeup, scars, tattoos, etc., then you may need to plan for two hours or more. Make sure your AD knows prep time is needed so that they can plan for each day of filming.

For a low-budget film, you may be asking actors to take care of their makeup and hair themselves. If so, take a look at each actor to be sure they didn't use to little or too much makeup. Be thoughtful with any corrections you make – they've done their best to comply with your directions. Ultimately, you want to ensure they look as much like the character as possible and if they are unclear as to how to establish that look, you or your art department will need to guide them.

If you do not have a makeup team on staff, purchase makeup powder and a mirror to keep on set so someone can lightly dust the actors face to keep beads of sweat from making them look "shiny" on camera.

Director Setting First Shot with DP

Once the lighting is in place and the camera is ready to go, the director look at the first shot with the DP to see if any adjustments that need to be made.

Audio Prep

Once the camera knows what position they will be in and where the actors will be, the audio department can move in and begin placing microphones. These may be wireless lavalieres (lav), shotgun microphones (mics), or whatever the audio mixer likes to use. The audio mixer and boom operators work with the camera operator to make sure that any mics are out of the shot. If they are running a hand-held boom, the boom operator needs to know the movement of the performers and the framing of the camera so they can keep the mic in front of the performer without getting on camera or causing a shadow.

The mixer will likely want to place a wireless mic on the performer. This may be suitable for some scenes but not for others. Check with the performer to be sure they are comfortable with the mic and make sure that it is not placed in a way that harms their performance or shows up on camera. It is not recommended to use only lav mics. Using both lavs and boom mics gives you the best options in post-production as lav mics can be easily hit causing large pops or scratching sounds when the actors are moving around the set. The better your audio recording on set, the less you will have to recreate the performance through ADR in post-production.

Rehearsal's Up

When the camera and lighting is ready, makeup and wardrobe have finished, and the actors are ready to perform, the AD will call for rehearsal. (This is not the main rehearsal, the main rehearsal should have taken place prior to filming where any questions from cast or crew can be answered. If none of the scenes have been rehearsed, the additional time on set will cost the producer a lot more during filming than during pre production.)

The crew should be quiet so that the director can talk with the actors and go over each scene one more time. If the director and actors have not been able to rehearse the scene on set during preproduction, they will now walk through the scene and chose various positions for them to move through the scene. For example, the director may have JOHN start on the couch, move to the window, the cross over to the kitchen. The couch would be John's "first position," which is where he would begin his action, the window would be John's "second position," and the kitchen would be John's "final position." These can be called "first position" or "one", "second position" or "two" and so on with the final position as "end." Collectively, these positions are called "marks" (thus, the phrase "hitting their mark").

While the actors are rehearsing the action, the camera operator and focus puller check to make sure that they have the correct camera settings and marks for focus so that the shot stays properly exposed and in focus during the action. The camera department also makes marks for any camera movement, especially if the camera is on a dolly or when a steady cam is being used.

When everything is ready, the AD calls "rehearsal action" and the performers run through the scene. The director makes any adjustments, and it is time to roll the first take of the day. Your 1st AD should make note of the time once you are ready for your first take. How long did it take to set up for the first shot of the day? One hour? Two hours? More? At this rate will you stay on schedule or do you need to make adjustments? Things usually move more quickly after the first shot is up, but depending on how long it took, you may need to make adjustments in the next days' schedule if you need to be into the first shot more quickly.

Slate it!

On the majority of film sets, the audio and the picture are recorded separately. To easily synchronize these two during editing, your camera department needs to "slate" the beginning of each take. The slate (AKA: sticks) is the clapboard that has on it the name of the film, the director, the DP, the scene number, the date, the frame rate of the camera, and any other important camera data that may need to be referenced later. Just before the director calls action, one of the camera assistants (or on a smaller set, the AD may perform this task) puts the slate in front of the camera and calls out the scene and take so that audio can hear it and then claps the board.

Picture's Up

First take of the day. The AD makes all the calls except for "action," which is for the director to do. The AD calls out "quiet on the set" and waits for the set to settle. This call should be relayed through the walkie-talkies so that everyone on set knows that the camera is preparing to roll. No one should be moving around or talking. AD - "roll audio." Audio will call out "speed," which means they are rolling. AD - "roll camera." The camera operator will say "rolling" when the camera has begun filming. The AD then nods to the director and the director calls "action."

If there are stunts, special effects, or other movements happening, other calls may be made prior to action. There may be a "stand by cars" for car movement, "action on cars," or if there are background actors, the AD will call "background action" prior to the director calling "action." The last call in the series is for "action" from the main actors by the director. If you are working with animals, especially horses and dogs, they may start to anticipate the action and move before you want them to. If this is the case, you may need to adjust the terms you are using to call for action to trick the animal into performing at the right time.

When the action is complete the director calls "cut," and the AD says "clear" loudly so that everyone knows they are clear. The call of "clear" is also repeated through the walkie-talkies to the rest of the crew so they know they can resume working. Sometimes, the director is not loud at saying cut and instead may say "good" or "ok" instead. The AD needs to ask the director "was that a cut?" and the director will respond with a yes or no. If yes, the AD will call "cut." The completed shot is also called a "take."

If the director wants to do "another take," (the actors doing the scene again) the AD says "going again" and then tells the actors and crew "back to one" or "first positions," which means all the actors return to their first position as does the camera if the camera moved. If the director liked the take, then the AD calls "moving on," which means they are moving to the next shot in the scene.

Monitoring What is Happening in Front of the Camera

While the action is taking place on set, it can be really easy to get caught up in what is happening around you. It's fun to watch the actors from different angles, but the only angle that really counts is the one that the camera is seeing. For this reason, you need to be sure that you have a properly calibrated monitor on set at all times. The producer, the director, and the script supervisor need to watch every take on that monitor and not try to watch from another angle. This monitor(s) is referred to as "video village."

Each shot should be monitored carefully to be sure that what you are getting is exactly what you want. Actors' performances, wardrobe malfunctions, brand labels showing up where they should not, camera mishaps, and boom mics entering the shot all should be carefully watched by the producer, director, and script supervisor.

If for some reason the camera is moving in a way that makes it difficult to tether to the video village, have someone from the camera department arrange for a wireless monitor for the director and the script supervisor. This may sound simple, but if you can't see what you are getting, you will not know what you have. This is not something you should be guessing at nor should you have to waste time after every shot to re-watch every take. This will greatly slow down your filming. If absolutely needed, re-watch the take, but don't make it a habit or you will fall behind schedule.

The Watchful Eye of the Script Supervisor

Another reason the production team needs to set up a monitor is so the script supervisor can see exactly what is being shot and make notes on their copy of the script. They need to mark where each shot begins and ends, who was on camera, what the take number was, was the shot good or not, were there any mistakes on the take, was the shot wide, medium, close, over-the-shoulder, was the take good for the camera and good for audio. The director calls out "circle that one" if they liked the take (these are called "circle takes"). The script supervisor circles that take number and will, in addition, mark any changes to the dialog by the actors.

The script supervisor can be an amazing source for continuity between shots as they pay attention to everything on screen. They often note if a performer moves from right or left, if they were carrying something in their hand, etc. They should also watch for any inadvertent labels, water bottles, soda cans, or other uncleared objects that make their way onto set.

Monitoring Audio

Your audio department should supply you with wireless headphones that are tied into the audio mixer's console. This allows you to correctly monitor the audio for each take. There should be a headset for the director, script supervisor, and producer.

Recording great audio in the field is essential, especially when doing a low-budget film. This may not be possible for all shots if you are filming an action movie, and you may have to do some ADR after the film is shot. The problem for smaller budget films is that the ADR process is often time consuming and expensive. In addition, you may be hard pressed to get the same performance from your actors.

If an audience can't hear the dialog between the characters, the film is lost. If you have to cut the budget down, don't hire a bad sound recorder. It will cost you thousands of dollars to ADR all of your performers' lines in post and without good sound, your film will likely be a disaster.

When possible, mic all the actors who will be speaking on camera. This may be challenging when you have several actors on screen at once, but you will pay a lot less for two sound engineers on location to capture all the audio than several days of ADR in post. If you have limited mics, and if one or more of the actors are facing away from the camera, you may be able to only mic the actor(s) facing the camera.

Ingesting Digital Footage

Some productions still use film but most likely you will work with digital media. Each camera system has a different way of recording the media, some on tape, some on hard drives, and some on flash cards. Whichever format you have chosen, your post supervisor and the DP or camera operator needs to work out system as to who takes the footage from the camera department and how it gets to the editor or the lab. Any footage like film or tapes that are sent to a lab, or transferred on set like flashcards or hard drives, should also be recorded for the production report.

If you use reusable flash cards or hard drives, be sure that all the footage is copied and examined by your DMT or the editor prior to returning the cards or hard drive to the camera department. Any errors on the cards or drives should be noted and immediately reported to the camera department.

If you use digital media for recording, then the DMT is one of the most important technical jobs on your set. Every piece of footage shot comes through this crew member. Do not save on your budget here by hiring an intern or an unskilled computer operator to transfer your footage. If this stage is not handled properly, everything you shot can be lost.

Once the download has been completed and copied to at least one additional hard drive, the assistant editor or the editor should check every single take to be sure that none of them has been corrupted. No flashcard or hard drive should be deleted or returned to the camera department until each take has been verified. Color temperature and video levels should also be checked for accuracy with any discrepancies relayed to the DP.

Editing Prep by the Assistant Editor or Editor

One of the great benefits of using digital media is that you can begin to edit footage as soon as it's shot. Once the DMT has checked the takes, they hand over the main drive to the assistant editor (AE). The AE brings each shot into the edit system and marks each take properly to match the numbers on the slate. The assistant editor also receives from the audio mixer the audio that matches the takes they were given by the camera operator.

The AE will then match up the video with the audio from the field mixer and combine the clips so the editor can look through each take and begin editing the film. If handled properly with a skilled AE and editor, you may have a rough cut of much of the film by the time you finish shooting. The benefit to this is seeing if you missed anything that needs to be picked up before you wrap filming.

If you are not using digital media but are shooting on film or video tapes, your editor will get the drives back from the lab one or two days after the shoot day. The editor should go through all the footage to see if there were any problems and report those issues to the DP.

If you are working on a smaller budget and can't afford an assistant editor, make sure your editor knows how to set up the footage and prep it for the edit. Some editors only focus on editing and don't have the same technical skills as an AE.

Behind-the-Scenes Photos/Video for Marketing

While you are set up to shoot scenes that may be really good for marketing, have your behind-the-scenes photographer step in and take a shot from the same angle as the film or video camera. Shots from a still camera will have a much higher pixel count and give you much cleaner images for promotions than trying to pull stills from the movie later in post. An HD frame of video is only 1920 x1080 pixels. A still camera can take 10,000 x 10,000 pixels or more. If you are using a camera with a 4k or 5k image, you may be able to pull some good stills, but don't count on it. Your actors may move in a way that works for a moving image, but they may not have the right look for a promotional still when the picture is not in motion. Have them pose properly for a few seconds, snap the photo, and move on.

You should regularly download the images from the photographer onto a separate promotion hard drive. You can then decide which ones you want to use for promotion while you are still filming and which ones you want to hold on to until after the film is ready to be released. Don't let the photographer leave that day of filming without giving you a copy of the card they shot on.

Taking Breaks

Whether or not you are working with a union crew, it's important to take breaks and give your crew a few minutes to grab coffee, a snack, or use the bathroom. When on a union film, breaks are required at set lengths and set times or your film may be penalized. Your AD should be familiar with any union rules and make sure that they are adhered to.

Shelter

If you are filming inside or in a studio, you may already have an area set aside for the cast and crew to sit and have breaks and be out of the weather. If you are filming outside, you need to provide trailers or tents to make sure that people can stay out of the , rain, or cold. Shelter from the weather is not only a comfort issue but a safety issue, especially if you are filming in extreme conditions.

Bathrooms

If there are not adequate bathroom facilities where you are filming, you need to bring in "honey trucks" or "honey pots." These are portable toilets and can range from very simple to elaborate. Some have just a simple toilet, others are fitted more like a normal bathroom with a sink and mirror.

Catering

The catering department should prepare for meals one or two days in advance. If you use a catering service, the head of catering will call into the service in the morning with an accurate head count for the day's meal. On a full 12-hour day of filming, you must provide two hot meals for the cast and crew, including breakfast and lunch and craft service items to supplement during breaks. If filming goes into overtime, you need to provide another hot meal in accordance with union rules. If your film is non-union, we recommend that you use the union's rules for meals as a guideline.

Make sure the catering department has checked with all the cast and crew for any dietary restrictions or allergies. Where possible, meals should include a salad, vegetables, a hot plate of some type, and a simple desert. Be careful with meals heavy in pasta and breads as the crew will be lethargic after lunch.

Meals

The AD needs to call lunch no more than six hours after the first cast and crew call. Anything after that and you will incur late lunch penalties if you are working under a union agreement. Unions require a one-hour lunch and that their members mark on their sign-in sheets the time they went to lunch and the time they went back to set. You will be charged meal penalties if you don't break at the correct time.

Aside from union rules (and even if the film is non-union), it's not a good idea to wait more than six hours to call lunch. People are working hard for you, and you need to give them a break in the day so they can eat, relax, and recoup. The AD should keep track of the time so that when it gets close to time to break, they can let the director know and the director can stop production at a convenient time prior to the six-hour mark.

Depending on the size of the cast and crew, you may need to stagger the lunch so that you can get everyone through without shutting down for two hours. Have your AD look at the day's schedule and work out the best way for the cast and crew to take lunch in a way that maximizes your schedule.

To decide who goes to lunch first, look at who is going to be needed on set first. If you have crew members who have to get back out quickly, don't make them go last in line. Let them eat first so that you aren't holding up the film while you wait for them to have their full break. The AD first calls lunch and then marks the time when the last person gets their lunch. This marks the beginning of the one-hour break unless you are staggering lunch so some crew members can start back before the others.

If you are on a tight catering budget, you may want to have a meal ticket system for your cast and crew so you don't end up with a lot of unexpected or uninvited guests eating your food. This can sometimes be an issue if you are filming in a public place as catering may not be aware of who is part of film cast and crew and who isn't.

Security

If you are filming on a city street, you may be required to have police to keep your crew and the public safe. Even if you aren't required to have police on set, you should see if security is needed. If you have a named actor, they may attract attention from the press or from a local crowd that could hinder filming.

If you have a budget for additional security, it can be helpful to have one or two security officers on standby for any additional issues on set. Guarding equipment and stopping disruptions from wandering members of the public should be part of your preparation for a smooth-running set.

If you have a small set and can't afford security, go over set rules carefully with your cast and crew, keep visitors away from the set as much as possible, and lock up the equipment if no one is around to watch it.

Visitors

Visitors on set should be kept to a minimum. It's fun to be on set and see how a film operates, but this is a place of work and should be respected as such. Anyone visiting the set should be made aware of set operations and rules of conduct. If they hassle the cast or crew, have your security team ask them to leave. On a small budget where you cannot afford security, make people responsible for anyone they bring on set and remind them that the set is a work place. Any disruptions and delays can cost the film a significant amount of money.

Often investors want to visit the set. If this is the case, set up a time that you can personally meet with them and escort them around. A good way to do this is have them arrive during lunch, make some introductions when the set is quiet, and have them stay for some of the scenes after lunch. If you have them come at the beginning of the day, it will be much harder for you to give them a tour as you will be busy running the set.

Burning Daylight

On set, time can fly by, and if no one watches the schedule, you can lose the day without getting everything you need. One of the AD's vital roles is to keep everything moving on set. If the crew or even the director is falling behind, it's the AD's job to remind the director of where you are in the day's schedule and where you are supposed to be. If filming gets too far behind, you may have to consider what needs to be cut from the film.

It is important that you get enough shots to cover the scene, so if you are getting behind, have the director first get what they absolutely need to tell the story and what they would like to have second. Give them a choice as to what to cut. Tell them, they can continue working on the shot they are on, but they will have to lose a shot later in the day if they don't move on. The director may decide that the shot later in the day is more important and move on.

Martini Shot

The last shot of the day is called the martini shot. You will usually hear a sigh of relief when the AD calls martini shot. The sigh that is the loudest may be from you.

Signing Out

Before they leave for the day, all union actors sign out on an exhibit G sheet while non-union cast and crew sign out on the non-union time sheets. The sign-out sheet for the nonunion cast and crew is to help keep track of payroll while the union paperwork is required by the union. One of the AD team should be available to make sure that everyone signs out.

Payroll

Make sure that all the cast and crew have filled out their sign-in and sign-out cards and that that information is passed on to the payroll company or to your accountant. Cast and crew expect payroll on time in accordance with their agreement with you. Payroll usually takes a week to process the prior week's information and send back paychecks. Those checks can be mailed to the cast and crew or handed out on set.

Camera Reports

While filming, the camera department should keep track of each take and file a camera report at the end of the day. These reports will be filed with the AD for the production report and later given to the post supervisor for use during post-production or for any reshoots.

Audio Reports

The audio department should also keep track of every take and file a similar report to the camera report. This report is usually handled by the mixer and should be filed with the AD then later given to the post supervisor.

Prep for the Next Day

As set wraps for the day, the AD team's work is not complete. Often, the ADs can be the hardest working members of the team, so make sure you have someone on board as your 1st AD who is experienced and easy to work with. Also, make sure there is some food still onset for the ADs as they wrap the day.

While filming, the 2nd AD begins to prepare the call sheet for the next day. Once filming is done, the 2nd AD gets a list of shots from the 1st AD that did or did not get filmed and makes adjustments to the call sheet. If you got through all the filming for that day and finish on time, the call sheet can go out as everyone is leaving set so that they know what to expect. If there are major changes because of missed shots or the call time needs to be pushed back to stay within a contractual turn-around time due to a late finish, the call sheet may have to go out later that night through email. (Turn around is the time the cast and crew leaves the set at the end of the shoot day to the time they report to set the next day. Union contracts require a certain rest period between times that a cast and or crew member can return to set.)

Having gathered all the information from the department heads, the AD team puts together a production report for the day.

Production Report

As part of their duties for the day, The AD fills out a production report. This report is often required by the studio, guilds, unions, bond company, and possibly your investors. The production report lays out exactly what happened during that day of filming. The front page should contain the production company name, the name of the film, the name of the director, producer and line producer, and or unit production manager. It should also have the total number of production days and which day today's report is on. This report includes notes from the script supervisor, a report from the camera department, audio department, the exhibit G's from the union actors, and the extras breakdown (i.e.: how many extras, in and out times, pay rate, and if there is any overtime.)

On larger films, the production report also includes a list of the entire crew by department, each person's in and out times, meal times, and whether there is any overtime. It also lists the location, any special equipment rentals, and any incidents on set.

Watching the Dailies

An important final duty and a good way to unwind at the end of the day is to sit down with the director, and if possible the DP, and watch through some or all the dailies. Dailies are the footage you shot that day. You can use either the hard drive that your editor is working on or the copy hard drive that you were given by the DMT.

How does the action look? Is the lighting right? Are you getting the coverage (i.e.: shots or angles) you need? You can discuss the look of the film and decide on any changes for the following day.

Cleaning Up

As your crew and cast leave for the day, ask everyone to pick up after themselves so that they don't leave a large mess for someone else to pick up after. If you are coming back the next day, you won't want to have to deal with a mess. If this is your last day on location, you should make sure that everything is cleaned and left in good condition.

Insurance

If anything is broken or damaged during the shoot, mark it down for insurance coverage. If anyone is injured during the day, contact your insurance company and find out what their procedure is to cover the injury.

Sleep

When you lay down that night - as reflections on that day's filming fill your mind only to be greeted by thoughts of what is to come - you may find it hard to sleep. As important as it is to be prepared, it's just as important to be rested. Don't let your crew stay out too late drinking, and get as much sleep as you can so that you have the energy and patience to lead the next weeks or months of filming.

JULIA VERDIN and MATT DEAN

"Anyone who has ever been privileged to direct a film also knows that, although it can be like trying to write 'War and Peace' in a bumper car in an amusement park, when you finally get it right, there are not many joys in life that can equal the feeling."

– Stanley Kubrick

Chapter 17

Production:
Working with Actors

It can be really easy on a low-budget film to want to push everything along faster and faster so that you get in every shot you think you need. We have found, however, that the film can suffer greatly if you don't give the actors enough time to present to you the best possible moment on camera bringing the characters to life. There have been times when we've looked back on filming a scene and wished we'd been able to give the actors another take, and if you miss those moments when you edit the film, it's too late. Finding the balance between capturing great moments and having all the shots you need on a short shoot schedule is very challenging, and it's why producers who know how to manage people and time are worth their weight in gold.

Working with Actors

One area you want to allow plenty of time for is giving your director and actors room to be creative. These performances are what will live in your film for better or for worse. A year or two after filming, you may not remember why you didn't have time to shoot something, but you will remember a performance that was or was not exactly what you had hoped for.

To start, actors need a quiet space to get into character and prepare themselves. If you are using SAG talent, you will be contractually required to provide your cast with a private dressing room or trailer. If you are hiring a star name actor, then their agent or manager most likely will insist on a trailer for them as part of their contract. If you have a smaller film and cannot afford trailers for the lead actors, you still need to make a comfortable space for them. This should be properly cooled or heated, out of the weather, and away from the storage of gear or crew areas. This is not because the actors are snobs, but because they may need to prepare themselves for their performance and being interrupted by crew members may disturb that process.

An uninterrupted space is especially important if your actors are performing an emotional role. Whether they are playing a villain or a distraught mother, the role may take a lot out of the performer, and you need to be sensitive to their needs. If they decide to mingle with the rest of the cast and crew, that is up to them, but they should be able to make that choice for themselves and not have that choice made for them by not having anywhere to retreat to.

Part of the instruction to the cast and crew should be for them to be careful about starting conversations with actors between takes. If the performer starts the conversation, then fine. However, many times between takes, the performer tries to stay in character, which may make it difficult for them to talk freely with crew members. If an actor is sitting quietly, it may be that they are emotionally trying to tap into their performance and should be left alone to do their job.

Before calling an actor to set, make sure that everything is in place. Let them know if they are just coming out for a run through or if they need to be ready for the performance. If it is time for the performance, make sure that everything is ready and don't call them out if the DP still has 30 minutes of lighting left to do. Making an actor sit around on set can cool off the performance they were prepping in their trailer and can often make them irritable.

When the director is on set rehearsing with the actors, instruct the crew to keep the noise to a minimum. Usually the AD will call out "rehearsal's up" when they are getting ready to rehearse. This means that everyone needs to be quiet. If for some reason the AD does not call for rehearsal, the crew still needs to be mindful of the director. Remind the cast and crew that this is a work place, and idle chatter should be kept in the break areas so that people can work.

To further help performances, be mindful of the mood on set. If you are shooting a comedy, joking around on set may be appropriate. If you are filming an emotional scene, keeping a somber mood may better help the actors. If you are filming a love scene, keep the number of crew down to a minimum and keep out visitors. The day that your actors are asked to perform nude is not the day to have your investors and their cousins visit the set. For any racy or risky scenes, actors find it helpful (and often require contractually), to have a closed set for these type of shots. Respect the needs of the performers and they will give you the performances you need for a quality film.

As shooting progresses, it's important to notice how each actor works best and make use of that on the set. Talk with the director if you notice that one actor always gets their best performance the first time around. This way, you can have the camera on them for the first take and then focus on the other actors on subsequent takes. If you are filming with a named star on a high salary, it would be appropriate to get their close-ups first, then their coverage second and the other actors after. If for some reason you run out of time, it is less expensive to re-shoot a close-up of the other actor than pay to bring back the name actor who will probably be on a higher salary.

Once the camera is rolling, don't let people fiddle unnecessarily with things behind the camera. Any movement and work taking place other than needed camera movement is distracting and unfair to the actors who are trying to perform. If lights need to be moved or if someone needs coffee, do it between takes. If something major needs to be adjusted, have the director call cut as the take won't be good anyway and you don't want the performers wasting their energy on a dead take.

If between takes an actor needs something from their trailer or they need coffee, or anything else, make sure there is someone to help them. Don't let anyone talk poorly of a performer because they need help with something. Simply getting up for coffee may take the performer off set and out of character at a time when that is exactly where they need to be.

In regards to performances, the only person who should be giving them direction is the director. Too many voices cause too many problems. The DP, the script supervisor, the key grip, or anyone else should not be giving performance advice or notes. It isn't that they don't have good ideas, they might. The problem is that the director knows (or should know), what they want and other input may not match. If someone has a suggestion, they should give it to their department head, who can pass it on to the producer or the director as they see fit. The only people who should be commenting on what is on screen is the DP and the script supervisor and they should make their comments to you so you can pass it on at the appropriate moment or to the director directly. This way, all of the instructions to the performer come from one voice and the director is not dealing with a lot of distractions.

If the actor asks you about their performance, and they often will, tell them they are doing a wonderful job. If you do have any comments or suggestions, you should also take them to the director. This isn't because you don't have great ideas, it's because the director may want something in particular that your suggestion may counter-act, and it is important that the actors have trust in the director to guide them in their performance. Speak to the director if you have a problem with where a performance is going and if needed, ask for one more take in the way you think it needs to go. You need to trust the director that you hired. There may be times however, when you see something they are not getting in coverage and you may need the additional material when you get to the edit suite. If this is the case, be careful how many times you ask for this as you may create a conflict with the director.

If you are having problems with the director connecting with the actors, find a quiet place one on one to pull them aside and voice your concerns. This can often be an issue with first-time directors who are trying to find their style. Try to find a solution that doesn't embarrass them. Some directors work better with actors than others. Sometimes you'll find that your director is better at technical aspects and visual style than with getting performances from actors. If this is the case, than after complimenting the director on their visual accomplishments, ask them if they would be comfortable having an acting coach work with the actors. The acting coach could help relay the director's vision while insuring a great performance from the actors. Some directing teams work this way with one of the team members working with the actors and the other calling the visual shots. This, however, is something you should preferably work out during rehearsals or through speaking to the director about their strengths when you hire them, rather than waiting until you are on set.

If you are a director/producer and you find it difficult to communicate your vision to the actors, it's a good idea to take some acting classes prior to filming so you can learn the actor's language. Each acting teacher or coach is different, but much of what you will learn in those classes can help you understand what the actor is trying to do, and how to help them understand what you are looking for. Not everyone is good at everything, and it's important for you to be realistic about your strengths and weaknesses. If even after some classes you still have trouble, consider bringing in an acting coach or a directing partner who can help you achieve the best performances possible.

If an actor isn't sure what the director wants, they may begin to feel insecure with the direction their performance is going and try something that doesn't fit with what you know is needed. Actors don't want to look bad on camera, and they don't want their performance to suffer. So if they don't have clarity, they will find a way to create clarity. To save yourself a mixed performance in the film, make sure your director knows what they want and take them aside if necessary to help them find it.

Between takes, make sure that the AD organizes assistants to have water and snacks available to the cast and crew. If the crew needs to reset a shot, the AD should find out how long the reset will take. The camera department will know if it will only take a few minutes or if it will take much longer. If it's going to take a long time to rest, the AD should release the cast to their trailers so they are not left on a set under the hot lights or where objects are being moved around.

Working with Extras

Rules for proper etiquette for extras is the same for the rest of the crew. They need to know where they need to be, who they are answering to, and what to do between takes. If you hire a group of extras that are used to working on films, they will hopefully already know how to behave on set; even so, it's a good idea to run through what you expect of them. On a larger budget film, you may need to hire an extras wrangler or have them take orders from the AD team. When the extras are not needed, there should be a holding area or an area for them to rest where they are not in the way of the crew.

Extras should not be allowed to leave set during filming as they may disrupt continuity in the film. If they need to leave for some reason, they need to tell the extras wrangler or the AD that they are leaving. Any extra who cannot stay for the duration of the scene should not be placed in that scene.

If the extras need wardrobe and makeup, be sure that you have adequate staff to handle the work load and that you have a holding area large enough for them. Additional snacks, water, and food may be needed for the extras. If you are dealing with a large number of them, it is a good idea to have a separate craft service table just for the extras. As with the other actors, be sure that the extras wrangler, extras casting department, or the AD team has had the extras sign all releases and other paperwork before coming on set.

"I would travel down to Hell and
wrestle a film away from the devil
if it was necessary."

– Werner Herzog

Chapter 18

Production:
Leadership

Scene: It's night in front of a large stone building. Inside a police car, the actor waits for their cue. A strong overhead light mimics a streetlight and the rest of the building fades into the night. The AD calls "Stand by" and the set quiets. "Cue rain" and suddenly the street is flooded with a downpour of rain from the sprinklers overhead. Several voices call out across the set. "Roll audio." "Speed!" "Roll camera." The cameras click on. "Rolling." The director looks at the monitor. The camera has framed the car window beautifully as the actor prepares to light a cigarette before stepping from the car. The director waits a beat and then calls "Action."

You grin as you snap a picture in your mind of this moment. This is why you are here. From your perfect vantage point, you absorb the ambience of the lights, the cameras, and the talented actors. It's heaven, frozen in a moment of time.

Suddenly, your bliss is shattered as your production assistant taps you on the shoulder. Something is wrong. The catering didn't arrive on time, the actor for the next scene is sick, the film is going over budget...

Sigh.

There have been a number of times when we have been happily filming a scene and were interrupted by some disaster on set. From catering that is late, to trouble with a cast member, to a broken camera, something will and always does go wrong. Meanwhile, everyone relies on the producer to keep everything operating properly so that the director and the actors can continue to create the "magic" you desperately need to make the film work.

Leadership

Finding your style of leadership means being comfortable with who you are, even if you aren't comfortable yet with what you are doing. This may be your first time producing, and much of the processes may seem overwhelming. You may begin to feel the weight of responsibly from handling other people's money, time, and efforts.

It's important for you to find a way to relieve the stress you may feel on something other than your set and your crew. You may need a quiet place at night or in the morning to gather your thoughts before you attack the day. Whatever you do, know that the temperament and working atmosphere on your film stems from you.

In this chapter, we are going to going into a little more detail on some of the things we talked about in chapter one. As a producer, you are required to be many things during the course of the production. While filming, you are going to need to acquire or hone your leadership skills as you discover how to be a better visionary, manager, cheerleader, and diplomat.

Manager

The largest and most demanding of these roles is the manager. Here you need to establish the rules that you expect people to abide by as well as set a good example for them to follow. To set up the code of conduct while filming, it's important on the first day of production to have the AD go through the set protocol and give a safety lecture. This is especially important if you are producing a small-budget film with relatively new crew or inexperienced crew and cast members on set. These people may not be aware of proper protocol, and it's important not to assume that people will know how to conduct themselves.

A good check list the AD should go through is:

1. Give the actors their space to work with peace and quiet between takes.

2. Cellphones and walkie-talkies off during takes.

3. Be quiet when "quiet on the set" is called and don't talk or move again until "clear" is called.

4. If any cast or crew leaves the set for any reason, let the 1st AD know. This includes going to the bathroom as people may be looking for or wondering where you are. A common verbal code for going to the bathroom is "10-1," rather than saying going to the bathroom.

5. When confirming instructions, especially on the walkie-talkies, use "copy that" not "roger." Someone on the set may be named Roger, which is why "copy that" is used.

6. No one working the set should wear open-toed shoes. There are many heavy objects on set, and there is a danger of people's feet getting hit by something falling or stubbing a toe on a light stand or other gear.

7. Make sure that crew members working on the lights have protective gloves. Some of the lights are VERY hot.

8. If cast or crew members are not assigned to work with certain equipment, they are not to handle that equipment. There may be ways of moving things they are not aware of and could break something or injure someone.

9. Everyone should sign in and out when arriving on set and leaving set at the end of the day.

10. No photos or video on set unless approved by the producers.

11. No visitors without permission.

12. Do not discuss the production, release any publicity, or post on social media anything about the production without permission.

13. Pay attention when on set. Watch for cables, booms, sand bags, or other equipment on the ground. Also watch for low-hanging lights.

14. Crew should wear dark or muted clothes. Do not wear white or anything reflective as it can affect the lighting if you are on set.

15. Put things back where they belong if they are not in use to keep set clutter down.

16. Do not walk or stand in front of actors' eye lines when they are rehearsing or shooting a scene as it can be very distracting for them.

17. No alcohol or drugs on set.

Basic set codes and phrases.

1. "10-1" going to the bathroom

2. "Talent" refers to the cast

3. "Striking" means to turn on or off a light. When you hear "striking" don't look toward the lights.

4. "Hot set" refers to an active set where you should not touch or remove anything that you are not assigned to touch or remove.

5. "Crossing" means that you are crossing in front of the camera and should be said by anyone who crosses in front of the camera.

6. "Points" or "hot Points" is said when someone is carrying an object with sharp points like a tripod or a light stand.

7. "Stinger" is an extension cord.

8. "C-47" is the name for clothes pins often used for holding lighting gels on lights. Why did we include this on the list? Because most

people on set think it's cool that something as mundane as a clothes pin has a name like "C-47." Only in Hollywood.

When on a smaller set, it's temping for people to help out in areas that are not their department. While it's great that everyone wants to pitch in, make sure that the department wants the help and that the people volunteering know what they need to do. Sometimes overzealous volunteers or interns can actually get in the way of a well- tuned crew. If someone isn't sure where to help, ask all the departments if they need help and assign them to that department. Don't let someone who has nothing to do wander around set. They will inevitably get in the way.

One of the best ways for you to get the pulse of the set is to stop by the wardrobe and makeup departments. Actors often spend several hours here having makeup applied and fitted for their costumes and they will often talk freely about everything on set. Here you can get a good feel for the mood on set and if anything is going wrong. If everyone here is excited and happy, things are going well. If the air is filled with complaints and frustration, see what needs to be done to set things straight.

Once "picture is up" on the first day, the beginning of filming, it's the producer's job to identify and solve problems as they occur. Or better yet, try to identify small problems before they become large problems. Rely on your staff to help solve problems in their department. Sometimes they already know what the answer is and just need to be sure it's what you or the director needs. Do what you can to solve all problems without involving the director so that they can work with the actors. If a problem needs the director's attention, wait until a break in the action before you approach them.

When a problem happens:

1. Get clarity.

2. Find out what your options are.

3. Act in a way that most benefits the picture.

Get Clarity

After taking a breath, get clarity as to exactly where the problem is coming from. It may be that someone has just misunderstood what the issue really is. Often problems stem from miscommunication or hurt feelings. You won't know how to solve the problem until you get to the heart of the issue. Is the problem something that is re-occurring and if so, why? Is it just late in the day and people are tired? Or is there a larger issue at hand?

Find Out Your Options

If the answer to the problem isn't clear to you right away, get the opinions of the team leaders around you. You hired them because they are good at what they do. If it is a legal question, union question, technical question, logistic issue, or an issue requiring some other area of expertise you don't have, talk to that department before making a decision. There is strength in leaning on the leaders you hired. This is the time to trust your team and find out what the best options are so you can make an informed decision. If you are working on a low-budget film and have to make the decisions yourself, have some people you can call to ask for expert advice and take a few minutes to consider your best options.

What Will Best Help the Picture?

The best solution may or may not be clear, so find the one that will best help the picture. This may sound simple on paper, but if you are faced with the decision of getting a much-needed shot or going overtime by five minutes, get the shot and worry about overtime later. Five minutes of overtime may well be less expensive than having to bring everyone back to that location if you are not able to cut your story together without that shot.

If one of the cast members is having emotional difficulties with the scene, taking a 15-minute break to help them find the right emotional place may be what is needed to make the story and ultimately your film connect with the audience. If this scene and the subsequent break are taking too long, your 1st AD may try to push the director to complete the scene so that you don't get behind on the day. At this point, what is most important is the total quality of the film. You need to assess the importance of the scene, the importance of this particular performance, and whether spending more time on it will give you what is needed.

Visionary and Cheerleader

Do your best to learn the crew members by name. People like to know you care enough to learn their names. This may not be feasible on a large set, but do the best you can.

Take time during filming to remind everyone of what they are doing and why. Keep them excited about your vision for the film by praising their work. Don't just assume that people know you are grateful for what they do. Let them know that you have faith in them to accomplish whatever their job requires. While you are there, see if they have everything they need to do their job well; however, don't take a lot of time for questions and answers as many of the crew members will need to get back to their work.

Your crew, cast, and director will look to you to keep them inspired. The people you hired came on board your project because they believed in you and are excited about your vision. They will work hard for you as long as you keep them inspired and treat them with respect. This becomes particularly important when you are producing a smaller budget film and the people you have hired are working beneath their normal rates. Help keep that vision going by respecting their time and energy and encouraging them along the way.

Diplomat

By setting up a clear line of communication between yourself and the department heads, you insure that you know what is going on everywhere on set and how to deal with any problems that arise. Each department should answer to their department head who answers to you. Each person should be accountable to the head of their department so that there is no miscommunication; however, let the crew know that they can always come to you if there are problems that the department heads can't solve.

The crew should not go to the director with questions as the director needs to focus on the creative process. Taking up the director's time with day-to-day operational issues is not the best use of their time and can distract them from their creative energy and focus.

Creating a good work environment for everyone is vital to the creative process. If you find that a member of your team or a production head is yelling at people when the situation could be dealt with in a better way, take them aside and find out why it happened and what can be done to fix the situation. Yelling on set not only disrupts what is happening for that worker, but disrupts the energy of everyone around. If the actors are trying to get into their role and they hear crew members fighting, it may take them out of what they are trying to do thus hurting the entire production.

The creative space can be a fragile one, and it's up to the producer to help create and maintain the space that the director and the actors work in. If you create good working rules and boundaries from the beginning, it's easier to maintain them along the way. Making sure that everyone knows what you expect will help keep things in check, but know that as the days get long and tempers get short, you need to keep your eyes on any issues that flare up and calm any situation before it gets out of hand.

Some people easily panic over the smallest issues, and it's important that you keep a level head about whatever comes up. If you panic, so will all of those around you. If you notice a problem with a particular individual where they are overly dramatic and get other crew members worked up, you may want to talk with that person privately, and if that doesn't work, look at replacing them.

Act out of a place of calmness rather than the heat of the moment. Good decisions are rarely made when someone is emotional. On long days, you too will be tired and you may need someone to remind you if your temper is getting short. Try not to vent your frustrations on set. Instead, have someone off set you trust and can call and vent your frustrations to. This person should be someone who can calm you down and tell you if you are overreacting. Your production team relies on you to solve all problems professionally.

Making Smart Decisions

There is an old saying in the military when it comes to hard decisions and life choices. If you are fighting an enemy and you have a long battle ahead of you, think of each problem as a hill with the enemy on top of it. Then ask yourself, "Is this a hill you want to die on?" In other words, is this problem so monumental, so important that you are willing to die for it? If not, move on. If so, stick to your guns and fight it out.

Small issues on set can lead to bigger problems if not handled properly. Things come up that you did not anticipate in pre-production, and a rash decision can have a lasting effect on the film production. You may get into the edit suite a few weeks down the road and wish that you had taken just a few more minutes to think something through on set.

Often, no matter what size your production, you wish that you had more time for a shot, more time with the actors, or more time to set up. Sometimes this leads to rushing into something you haven't had time to think about. Something will not go exactly the way you had hoped, but you have to learn what problems you can live with and which ones you cannot. You may not be able to get everything you want. Some areas of the film are more important than others, and you have to learn what you can cut when the day gets too long.

Sometimes on a tough shoot day, you may be required to keep people working longer than expected. If it looks like you are going to have to keep people longer than agreed upon for the day, you need to let them know what is happening and ask if it's OK that they stay longer. Some people may object to working overtime, and if you do this too often, especially with a low-budget crew, you may find that people won't stay.

If you do have to go into overtime, make sure you are aware of and abide by applicable union or government laws pertaining to overtime, and also be aware of how it will affect your budget. You may be required to provide an additional hot meal, but if you work people into overtime, you should want to provide this to them even if it is not required. Keeping a crew fed and praised for their efforts keeps them happy.

Per union rules, if you have to keep a union actor or a union crew worker on set more than 12 hours, you have to ask them permission, you have to pay overtime, and you have to push their time back the following day. This "push back" is called "turn around." Union actors require what is called a 12-hour turn around, which means if they leave set at midnight, they cannot be asked to comeback to set until noon the next day without incurring fees and penalties.

It's important to give people enough time to get enough rest and come back to work fully charged and ready to go. If you try to run a set on 14-16 hour days for six or seven days a week and four weeks in a row, people will walk off your set. Try to keep your set to 10-12 hours of work at most. If you need to do a couple of 14 or 16 hour days because of limited time at a location, you won't get as much push back or rebellion from the cast and crew as you would if you normally keep 10-hour days. In addition, an overworked crew can more easily make mistakes, and a tired crew increases the chance for injuries and poor production quality.

PART V
FINISHING THE FILM

"We shall neither fail nor falter; we shall not weaken or tire.
Give us the tools and we will finish the job."

– Winston Churchill

"Movies aren't released, they escape."

– George Lucas

Chapter 19

Post Production

Post-production is where the final version of your film emerges. The version you had on the pages of the script may look different from the one that you shot, and the one you saw in the monitors on set may look very different from the one you see come to its conclusion in post-production. Here is where you see which pieces of the film work and which don't. As you enter this stage, think back to why you are making this film as you determine which parts of the film stay and which go.

Patience can be a challenge in post-production as this stage can take significantly longer to complete than any other area of the film. If you haven't already started cutting while you were in production, it should take around one to one and a half months to cut together what is called a "string out" or a "rough cut" of your film, which means cutting all the scenes that you shot. Editing can then take another month or two of cutting with the director, making producer notes, notes from the studio, etc. Then there is the sound design, color correction, and delivery all of which can easily take six months or longer to complete.

During this time, it can be a challenge to keep yourself excited when you are several months deep into post production. Dealing with seemingly endless paperwork, watching the edit for the 50th time when you've lost all sense of objectivity, a daunting or expensive reshoot - there are a million things that can and will happen to take you off task. But don't be discouraged! You are almost at the end. Taking time to do post- production correctly insures that the picture you are making is going to look great as well as meet all the technical standards required to deliver and sell your film commercially.

While this process can be lengthy, a good producer won't take forever to finish the film. While it's important to get things right, too much time can be spent second guessing every area of the film. An objective view on the pacing, music, and acting is gradually lost as time goes on. To avoid this and to keep on task, a good producer sets a delivery date so that you have a goal for the film to be finished. There are many great films with small errors and when your film is finally released, it will not be the small errors or small victories that make the film a success or failure. Instead, success or failure will be based on the picture as a whole.

If upon completion you find that there are major problems with the film and not just minor ones, this is the time to rethink the edit or think about reshoots. It is always good to do a few test screenings with friends and people whose opinions you trust in this process. Have a mixture of industry professionals and people who are just movie lovers attend your private screening so you can get feedback. If all of them come back with the same comments about a certain issue, take time to think about how to fix those areas as best as you can.

Post-production is not an area to cut your costs beyond what is reasonable for your total budget. Post-production is used to add a level of production quality that can make the difference between a film that looks like a low-budget indie and a studio-level picture. From great editing, VFX, sound, music, and coloring grading, each area adds to the full scope of your film. If you have been wise in your handling of the budget throughout the filming process, you should have enough here to complete your film properly. If there have been errors, coming into post without enough money to finish properly can hurt the quality of the film.

Post Co-Production

Unless you have your own production company or post-production suite with editing, color correction, and sound mixing, you need to find a good post-production partnership. Preferably, this will be a company that you will partner with at the beginning of pre-production so they can be part of the budget, help you set up all of post-production, and help you prepare the footage as it comes off set each day. A partnership with a proven post house is extremely important as you rely on them to deliver a film that will pass quality control both domestically and internationally, as well as be of broadcast standard. This does not mean they have to be a large post house, only that they have the skills and expertise to properly handle your film. From the picture ingest, to editing, visual effects, to sound design and mix, to color correction, and final delivery, the more you are able to do in one place, the lower the cost will be and the more control you will have of insuring quality. As part of the agreement, make sure the post house guarantees their work and that they will make any fixes needed if the film does not pass quality control.

To find a good post partner, you may need to look to a larger city. If you live in places like LA, New York, Dallas, or Miami, you will have a lot more options. You also need to consider any tax credits you are counting on as part of your financing for the film. To maximize your tax credits, you may need to complete post-production in the state where you are getting your tax credits.

A good way to form a partnership is to talk with the owner or the manager of the company. Let them take you on a tour of their facility and talk about what they do there. Talk openly with them about the budget for your film and what you need done. They will let you know what it costs to work with them and if their costs are higher then what you have budgeted, see what can be done to lower the costs through shortening the amount of time for the edit, sound mix, cutting down on the VFX, or see if they will come in as a producing partner and take a deferment for some of their services.

If you have to cut back on the amount of time spent in post to insure that you stay on budget, make sure that your post-production company partners allow for at least a minimum amount of time for each service so that you are assured of a finished film. An all-in-one deal where they provide all the services for one cost may insure that you stay on budget and have a finished picture.

If the company is willing to defer their costs, have in writing the value of each of the services provided and a clear path for recoupment on their goods and services. With a contract in place, there is no confusion or a larger-than-expected demand of funds when the picture begins recouping the investment.

For lower budget films, one of the best ways to lower these costs is not to edit at the post facility for the entire cut of the film. If possible, have the editor string the film together at home using the same edit system you will master on, or at a smaller facility where you don't pay full price for an edit suite for one or two months. When the film is ready to enter the final stage of editing, bring it back into the post house for the online edit, color grading, audio mix, and mastering.

Duties of the Post Supervisor

The job of post supervisor is similar to a line producer's position as it is the management and oversight of post-production. Post-production deals with many technical issues that a producer needs to be aware of. If you are producing a lower budget film, you may have to take on the duties yourself. In this case, you need to get familiar with each stage of post. This is not an easy task and not recommended if you are trying to deliver your film to foreign markets. If you partner with a post-production company, that company may assign a post sup to you to insure that their post budget and service time is handled properly.

The post sup presides over everything from the editing and data storage, to post contracts, and all the deliveries to the distribution company. They should have a knowledge of post facilities, color correction, quality control (QC), audio, VFX, music, contracts, and current delivery standards for the major distribution companies.

The first job of the post supervisor is to look over the post-production budget and evaluate if the budget is correct for what your needs are. They then create a post- production schedule predicated on your release date.

The schedule will include:

1. Date of first assembly/string out (one-two months)

The string out time may overlap with production if you begin editing while still filming.

2. Delivery of the director's cut (If director is a DGA member, you are required to allow them 10 weeks to cut their version of the film.)

3. Producer's notes (2 weeks)

4. Editing of producer's notes and final review and feedback from screenings (two-three weeks)

5. Date for locked picture

6. Date for completion of visual effects

7. Completion of color grading (two days - one week)

8. Identify and hire a composer or other music source like a music library. (four weeks+)

9. Sound design schedule (one-two months)

10. Actors ADR (time variable depending on need)

11. Sound pre-mix and final mix schedule (one week)

12. Creation of main and end titles. (one week)

13. Online edit (bringing together the highest quality color corrected version of the film for the release along with the VFX, main and end titles, final sound mix) (two days - one week)

14. Date for mastering of film

15. Completion of producers delivery book/ Bible

This includes all post paperwork needed for delivery to the distribution company and can take several days to several months depending on how well everything was kept track of and duplicated during the production stage.

16. Creation of any deliverables needed for distribution. (Including any promotional material.)

The Post-Production Process

1. Choosing the Edit Format

You will already have chosen the editing format in pre-production. Post-production is where those choices are put to the test. Are you shooting on film? Tape? Hard drives? Each has its own issues that must be handled differently. The post department will have to determine the best edit system to use according to the budget and what the post house is set up for.

Film

If you are using film, then your post-production work flow and costs need to consider the extra time and money for the film to reach the lab, be developed, have a print made, scan the film with a 2 or a 4k scanner, and send those digitized files to a hard drive and into a format that fits your selected edit system. The field audio can be married to the video at the lab or by your editor. It costs more to have the lab do it. If you decide to go back to film after cutting the film, there will be additional time and costs for taking your EDL (edit decision list) from the edit system and having the film physically cut from the prints. The film then needs to be color graded through a film lab and sent to print.

Tape

If you are using tape, you will send the tapes each night to a lab or post facility that will ingest the tapes into the edit system that you and your post supervisor have chosen. The drives will be copied and sent to you and your post supervisor while one is kept in storage for safety.

Hard Drives and Flash Cards

Unlike film and tape, hard drives and flashcards are reused on set and so there is no "original" material to work with in the edit. Your team should have copied all the footage to a producer's drive, a main edit drive, and a backup drive. After filming, the three drives should never be in the same place at the same time so that there is not a chance of losing all of your footage.

Work flow for cameras that use high-quality files like 4k and higher, may take longer to transfer and verify than cameras that use 2k files and under. In addition, with image files like those of the *RED* camera, you have many opportunities to change the look of the image when you prepare the footage to go from the *RED* into your edit system. This is something you do not need to adjust until after the edit is complete.

2. Dealing with File-Based Systems

File-base cameras, which have taken over much of the industry, come with their own set of problems that if not handled properly, can mean damaged and irretrievable files. Make sure the post team is clear about how they ingest material from the camera into the edit system and how they back up the material. With some file-based cameras, you may only have a few cards that need to be reused on set. If this is the case, be sure that the DMT or the editor have copied each file twice and have checked to be sure there are no errors before any of the original material is deleted and the cards reused.

3. Ingesting Picture and Audio Files

No matter what format you are shooting on, film, tape, file-based formats or others, you need to ingest that material into the edit system. Film is scanned in, tape is put through a tape machine and captured into the edit system, and file-based formats are brought in directly or transcoded to work with the edit software. The work on ingesting the material and preparing it for the edit session is often handled by an assistant editor, leaving the creative work for the editor. If you are working on a smaller budget, you may not be able to afford both.

The quality at which the picture is ingested depends on how the post supervisor likes to operate and the capability of the edit system. Chances are, you will be work on what is called an "offline" edit, which means that the material is brought into the edit system at a lower quality than the master. This lower quality allows for a faster working edit system and less time to transfer materials. When the edit is complete and the picture is locked, you go back to the original files, tapes, or film and recapture only the pieces needed at their highest quality.

Audio files are also brought into the edit system, though they will most likely not need transcoding into a different format. To help your editor, make sure that the audio field recorder marks each audio clip with the slate information. On a smaller set, this may mean they have to take the material home and mark it each night to bring back in the morning. If this is the case, make sure to get a copy of the material before they leave and then recopy the material with the corrected slate info. If possible, have the field recorder mark the takes during the day so that they don't leave set with the material.

4. Pairing Audio and Video

On most productions, your audio and your video are separate. You have an audio recorder with a boom and some lavaliere microphones and they record to a separate device from the camera. The audio and video then need to be ingested and paired together. Here is where time code (a code written into the video and audio signal, which allows the user to sync the video and audio) and/or a clapboard come in handy. If your camera did not record any sound, which some high-end cameras do not, you will use the clapboard to line up the clap sound with the image. If your camera does record sound, it is possible to use software like *Pluraleyes* to match the audio and video. Software like this is not always accurate in paring the audio and video source so if you are using it, double check to be sure everything lines up properly.

This is one of the first places that a copy of the script supervisor's notes comes in handy. Here, the assistant editor or editor makes sure that all the takes are in the system and nothing is missing. They may mark or color the "circle takes," which are the ones that the director liked while on set.

5. Beginning the Edit

The rough assembly or "string out" is where all the scenes are strung together in the way the film was scripted. This is handled by the editor who uses this time to get familiar with all the material. The editor compares each take with the script notes from the script supervisor and tries to use the parts of the takes that the director liked. Using their best judgment, they cut for pacing and emotional impact, but they should wait to cut out any scenes until after everyone has seen the string out.

Depending on notes from the director, the editor may or may not add temporary music at this time. If the director has a particular piece of music in mind, they will suggest to the editor that this is what they are looking to use for a scene. Music can be helpful for pacing, but can also be constraining for a composer later. Once the string out is complete, the director, producers, and studio take a look at the film to see what works and what does not.

A great editor knows how long to stay on someone talking or cut away to a reaction shot and how to best deliver an action scene or find a touching moment in an actor's performance. Editing turns the audience into a third person in the room, watching an event unfold. If you were in the room watching the scene, where would you want to look next? The ceiling, the floor, the person's hand as they grab a glass and turn toward the window or would you want to move closer to them as they whisper something important?

6. Editing in Reels

Editing in "reels" began because a film reel could only hold a certain amount of film footage relating to a certain length of film. Today, that is used much less but it is still a good idea to cut in reels, which means cut around 15-20 minutes of your film on one sequence and then put the next 15-20 minutes on a new sequence. Upon completion of the edit, visual effects, and sound, the picture is combined into one reel when you create a digital master of the film, but in the meantime, it's easier to keep track of 15-20 minute sections of your film than to have one long edit for a 90-110 minute long picture (or longer).

This format is helpful when dealing with audio mixes and color grading. Smaller file sizes and smaller sections of the film make it easier to work on each piece without having to deal with all the film at one time. In addition, this helps keep costs down if you end up making changes after you have "locked" the picture.

For example: Say you have completed editing the film, which means you have a "locked" picture (i.e. there are not supposed to be any more changes to the edit). You now hand off the picture to the sound mixers and color correction who begin to do their work. After finishing their work, for one reason or another, you realize you have to make a change to the editing of the film. If the film is cut in "5" reels and the edit is in reel "2," all you have to do is reopen reel 2, make the changes, and send it back to the mix house and color house. This is a small change to only 15 minutes of the film. If the film is not cut in reels but is one long file, the entire picture has to be opened up, which will cost more money than just opening up reel 2.

7. Director's Cut

After the string out, the director takes control of the picture and cuts the version they intended. They may work with the editor or if they know how to edit, they may cut it themselves. DGA rules are that the director gets 10 weeks to cut the film, but if the project is non-union, you can work out a deal with them on how long they are given to complete their cut. The director should have a strong vision for the film and should be given enough time to see this vision materialize while keeping in mind the delivery date. Give them a chance to do their best work before making any suggestions or changes.

8. Producers/ Studio Notes

Once the director has their cut of the film, the producers get around two weeks to make their notes and determine if there needs to be any changes to the film. Many directors don't like having the film adjusted by the producers, but it is the producer's responsibility to make sure the film adheres to the reason they were producing this film in the first place, and if the director's final vision doesn't accomplish this, there may need to be some changes.

The producer may also get notes from the studio or distribution company stating that something is too long, too gory, too much nudity, or there may be story points that are not clear. These notes usually relate to the sales potential of the film. Some of these notes may be helpful and others may not. While considering the director's artistic choices, the producer has to decide which of the studio's notes to keep, and which ones to lose. If the studio has "final cut" of the film (meaning they have the last word), the producer may be forced to make the changes whether they like them or not.

9. Screening for Industry Friends / Associates

At this point you may want to screen the film for several people who have never seen it and are not familiar with the story. Getting a fresh set of eyes on the picture helps, as you and the rest of the team have seen several versions of the picture. These should be people you trust will not share the film with outside sources or the media and should be people you trust to give you an honest and insightful view of the film. It may surprise you which scenes work and which do not when being watched with fresh eyes.

10. Locked Picture

Once the notes are complete, you now have a "locked" picture, meaning there should be no changes from this point forward. This allows your VFX department, your music and sound department to begin syncing their work to the picture. If you make changes after you lock the picture, it can cost you in time and money as each department has to make changes.

Once your picture is locked, you send out a reference movie for each reel of the film. This needs to have a sync marker at the beginning and the end of the reel so that the audio department can make sure the audio and video is lined up properly for their session. The editor checks to see what type of reference video file the audio department wants to work with.

11. Visual Effects

If your film has extensive visual effects, you need to prep them in pre-production. By the time you get to post-production, you should have all the plates and any live action pieces already shot and being processed (plates are backgrounds for the VFX, which are shot on location). The editor can cut in any live action pieces or VFX pre-visualization pieces so the director can get a feel for pacing while the VFX are being completed. The final VFX shots are dropped in when the editor puts together the "online" version of the film.

It's important to have a good VFX supervisor who understands the workflow and knows how long shots should take to complete. Their job is to work with the editor to be sure the VFX artists are working from the best quality picture possible. The supervisor hands out each shot to VFX artists and keeps them on task for completion. It's a good idea to keep the director in the loop and continually check to be sure that shots are coming together as planned.

If VFX can't be done well, then it's better to take them out of the film. Unless the film is supposed to be cheesy, it's better to use mystery and misdirection than try to pull off a really bad visual effect.

12. Music

You may bring a composer in early to the process, but it is likely they will not be needed until you have a rough cut/string out of the film. It's then that they can begin to get an idea of the characters, the pacing, and the mood of the film so they can begin to work on composing music that matches. The director should have an idea of the basic feel they want and may have some samples of music they like.

When looking for a composer, find one who has done films similar to yours in the past or whose music has a tone similar to what you think works well. If you are working from a very low budget, one of your options includes purchasing inexpensive pre-made music online. You can find any style and theme from horror, to drama, or comedy, all at a reasonable cost. In addition, there are several music library companies that will work with independent films and low budgets. We've worked with several who will, for a very reasonable flat fee, open up their entire library to a filmmaker.

A well-scored film can make a huge difference to the performances, the emotional beats of a scene, suspense, atmosphere, and the overall mood of the film. Finding someone who understands the mood and vision for the film is paramount. If you are unsure of who you would like to use or you have a limited budget and have to take a risk on a less experienced composer, we recommend you have several composers give you a sample score of one of your key scenes to help you decide who to hire.

13. Music Supervisor

Additional music for your film may be found through a music supervisor. This person oversees any of the prerecorded music used in the film. They should have a library of new bands that may fit your style or they will handle the licensing of any already-published bands that fit your film. This also includes any songs used as part of the soundtrack or any songs that your characters are listening to on screen. Either you or the music supervisor needs to make sure that you have sync performance agreements with the bands and their record label. If you cannot afford a music supervisor, this duty falls to you, and you need to be sure that you have the correct paperwork from your lawyer.

If you are working from a limited budget, one of the best ways to get music for your film with little to no cost is to contact music managers in your area or in a large city nearby. Many managers carry a number of different bands who all need promoting and may let you use their music for free. Your film may be the chance they are looking for to further promote their music. In this case, rather than pay them cash, you pay them in trade for promotion along with the film. You can then post them on the film's website, social media page, or even use them in the trailer for your film. Each of these areas helps expose the band, which can often be worth a lot more than paying a small fee for usage of the music. Make sure your contract with them allows for use of the music in all territories worldwide, forever. Anything less than that and you will have problems with distribution.

14. Audio

If the post house you are working with does not have a sound stage for mixing, you need to partner with an audio house. It's better for your budget if you can find an all-in-one location, but this is not always possible. The audio facility should have a place to record ADR, Foley (footsteps and the sounds of the actors moving and interacting in the scene), dialog editing, sound design, and final mixing.

The audio supervisor oversees and coordinates all the audio work in the picture. They work with and answer to the post supervisor and schedule all audio sessions, including the audio editors who work on dialog editing, the Foley artists, ADR sessions, and the final mix. Led by the audio supervisor, the audio team should consist of an audio editor, sound designer, Foley artists, and mixer. If you are working on a low budget, these may all be one person, but each role is important.

Dialog Editing

Dialog editing is the first step before any ADR is recorded. The dialog editor goes through the film to see what audio can be cleaned up and which must be replaced. To save money, you may have an assistant editor set up the dialog properly before handing over the audio files to the audio house. This can be done by keeping dialog on separate tracks from any music or sound effects you have added to the cut of the film.

ADR (Additional Dialog Recording)

ADR is used when the audio recorded in the field is not a good enough quality to be used in the film. This may be because of additional noise on set or dialog in an action scene or for any other reason. Where possible, you should keep this to a minimum as it can cost a lot to get your actors back in and can take a significant amount of time to record more than just a few lines. Not all actors are good at doing ADR, and the performances do not always match what you get in the live performance. If your actors are SAG, you have to pay union rates to have them back in the studio to record their parts. With studio costs and union rates, recording additional ADR can easily get very expensive if you need a number of your cast for additional lines of ADR. If any of your actors are not local , you may have to incur travel expenses or find a local ADR facility where they are based and have the director give them ADR notes and listen on a video link from your post house.

Loop Group

"Loop group" is the title given to the people you bring in to cover voices that are not covered by the main actors. This can be anything from background noises of crowds, to voices on the phone, and sometimes even covering "sound-a-likes" for actors you were unable to bring in for an ADR session. There are companies that handle loop group artists, but if you are on a low budget, a possible solution is to form your own loop group from actor friends who have experience looping. Good looping is an art so if you need looping, look for people who have experience otherwise it could end up costing you more time and money with your ADR facility. Some loop group artists are union, so you need to follow union guidelines if your film is union signatory.

Foley

Foley is the creation of sound effects made to replace the sounds made on set as actors do business in the scene (i.e. walking, opening and shutting doors, etc.). The name "Foley" comes from Jack Foley, a sound artist who worked for Universal Studios during the switch between silent films and sound pictures. A Foley artist is the performer(s) who watches the film on a large screen and re-enacts the movements made by each person on screen, live. Most Foley stages have a large number of objects they can use to recreate the sound of walking on different surfaces, doors, glass breaking, cloth movements, etc.

A basic Foley pass should take three days to a week, depending on how complicated the film is and what your budget is. If you have a low budget but you still have to deliver a full M&E (music and effects) track for foreign distribution, budget in at least a half day for prep and one full day for recording Foley. You won't get the precise work needed on a better quality picture, but at least you will have a full track of effects, which is what foreign distribution looks for. If you are missing footsteps, doors closing, etc., the film won't pass foreign delivery quality control (QC). When checking to see if you have a full effects track, turn off all the dialog and watch the film. If there are any sounds missing, make sure the audio house fills those places before mastering the film.

Sound Design

Sound design is the overall tone and audio tracks for the film. It is the general background as well as specific sound for objects like cars, planes, etc. A great sound designer adds much depth to the film and can make the difference from a low-budget picture and a studio film. Great sound makes your film "look" better where bad sound will make your film seem small and cheap. If you cannot afford to have high-end sound design for your film, one way to cut costs is to have a sound editor cut in prerecorded sounds from a sound effects library. The rights for sound effects purchased from a library are usually covered for use general use in a film, though you will need to check any rights or restrictions given by the company they are purchased from. Though the sounds won't be original, they can still be effective.

Audio Mix

The audio mix starts once you have all Foley, dialog (including ADR), sound design, and music ready to go. A pre-mix is done first where basic sound levels are set and the director comes in to work with the mixer and helps set the proper levels in each area of the film. Once the pre-mix is done, the final mix is prepared and the director, producers, and the studio should be in the room to make notes and comments on the picture. Once all the notes have been addressed, a final mix is prepared.

A festival mix can be used if you are not ready for a final master of the audio. This often happens if you have music that you have purchased the rights for festival use only and you are hoping that the distribution company will help you pay for the full rights to the music for distribution. This is not recommended as it can cost you more to go back and do a final mix later when you have the final music. In addition, if the distribution company can't or is unwilling to pay for additional licensing of the music, you will have to find alternative music and pay an additional amount to go back to do the final mix of the film.

Exporting

Exporting the audio master in preparation for the mastering of the film should happen with the specifications of the studio or distribution company. You need a stereo track, a 5.1, 7.1 (or larger depending on playback intentions) surround track and a M&E track, which separates out the music and effects channels. This is done so that when the film is sold to a country that has a different language, the sales company can dub the film into that language. Without a full M&E track , you won't be make many foreign sales and will lose out on the money that could have been generated. You may also need additional digital tracks for theater releases or VOD releases, but you need to check with the studio or distribution company for those specifications. If you don't have a distribution company, be sure to keep a copy of the mix session so that it can be opened later for any changes or new mixes.

If you need a Dolby, THX, or other licensed master for a theatrical release, you have to get licensing and pay the corresponding fees. Check with your distribution company to see what is required as these standards change and new formats are emerge, and see if they will cover the cost.

15. Titles

There are two types of titles. Main titles and End titles. The main titles are usually at the front of the film and consist of your lead actors, screenplay writer, director, producer, composer, DP, production designer, and costume designer. Depending on your contracts with your cast and crew, that list may be adjusted. The end titles are traditionally all of your below-the-line crew credits including: supporting cast, stunts, extras, AD's, production staff, post-production staff, music, suppliers, union logos, and copyright.

The director should have input as to what type of titles they would like to see. The post supervisor works with a title artist to insure that the titles are created with the proper specifications to be included in the online version of the film. (Online, in this case, refers to the version of the film just before creating the master, and not an internet version of the film.) For foreign delivery of the film, you need one version of the picture with titles and one without as the foreign country way want to replace your titles with one in their language.

If you have any contractual billing agreements for the actors, crew, or suppliers and your production partners or distribution company, you need to be sure that the order and size of the titles comply with your agreements. To include the *Humane Society* logo, you need to contact the *Humane Society* and request a unique ID for your film. Check what other contractual agreements you have regarding the logos for titles. If you are under any union agreements, they require their logo to be added to the credits and will supply you with it. If you want MPAA rating and logo for the film (Motion Picture Association of America), you or your distribution company need to contact the MPAA for specific guidelines. Only films released for theatrical screening need to have a MPAA rating, and there is a cost to have the film rated.

16. Online Edit

If you have been working from an offline or lower quality version of the film, you will create the "online" version of the film prior to going into color grading. This is done by taking the edit decision list (EDL) from the editing software and using it to gather only the needed high-resolution versions of each shot that make up the picture. The online process can take place through your editor or can take place through the colorist. Whoever does it, this version is needed before the colorist takes on the picture. At this stage, all picture elements need to be added back into the film. Any titles and VFX need to be added into the picture before going to color correction.

17. Color Grading/Color Correction

There are two names for the color process of your film. Color grading, and color correction. Color grading is the process of adding color schemes to the picture to add tone and mood. Color correction is the process of making sure that each shot matches the shots in the scene around it. Though the terms are sometimes used generically as color correction, there is a difference in the intended results of each process.

Color grading should be a service provided by your post-production partner. If this is not something they offer, find a color house that is able to give you a delivery that will pass quality control.

The colorist should have a strong understanding of color grading and stylizing the film. If you doubt the importance of color grading, watch untreated footage from some of your favorite films in the behind-the-scenes sections. The original footage lacks the emotional impact of the final master. Why? Color, black levels, and style are all finalized in the color grading process. Most likely, your director of photography will want input at this stage. They will have shot the footage in a certain way to achieve a particular look. Have the DP and the director go through the picture with the colorist and tell them what look they were going for. At a minimum, do a color correction pass so that the color matches from shot to shot. Even if you can't afford to spend a week color grading, at least take the time to be sure that the film is consistent.

There are different standards for acceptable video and color levels depending on whether your film is being delivered for theatrical release or TV broadcast. The color correction house you are working with should know these standards and be able to deliver a picture that fits the needs of distribution. If you cannot afford to do color correction pass for both a theatrical version of the film and a broadcast version, you must make sure to have the broadcast version. Without it, you will not pass quality control for broadcast which will likely be your largest sales.

18. Mastering

Several masters of the film need to be created from the audio and video master. Each master is made to the specification of its use. You may need (1) a domestic master with the full audio tracks in stereo, surround, and digital audio, (2) a foreign master with textless title sequences and M&E tracks for dubbing, (3) a master for *Blu-ray* and DVD, (4) a screener master with a watermark used for sales screenings and festival screenings. You may also need masters for theatrical releases, VOD releases, and mobile device releases; however your domestic master covers most of those and your distribution company can meet those needs when they arise.

19. Quality Control Report

Depending on the deal you make with your distribution company, you may be able to get them to cover the cost of a quality control (QC) report. A QC report is done to make sure your film passes the quality control of foreign and broadcast delivery standards and should be performed by a recognized company. Check with the distribution company to see if they have a list of approved QC houses they require you to use. Failing QC is often used as a reason for companies to refuse delivery (and payment) of a film, so getting the report from an industry-recognized house always helps avoid disputes down the road.

To help the film pass QC, make sure your colorist understands the QC process and can watch for and correct any levels that may be off that will make the film fail the QC process. You can also help insure the film passes by having the digital master of the film processed through a limiter, which will keep the high and the low levels in their proper place. It is always a good idea to have an agreement with your post house to ensure their work is of quality to pass QC and they will make any fixes necessary at no additional cost to you. Passing QC for broadcast is also the same standards for VOD and other digital releases. If your film is however, not going into broadcast, you may not need to pass QC at all.

PART VI
RELEASING THE FILM

"We shall not cease from exploration
And the end of all our exploring
Will be to arrive where we started
And know the place for the first time."

– T.S. Eliot

"Success is not final, failure is not fatal:
it is the courage to continue that counts."

— Winston Churchill

Chapter 20

Distribution and Self-Releasing

We've worked on a combined total of over 50 feature films and have worked with both good and bad distribution companies as well as tried our hand at an independent release. Some companies have been honest about the recoupment money and payments, while others have been rather evasive or have gone bankrupt and completely disappeared. Through all of this, we have found a few steps to help find better and hopefully more reliable companies to work with. At this point in production, you hopefully already have a company working with you and if that is the case, you are ready to move on to preparing the delivery items. If you have yet to find a distribution company, here are some things to help you understand the distribution process and what to look for.

Distribution

To get your film distributed worldwide, you need to either find a company that does both domestic and foreign distribution or a domestic distribution company and a foreign sales agent. Sometimes, you may even divide this up further by going to different companies for theatrical distribution, VOD distribution, DVD/Blu-ray distribution, TV, and Pay TV and all other ancillary media.

A distribution company may choose to buy your film but more often they will license your film for a certain period of time, which gives them the rights to distribute the film through their outlets. These outlets may be: VOD platforms like iTunes and Amazon, hard copies like DVD/and Blu-ray for Wal-Mart or other retailers, broadcast outlets like cable TV including HBO, Showtime, Lifetime, TNT, etc., or even airlines and college screenings. A good distribution company has numerous outlets and relationships where they can easily reach out to buyers with your film. If the distribution company is smaller and has yet to build these relationships, they may sell your film to a larger company that already has output deals in place and will take a cut of those sales (i.e. they are the middle man).

How to Meet a Distribution Company

A good way to meet distribution companies is to attend a film market like the American Film Market (AFM) in Los Angeles. There, you can meet the distribution company sales and acquisition people face to face. They may not have time to answer many of your questions at the market, but get their business card and contact them as soon as the market is over. These are extremely important relationships to nurture both for your current film and any film you hope to produce in the near future.

If you have a hard time getting meetings with distribution companies, you may want to hire a producer's rep to help you. Most producer's reps charge a commission fee, which ranges between 5 to 10 percent of the sale. They may also want to charge for expenses so you need to work out the details of what those entail and put a cap on how much can be spent. Major agencies like CAA, ICM, WME, UTA and Paradigm also may be interested in representing (aka: repping) your film. Some entertainment legal firms also rep producers and their films.

As we discussed in an earlier chapter, another good way to get some recognition for the film and possibly pick up good distribution, is through marketing and film festivals. Distribution companies pay attention to the larger festivals like Berlin, Sundance, Cannes, Berlin, Telluride, Tribeca, Venice, and Toronto and are always looking for good pictures to pick up.

To get distributors, sales agents, and producer's representatives to see your films, it is a good idea to set up a screening or two that they can easily attend. You may want to rent a comfortable screening room, which can cost between $300 to $2,000 depending on size and location. You can then email any of your connections a flyer and a trailer for the film. It is helpful if your cast, crew and friends can attend the screening as you want a supportive atmosphere for the picture. If you have notable talent in your film, and if they attend the screening, you may want to mention this in the flyer as if may help increase attendance. Making the screening a large event with a reception afterward may also increase the chance of distributors attending.

In the event you are not able to get busy people out of their offices or away from their home life to attend your screening, or if you don't have the right connections to reach them and get them to attend, sending out a screener and a press kit can be another way to reach them.

Not all distribution companies are going to be right for your film. Some handle only A-list features with known actors while others may focus on independent horror, action, or family films. When you research companies to approach, take a look at some of the movies that you consider a similar quality and style. Who is distributing those films? Make those the first people on your contact list. As you talk with producer's reps, use the same approach. Which ones have good relationships and have sold films similar to yours?

Preparing the Film for Screenings

To show your film to distribution companies, you need to have screener copies made of the film. For a theatrical screening, determine what format the theater/screening room uses to play the film. Many theaters can take digital files or even DCP (Digital Cinema Projection) files. True DCP files can be expensive to make and may not be needed for small screenings. They are, however, the most reliable source and best digital quality for large screenings. Digital playback files can vary in size and reliability with each depending on the playback device and the ability of the projector to play the format. It's not recommended to use a burnable DVD as DVD's are not always reliable. Blu-rays are more reliable than DVD's, but these too can have issues. As a final option, you may be able to use a reliable (though outdated) tape format like DigiBeta or HD cam. Whatever format you go with, test it before your have a room full of distribution representatives waiting. If something is wrong with the file or wrong with the way it plays in their system, you need to know a few days in advance so you have time to make changes.

How to Know a Good Distribution Company From a Bad One

Having worked with a large distribution company that went bankrupt and others who found ways to hide fees and sales, we cannot stress enough just how important it is to research a distribution company before signing with them. Even distribution companies with big names and big films can have trouble. Your best bet before signing a contract, is to contact several producers of films that the distribution company is carrying. You can usually find their contact info on *IMDB pro*. Ask them how they have been treated and if the distribution company has been honest and forthcoming with them. Many producers are happy to talk about their experiences and whether or not the distribution company has kept their commitments. They may even have good recommendations of great companies they've worked with. If you get one producer who isn't happy, it may just be that their film did not perform well. If you get several producers who aren't happy, then stay away from that company.

If the company is giving you big numbers and much high praise for the film, ask them to back up their projections with numbers for each territory and see if they are willing to be accountable to those numbers contractually. If it sounds too good to be true, then it is. You need someone who is excited about your film but not someone who is just going to tell you what you want to hear.

You can only sell your film for the first time once, so take your time and make informed choices. Don't rush into a contract with a company without getting references and having the contract reviewed by an attorney. If the initial distributor is not able to sell your film, it can be expensive and time consuming to get the film back. In addition, there are only a certain number of buyers in the world. Once a buyer has seen your film and if they passed on it, or if your film has been around the market year after year, it is perceived as tarnished and a second seller will have a difficult time selling it.

If you do have problems with your distribution company and you have to get your film back, there may still be hope for it. The best solution when re-approaching the market with an older film is to: redo the art work, make a new trailer, and if possible recut the film so that you can make it a "re-release" such as a director's cut or extended cut. This may breathe new life into your picture.

How to Know if You Are Getting a Good Deal

The initial value of your film is based on the areas we discussed earlier in the book: genre of the film, known actors, and the quality of the film. If you have high marks in each of these areas, you may get a sizable down payment (i.e. minimum guarantee) for the film. Any money the distribution company pays the producer up front is charged against any sales that are made. For example, if the distribution company pays the producer $100,000 as a down payment (i.e. a minimum guarantee or an advance) on the film, they will take $100,000 out of the first sales that they make. Depending on how the distribution deal is structured, the producer may or may not see any money after that minimum guarantee due to additional fees that the distribution company charges against the film. These charges can include cost of promoting the film, attending the film markets, and any additional delivery items that they need. When possible, the producer should get as much money up front and at least enough to cover the investors' initial investment in the film.

If you don't have high marks in genre, actors, and quality, your best is getting a decent split from the US distribution company. A 30-40 percent to them and 60-70 percent to you is reasonable, especially if you can get them to take the film without adding marketing costs on top of their percentage. You also want to find out what direct output deals they have arranged with companies like Wal-Mart or Target, or in what areas they might be going to other distributors who may also charge a fee. It's always important to get really clear information on what percentage of revenue will come out before you see any money. Keep in mind that each company that the film is handled by takes out a cut of the profits.

For example: If a small distribution company (company A) is too small to directly go to iTunes to sell the film, they have to use a second company (company B), plus iTunes is taking their cut, you are left with a very small percentage. e.g.: The film sells for $10. iTunes takes 50 percent leaving $5.00 Company B may take 20 percent, leaving $4.00. Company A then takes 40 percent leaving you $2.40 to split between the investors and those who have points on your film. At this rate, it will take 50,000 sales of the video on iTunes to make $120,000 in profits. If your investor gets 50 percent of the film until they are paid back plus interest, then this only pays $60,000 toward their investment. You need to ask yourself if you have enough people interested in the film to make enough sales to pay everyone back. If 1 person in 100 buys your film after hearing about it, to get 50,000 purchases, you need to reach 5 million people. This model clearly illustrates that digital sales alone will likely not pay back your investors. On budgets higher than $100,000, you need multiple TV, VOD and SVOD sales worldwide to cover your investors and pay yourself and your team profits.

Advance Payment Against Sales

For larger budget films with known actors or a known director, the distribution company may pay you an advance. An advance, also known as a minimum guarantee or an "MG," is a payment based on what their sales team thinks the film will be able to do for them and the amount of the advance is taken out of the initial sales of the film. On smaller films, the distribution company may just pay you a split of the revenue. The advance is paid upon your delivery of all the items on the delivery list in your contract with the company. If you are working with two separate companies, both foreign sales and domestic, try to get a payment from each, which will help pay back your investors.

Marketing Fees

In your arrangement with the distribution company, they may ask to take out marketing costs and expenses before they pay out the original investment and revenue shares. These marketing fees pay for posters, trailers, publicity, social media marketing, screenings, advertising, attending film markets, a publicist, and any other item associated with promoting your film, including possibly their overhead and staffing costs. Other expenses may include additional delivery items, E and O insurance (Errors and

Omissions) additional clearances, and any other item of delivery that you have not already supplied them and needs to be made to sell your film.

If the distribution company requests that marketing fees are taken out of the sales numbers, it's recommended that you have these fees listed and capped in your contract with them. Some companies may not like to have a cap on spending. You may need to agree that, if requested, they can go over the cap only with permission in writing from you. In this case, you will have to decide if the additional charges are a sensible and justifiable expense.

Delivery

As the market has changed, some delivery items have changed with it. We will go into this in more detail in chapter 21, but when first looking at a distribution company, find out what delivery items they look for so you can determine the total cost of your delivery. If you don't have a budget left for delivery items and if the company is not giving you an advance that will cover those items, find out if the distribution company is willing to pay for delivery themselves or can just have you deliver items when they are requested by a buyer rather than all at once. It would not make sense for you to have to deliver a costly item if buyers never need it.

Contracts

A good production attorney is extremely valuable at this point of the negotiations. If you could not afford an attorney for any other area of your production, consider putting together some money to have an entertainment lawyer look over your contract before you sign. This contract could tie up your film for several years or even forever and if there are errors in the contract that give you no power to hold the company accountable, you have no recourse if distribution goes wrong.

There are several items to watch for when reading over your contract. One item is sub-distribution fees. These come from companies that act as a middle man rather than having their own output deals. If your film is small, you may have to work with these companies. However, a company with its own output deals is better to work with as you won't have these additional fees.

Your agreement with the company is for a certain period of time, usually three-five years. To protect yourself against a company that is unable to sell your film during that time, you can ask for sales estimates that they agree to hold themselves accountable to, or include a performance clause in the contract that allows you to get out of the contract if they can't perform by making a certain amount of sales in a designated time period. If a company is unwilling to enter into a contract with a minimum estimate on sales or a performance agreement, they may not think as highly of your film as they claim.

The film business is notorious for finding ways to hide costs or using creative accounting to cover losses of one film with the revenue of another. To help guard yourself against this, put a cap on the marketing fees and expenses with a clause that additional cost must be approved by you so that these costs don't escalate. A right to audit is standard in most distribution contracts and insures that you can keep track of their costs and profits on your film.

Bankruptcy of the distribution company is always a possibility, even with the larger companies. To avoid any issues of ownership and to insure that you are not stuck if your distribution company goes bankrupt, include a bankruptcy clause where the rights of your film revert back to you if you have not been paid for your film. This clause should also include a phrase wherein the rights revert back to you if the company moves without warning or is unreachable for a given length of time.

Collection Account

To insure that funds are not being hidden anywhere, set up a third-party collection account at a bank. This third party collects revenue from all sales and then splits that revenue between all parties. The listing of these payouts is called a "waterfall agreement." This agreement should be put together by you and your attorney and include how each party is paid and at which stage. It also includes any residual payments due according to your union agreements, deferred payments, payouts to investors, any profit participants, payout to the distribution company, and payouts to you. The collection account then creates a collection account management (CAM) agreement, which is sent out to all parties to approve and sign.

Holding Distribution Accountable

The best way to hold your distributor accountable to their promises is to have points in the contract that they must meet to keep the contract valid. Performance clauses should not be a problem for a distribution company that truly believes in your film. These clauses should, however, be reasonable. It will take several months for the distribution company to prepare the sales team with a poster, a trailer, and other needed sales tools before presenting your film at a market. It then can take several months to see if some of the deals made at the market are going to come through. Even when the sales agent signs a deal with a foreign buyer, it may take months to get a deposit check and have the film sent to clear QC in that country.

Performance also depends on whether you are taking the film out theatrically. Theatrical releases can take more time to set up and may need to wait for the right window for marketing. In the past, DVD, VOD, and other digital releases used to always come after the theatrical. Increasingly independent films VOD either come out at the same time as the theatrical release or are released in a much shorter window. If your film is going straight to DVD/Blu-ray, it is reasonable to expect one international sale and several VOD or digital deals within one year. If the distribution company wants your film, they are counting on a lot more than this and chances are, if they don't have at least one sale in a year, they may not want to keep your film anyway.

Distribution Channels

Domestic Sales

In Hollywood, the term domestic sales refers to films sold in the United States and sometimes includes Canada as well. Depending on your film, domestic sales may help drive foreign sales. Because U.S. sales in the often drive other markets, distribution companies may want a limited theatrical release along with marketing for the film in the domestic market. If the theatrical release does well, it may help drive up the VOD and any DVD and Blu-ray sales. Because of the large number of films released each year, many VOD services no longer take films unless they have had a limited theatrical release. In addition, to be a "featured" film on many platforms like iTunes, Amazon, and other VOD services, your film has to play to at least 10-15 theatrical markets domestically.

Foreign Sales

If you have sold your film to a domestic distributor who only deals with the U.S. rights, you will need to engage a foreign sales company if you want to sell in foreign territories. They, like the domestic company, may or may not offer an advance on the picture and may take a marketing fee involving similar items to the domestic distribution company. If you do not yet have a domestic distribution company but secure a foreign sales agent, the sales agent can help you secure a domestic distribution deal but will take an agreed percentage of the deal as payment.

Much of the sales for your film are going to come from foreign buyers. These are the people your distribution company are going to be most eager to please. Foreign buyers purchase the rights through your distribution company to play your movie in countries other than the country of origin. They buy the rights to sell the DVD, Blu-ray, digital version, video on demand, and sometimes a theatrical release of the film.

Foreign buyers look for the same thing your distribution company looks for in a film. They come to a film market (like AFM or Cannes) with a quota and specific types of films in mind. They have cable, DVD, and digital sales to consider, and each market wants something different. They often want to know what type of a domestic release the film is getting before they commit to a sale. If your distribution company can secure a successful theatrical release in the U.S. market, your film will have a better chance in the foreign market.

The question most often asked is: "Who is in the film, and can they draw an audience in their country?" This can vary from actor to actor. Someone you may think is only a B-list actor domestically may be really hot in Germany or Australia, and someone you think is an A-list actor domestically may not pull a very big audience in France or Russia.

The next question is often: "What is the quality of the film?" Was it shot in digital 4k, film, or on a consumer camcorder? Many foreign buyers demand a high- quality production, meaning not just HD, but 4k. If you could not afford a higher grade of production, you may suffer with a ᴸ foreign sales price.

Finally, the foreign buyer asks: "Does the story translate into their culture?" This is the reason to be careful about the genre you chose to shoot. Many dramas and comedies fail this test. A drama set in Japan may not translate to the U.S. because of cultural differences. In the same way, an urban drama from Detroit may not sell well in Germany. Comedy is also difficult because something that is funny in one country may not be funny in another. When languages are translated, the jokes do not always work. An exception to this rule in comedy are the slapstick visual comedy style films, which seem to translate to multiple markets.

TV (Broadcast and Pay TV)

Broadcasters do not usually buy from producers directly. For any TV sales and releasing, you have to go through a distribution company or sales rep. This is often because they know that the distribution company can handle the delivery properly, and they don't want to deal with individual producers.

VOD (Video On Demand)

VOD services are places like *Time-Warner*, *Comcast*, and other pay-cable platforms. Almost all VOD services do not work with a producer directly. To get a VOD deal, you have to go through a distribution company or a digital aggregate. Some aggregates take a percentage of the film sales while others charge a fee to get your film in with VOD service and digital sales.

SVOD (Streaming Video On Demand)

SVOD services involve companies like *Netflix*, *Amazon Prime*, *Hulu Plus* and others which make videos available to their subscribers by licensing the film from your distribution company for a certain period of time.

TVOD (Transactional Video On Demand)

TVOD services are provided by companies like *iTunes*, *Amazon* and *Youtube* where customers buy or rent videos for a set price. Most of these companies do not deal directly with indie producers and you will need a distribution company or an aggregate to get your film listed with them.

Theatrical of Straight to Video or VOD?

Your film doesn't have to be at the top of the box office for a limited theatrical release to still be a big help to the film. It's been noted in *Variety* magazine that profitable films rarely open in at the top of the box office list and that a large number of films that gross significant profits overseas were listed as "losers" in the domestic box office. With roughly 85 percent of the film's earnings coming from cable TV sales and VOD, the theatrical release is often just a way to prop up the film with marketing, word-of-mouth and reviews.

If your film is not suited for a major theatrical release, a good option is to do what is called "Four-walling" or "day and date release". If your film doesn't have the cast or quality to support a theatrical release, you should find a distribution company that specializes in your type of film. They will know how to get the most out of digital sales worldwide so that you can see the best return.

Internet

You may be able to sell DVDs or Blu-rays of your film directly through your website, or through one of the numerous new platforms such as indieflix or Yekra which will split the revenue with the filmmaker.

If you have a short film, skit, or if your film's only purpose was a demo reel for you and the cast, a free Internet release may be the best way to go. Since you don't need to be concerned with the amount of money made for investors, you can focus on how to get the most views on the video.

Mobile Devices

Mobile device licensing works similarly to VOD services. You need a distribution company or an aggregate to facilitate these sales for you. Often, for mobile devices, you have to edit small sections of the film so they can be easily downloaded.

Self-Distribution

The route that might be right for some producers with a low-budget film is self- distribution. To be successful, this is a time consuming and possibly expensive route. You have to cover all the expenses yourself as well as take care of any delivery items that may normally fall under the distribution company. This can work if you have an extremely low budget to recoup, or if you have already established, or are currently establishing a following who wants to see the project or projects that create.

If you plan to make several films and distribute all of them yourself, you are essentially becoming a small distribution company and will be setting up a network of places to sell your film. In years past, these were physical locations like electronic stores and video rental stores. Now, you can generate a decent income from a digital release of your film and sales directly to your audience.

Some VOD or SVOD services may be difficult for indie producers to access. One exception to this rule is *Amazon's* VOD service. Through *Createspace*, producers can sell directly through *Amazon's* digital store. This is a great way to monitor the sales numbers and know exactly what you are making back and what marketing is successful. Because you can see how many people are buying or renting the film in a month, you can more easily tell if an ad campaign you ran is actually working.

"Four-walling"

This is a process where you rent out the theater and sell tickets yourself. Many independent films get off the ground this way. To get critics and press to show up, you must have the film in the theater for at least two weeks and sometimes longer. If you have paid for the theater, you keep the proceeds from the ticket sales. If you are able to negotiate a discount price for the venue, you might split the box office receipts with the theater. When possible, be sure to put aside free tickets for the press.

Start four-walling in one or two major cities, and one or two smaller cities. One good critic often influences the others. If you know you can get a good review in your home town of Toledo Ohio, start the film there. After a good review, it is easier to get good reviews elsewhere.

Four-walling takes additional advertising and marketing dollars if you
. It to attract and audience. What you get in return for four-walling is: a
review from critics, coverage from the press, a better understanding of your
audience and who likes the film, and a better position to get a good deal for
VOD.

If the screening goes well, you may be able to build a word-of-mouth
campaign to help launch the film into the next city. Numerous indie films
have built a strong following by starting in two cities and working their way
up to thousands of theaters nationwide.

Other Options

There are a lot of other releasing options for you and your distribution
company with new ones being presented constantly. Companies like *Redbox*,
airlines, hotels, and colleges are just a few additional options. Be creative.
Find where your audience is and look for a way to reach them.

Releasing for Educational Films

If your goal is not monetary gain but education of the public, your release
strategy may be a little different. You still want to market to the audience
you most want to see your material, but if you have the resources to give
away your film or make it available for a discount, you might look at giving
the film to schools, libraries, or just making it available online for free.

You may also consider taking the film around your local area or
around your country and screening it at theaters, churches, social centers,
malls, and other suitable venues to build awareness. Some of these may be
willing to pay you a fee to screen your film.

Festivals

If you want awards and accolades for your film, then you need to get your
film into festivals. If you have a short film and want to be eligible for the
Academy Awards, your film needs to be accepted at one of the qualified
festivals. The qualifying list for the Academy Awards changes so check for
the current list on the Academy Awards website.

Festivals can also be a good source for finding a distribution company and getting good marketing for your film, plus, they are relatively inexpensive. Even a small festival can reach hundreds if not thousands of people, many of whom will see your poster and trailer or come to your screening. If the film does well, the word of mouth from festivals can be a great asset in marketing your film.

One of the larger challenges of getting into a festival is that the major studios have descended on the better known festivals with their major releases. Having seen the benefits that a festival can have on a film's public awareness and the increase in sales, the major studios have turned many large festivals into their own private platform for releases. Sadly, this leaves less and less space for the smaller indie producers, which was why many of the festivals were created in the first place. Festivals receive thousands of entries and to be considered at one of the larger festivals (Sundance, Cannes, Toronto, etc.), your film has to have the perfect blend of art and star power or a really original unique voice. Even with increased competition from the studios, every year a couple of smaller films do manage to break through. Though it's good to keep your expectations realistic, if you have made a really special film, enter and see if you can get in.

Which Festival is Right for the Film?

Though not every festival is going to be right for your genre of film, every film should start with the major festivals and work their way down. Many of the major festivals want your film to premiere at their festival and won't accept the film if you've already premiered somewhere else. (A cast or distribution screening does not count as a premiere, but a public screening for press will.)

Being accepted at the major festivals does not guarantee that you will get a good distribution deal, but it does give you a better chance of having your film seen. The press that you can get out of a great festival screening makes it easier for you to promote your film and will raise its awareness in the general public.

Each year there are new festivals added to the list, and for smaller productions, these indie festivals can be a great way to reach out to the people who specifically like your genre. Currently, some of the major festivals that will get you the best exposure for your film and where you are more likely to get reviewed are: Berlin, Cannes, Toronto, Venice, Sundance, Telluride, Tribeca and South By Southwest. Each of these have great press coverage and strong attendance from distribution companies looking for new films.

With each passing year, some festivals gain in importance and increase their reach into the film world. American festivals to consider are: Santa Barbara, Palm Springs, South by Southwest (SXSW) Seattle, Los Angeles Film Festival, AFI, Hollywood Film Festival, and Cinequest. European festivals to consider are: Locarno, Deauville, BFI and Raindance in London, San Sebastian, Rome Film Festival, Karlovy Vary, Rotterdam International, and Edinburgh.

There are many great festivals that are not on the list, and you should check the current status of any of the festivals listed here. Your film may not qualify for the larger festivals, but the smaller festivals can just as effectively reach your market. Furthermore, some smaller city festivals can be very accommodating, especially if you bring some of the actors with you to the festival.

With thousands of festivals around the world, there is a wide range of genres covered and your film is bound to fit a number of them. From short films, to horror, to women in film, and animation, there are festivals to cover every topic and style. Being in a festival specific to your genre of film can also help with getting good press and fan awareness for audiences who are already fans of the genre. For example: *Screamfest* in Hollywood, *Fantastic Festival* in Switzerland or Toronto's *After Dark* get attended by distributors and press interested in horror films.

How Does the Film Get In?

Submitting a film for festivals is not terribly difficult, especially if you use a service like withoutabox.com. Websites like this allow you to digitally store all the information on your film and automatically place that info into the submission application for the festivals. Most festivals charge a minimal fee; however if you contact the festival directly, or if your distribution company contacts them, you may be able to get the fee waved in some circumstances.

With thousands of submissions every year, each festival hires a number of people to decide which films will be accepted. If you don't have a strong distribution company, the best way to insure that your film gets through to the head of the festival is to submit through a well-respected producer's rep or film publicist with some clout. They should have contacts at the larger festivals through prior dealings. Although they cannot guarantee that your film will be accepted, they can be sure that it is being seen by those in charge of the festival.

Known talent in your film can often be the deciding factor as to why your film is accepted at a festival. Each festival wants to have celebrities attend, and if your film has an actor or director the festival is interested in, chances are higher that your film will be accepted.

Another way your film can stand out is if it covers a topical or controversial issue. Film festivals are a great place for a debate on current social issues, and those who run festivals are often more attracted to films that dare to try something new and challenge the social norms.

Yet another way your film will stand out is if it is reviewed by a major film critic. A favorable review from a noted critic will gain additional attention. The more attention your film has, the more desirable it will be to the festivals. To be reviewed by a major film critic, the film must have a theatrical release or has to be reviewed in another major festival.

Even if you don't have a known talent, a producer's rep, a national critic review, or a distribution company, do not give up trying to get into the festivals. You may strike out at the larger festivals, but if your film has merit, it will find a lot more love and acceptance at the smaller festivals. Though a film can easily get lost in the crowd at the larger festivals, the smaller ones will often roll out the red carpet and treat the filmmaker to kind interviews and exceptional reviews, all of which are a great help marketing the film.

You're in! Now what?

If you are fortunate enough to get into one of the larger festivals, find out who is responsible for coordinating the press. Get a contact list of the press who will attend and email them with links to your site and your trailer and send them an invitation to the screening. The festival will also have a list of buyers who are attending. Get the contact list for all the buyers and send them a link to your website and the trailer and an invitation to the screening. If you need help, contact the people in charge of the festival and ask for advice on how to reach potential buyers. Festivals want to see their selected films do well as it helps promote the festival for the next year.

If your film is accepted into one of the major festivals and if you have a budget for promotion, you may want to think about hiring a publicist to help your film get attention and maximize the opportunity. Before you attend the festival, prepare yourself and your cast for interviews. Know what you are going to say about the film and have some key talking points. It's also a good idea to be ready to talk about your next project. If your film does well, you may be courted by buyers and distributors. Don't be in a rush to sign with any of them. Take time to read through the paperwork, and make sure your lawyer looks it over as well.

Conventions

Conventions are similar to film festivals, but here, you get to target the market that is attracted to your genre of film. The genres that fit best into this category are science fiction and horror. Sci-fi and horror conventions are big around the world and are a great source for talking directly to your audience.

If you are going to go to a convention and you have DVDs to sell, it's a good idea to rent a small booth or share a booth with another vendor. Here, the fans can come by the booth, buy a copy of the film, and get autographs. It's important, when possible, to bring some of the cast with you so that they can sign copies of the film as well as autograph photos. This can be expensive if you have to travel, so if you are on a limited budget, try to attend a local convention first to see what reaction you get from the fans. If you make enough in sales to cover the trip, look at doing another convention.

"We can lick gravity, but sometimes
the paperwork is overwhelming."

–Wernher von Braun
(Father of Rocket Science)

Chapter 21

Delivery

Not everyone likes the detailed paperwork involved with any business. Delivery of a film is full of paperwork and details. If you are not a detail-oriented person, it is important to have people working with you who are. These people are usually your line producer, production coordinator, script supervisor, accountant, and your legal team, to name a few.

If you have kept track of the paperwork up to this point, the delivery will be much easier. If you have waited until the last minute to get everything done, this stage will be much, much harder. There can be a large difference between the delivery demands of a larger distribution company and a smaller one. Smaller companies may not ask for all the same items that a larger studio does, but you should have everything ready anyway. Even if they don't ask for it right away, you are going to need the delivery items at some point, even if just to protect yourself.

Each of the items for your delivery list are going to cost time and money. When calculating the time for delivery and release of the film, consider how long it will take to put all the delivery items together. Likewise, look at the cost of the items and the cost in man hours, and be sure that it fits your budget. This is one more reason to be careful with how much money you leave for post-production and delivery.

Paperwork

Here is where hard work during pre-production and production pays off. If you kept everything in order and made sure paperwork was signed and duplicated while filming, compiling that paperwork is the final piece of the puzzle. All the paperwork you collected is to be combined into what is called "the producer's bible."

The Producer's Bible

The producer's bible is where you keep all the paperwork needed for delivery. Start with at least three large binders. One copy should be kept by the producer, one for the domestic distribution company, and one for the foreign sales company. The original signed copies stay in the book you keep, while the duplicates go to the domestic and foreign distribution companies. Depending on the requirements from your distribution company, they may ask for or require any or all the following items be included in that book:

1. Summary of the Film

You should already have this from your initial business proposal. If any of the basic story has changed or if you have a better way of summing up the film, this is where you use it. You need a log-line, a one-paragraph summary, and a one-page summary. These are used in press releases, promotional materials, and anywhere a description of your film is needed.

2. Technical Details

Here you list the year the film is being released, what the film was shot on, what the film is mastered on (film, digital, tape, etc.), the format (16x9, 2.33, etc.), the country of origin (U.S., UK, China, etc.) and the running time.

3. Chain of Title Documents

This includes any option agreements, life rights agreements, book rights purchase, and any and all contracts with the writer of the screenplay.

4. Certificate of Origin

The certificate of origin states the pictures title, lead actors, director and lead producer(s), and country of origin along with the running time. It is usually be signed by the producer and authenticated in some way. In the U.S., it is typically notarized by a notary public. You should check with your own legal team about this requirement.

5. Copyright Registration

Upon completing the film, you need to send in a copyright form along with two DVDs of the finished film. (As the requirements for this may change, check with the copyright office about the format they request and the cost for copyright registration.) Once you have received a copy of the paperwork from the copyright office, put it in the delivery file.

6. Title and Copyright Report

A lawyer needs to create for you a title and copyright report showing that your film does not violate any copyright laws.

7. Certificate of Authorship

This is only needed if you hired a writer to write a screenplay. This is a notarized certificate stating that the screenplay is an original work by the author or that it was written as a work for hire for the producer.

8. Final Main and End Credits

This is a list of the main credits and the end credits in the order they appear in the film.

9. Cast and Crew List

A full list of the entire cast and crew and their contact information.

10. Contracts/Agreements

If you followed the guidelines in our legal section, you will have a comprehensive set of legal agreements, contracts, or agreements with everyone you hired. Normally the first to go into your delivery book are the producer's contracts, the director, the writer, the editor, and the DP. Next, you'll have the heads of departments, and all above-the-line cast. You may also be required to deliver contracts on every cast member and every member of your crew so make sure not to leave anyone out. You may also want to organize everyone according to union or non-union workers for the purpose of the payout of benefits.

Make sure you have a signed contract for everyone who worked on the film (crew) and everyone in the film (cast including all extras) so that both you and they know exactly what they were to do and what they were to receive for that work. This way, you can avoid any legal issues that could hold up distribution of the film. This is an item that a smaller distribution company may not ask for, but you should have it ready for your own protection.

11. Union Paperwork

If you hired DGA, SAG-AFTRA or other union workers, you need to include all of their paperwork. This includes any contracts and sign-in/sign-out sheets as well as copies of all payments made. From time to time, paperwork can get lost with the unions and you may be required to furnish them with a copy, so be sure you keep a copy of everything, including the checks you write. You should also have clear lists of union members who worked on the film for each union. These lists can be used to calculate residuals.

12. Payroll Reports

You may well be required to show proof that all have been paid for all performer and crew services. If you used a payroll company, payroll reports should be included. If you didn't use a payroll company, copies of checks will suffice.

13. Location Contracts and Permits

For each location you filmed at, you should have a location contract or agreement. Along with that, if it was necessary, you should include any permits that were required by the city or state.

14. Music Licensing

Each piece of music you have in the film needs to have a licensing agreement. This includes the agreement for the score with the composer as well as any agreements for incidental music (music played by characters in the film) or by music cues or pre-recorded tracks. Each license should be indefinite for worldwide distribution or you will have trouble with distribution. You may be required to show proof of payment, so a receipt or a copy of a check is good to include with each agreement.

15. Music Cue Sheet

The music cue sheet lays out what music is in the film and at what point it appears in the film. It should be laid out with exact time code from the time the music begins to the time its ends along with the title of the composition and the artist. This includes the title of the composition, the name(s) of the composer and if they belong to a performing rights society, the name(s) of the recording artist(s), whether the music is instrumental, vocal, or instrumental-visual/vocal (performer is on screen). It also includes the name and address of the copyright holder and the name and address of the publisher that controls the recording.

16. Legal Clearances

Your legal team needs to go through the entire film and clear each location, or any object or logo that may have a copyright. If an item cannot be cleared, it may need to be removed from the film to avoid possible lawsuits or issues with distribution. You should also have signed clearance release forms for any brands, recognizable objects, or logos that appear in the film.

17. Script

You need to include a full copy of the final script as it was actually shot. This is used for dubbing purposes, which is why it's important that it is a final shooting script. This should be clean and without script notes. You should also include a copy of the script from the script supervisor with all of their notes.

18. Production Reports

After each day of shooting, the camera and audio departments should have handed you or the line producer/production coordinator daily production reports. This is an item that a smaller distribution company may not ask for, but you should have it ready for your own records.

19. Paid Ad Credits

This lists all cast and production credits that are to be given in paid advertising. This includes posters, disc covers, commercials, and any other advertising. This is created from the contracts you made with the cast and crew. It's a good idea to get help on this from your production legal services. If that is not possible, you can do it yourself by going through every contract and make a list of who is required to be included in any paid advertising and the size and placement of those credits.

20. Dubbing and Subtitling Restrictions

This is a list of any restrictions relating to the replacement of any performer's voice including the dubbing into foreign language.

21. Combined Continuity and Dialog List

A full dialog list of the film needs to be made for both closed captioning and foreign dubbing. This includes a line-by-line, cut-by-cut description of the film with time code. Where there is a cut or fade, the time code must be marked and the shot listed for what it is. Also, each piece of dialog and character moment must be described accurately and with matching time code.

This is a complicated piece of paperwork that must be done for the entire film and should be completed by a professional who knows how to properly format this paperwork.

22. Quality Control Report

A quality control report is almost always required for selling the film, and many territories will not accept the film without a cleared CQ report.

Hopefully, this is an item that the distribution company takes care of for you. If not, you can include the QC report in the producer's book.

23. E&O Insurance (Errors and Omissions)

To make sure that everything is covered in the film, even with all of your contracts and agreements, the distribution company will most likely require you to have an E&O policy. This way, if anything did get by, you and the distribution company are protected. E&O insurance gives you some protection from lawsuits alleging infringement of copyright, libel or slander, trademarks, unauthorized copying of ideas, invasion of privacy suits, plagiarism, branding or rights issues, etc.

Materials for the Sale of the Film

Materials needed for the distribution of films constantly changes. From physical films being sent around the world, to digital streams beamed directly into theaters, to the materials needed for marketing and promotion, the type of materials your distribution company requires fluctuates with advancements in technology. Get a complete list of what is required from your distribution company; however, below are listed some basic items that are likely to be required for delivery.

1. Hard Drive

In the near future, there may be alternate ways to get your master to the distribution company. For now, the best way is through a quality hard drive. Don't buy something cheap. This is the master of your film, and you should deliver it on a drive that is not going to give the distributor problems. If you have both a domestic and a foreign distribution company, you need two additional hard drives.

2. Picture Master

The master may be a tape or film, but these days it is usually a digital file. The hard drive should include the highest quality master of the film. The type of file format is determined by the distribution company, and they may require that you deliver a format for both foreign and domestic sales. Be sure to get a list of all of their requirements and make sure you your post-production partner can deliver those materials. Some of these costs can be extensive, so if you cannot afford them, try to get the distribution company to cover the costs of items as they are needed.

Tapes

The era of the tape is quickly fading. There are, however, still many countries that use tape format for delivery. You need to discuss with your distribution company whether they require a tape master or if they can make one from the digital master when and if they get a sale requiring a tape delivery.

Film

Film, like tape, has almost completely disappeared with digital projection taking its place. See if you need a film delivery before you go through the sizable expense of making one. You may not need it.

Edit files

In addition to the picture master, your distribution company may also require the edit project for the picture for additional editing for TV, foreign, or airline sales.

3. Audio Print Master

This should include a stereo audio track, surround sound track, and separate music and effects tracks for foreign dubbing (M&E). A Dolby or other encoded digital file and license may be requested if you plan a theatrical release of the film. You may also be required to supply the audio mix session for additional editing or mixes.

4. Digital Paperwork

You may also want to include any digital copies of the material you put into the producer's book, especially the summery of the film and the credit blocks. These are used by the distribution company for promotions, and it helps to have the material in digital form.

5. Screeners

If you have already created a screener, you can include the files for it on the hard drive. However, it is likely that the distribution company will want to add its logo and create its own version of the screener.

6. Trailer

You may be asked to create a trailer for the film and deliver the elements used to create it, including a picture master, audio master, and the edit project.

7. DCP (Digital Cinema Package)

The DCP is taking over where film is being retired. DCPs can be locked so that no one but the projectionist at the theater can unlock it. This cuts down on theft and allows for quick delivery and high-quality projection every time.

If you are taking the film out yourself to four-wall at theaters, check with the theaters to see if they can use a DCP file. If so, it will be worth the expense. Some theaters may still require film projection. DCPs can be expensive but are a lot less expensive than a film print and safer than Blu-rays or DVDs.

8. Music

On a CD as digital files, you may need to include the original version of all music in the film. These should be unmixed, without any dialog or sound effects over it.

9. Key Art

This includes any promotional material like posters or still images for marketing that you have created for the film. If the art is a layered Photoshop file, include all the elements so that adjustments can be made if necessary.

Advertising and Publicity Materials

The distribution company may want help promoting the film and may ask for several pieces of material to help. This may include:

1. Synopsis of the film

This should be in three versions. A short, one- or two-line synopsis, a medium- sized paragraph, and a long two-three paragraph version.

2. Biographies

This should include the main cast and the principal production team, (director, writer, producer) as well as any press articles about them.

3. Photos

Include between 80-100 approved images from the film as well as behind-the- scenes photos of the cast and crew.

4. Video Press Kit

This can be your EPK or an edited, behind-the-scenes look at the film including interviews with the cast and crew and clips from the film.

5. Billing Block

This is the block of credits that you see on posters or at the end of a trailer. The order of the names and credits is often determined by the contracts you made with the actors and principal production team. Make sure that you or your legal team carefully creates this item so that it does not conflict with those contracts.

"Courage doesn't always roar.
Sometimes courage is the quiet voice
at the end of the day saying,
'I will try again tomorrow'."

– Mary Anne Radmacher
Author

Conclusion

Movies can be an amazing expression of the best of all the arts. Poetry, music, painting, dance - the expression of these and so many other forms of art are limitless in the structure of a film. From the makeup artists to the set construction team and even the catering department (seriously, some of those people are artists with food), the entire entity of a film production is wrapped around the idea of creating a form of art - and art takes courage. Courage to put your dream out into the world for everyone to judge with their online critiques, awards, and pocket book. Courage to face your harshest fears and knowing that courage is being afraid and yet doing what you have to do anyway.

Now is the time to make your dream a reality. Producing is not easy, but it can be very rewarding, and you now have the tools in front of you to help you on the way. In addition to these basics of filmmaking, you need drive, ambition, and a spirit that is unwilling to give up. If no one wants to fund your first script idea, move on to the next one. If the first film you do isn't successful, try again. Learn from your mistakes, be a passionate but kind leader, and build a team around you that believes in you even more then you do.

Come visit us at successinfilms.com and tell us your stories of success or failure so we can all share in the experience of making film more successful.

Made in the USA
San Bernardino, CA
10 May 2016